The Theatre of Jean-Paul Sartre

DOROTHY McCALL

COLUMBIA UNIVERSITY PRESS

New York and London

Copyright © 1967, 1969 Columbia University Press
ISBN: 0-231-08657-1
Second printing and Columbia Paperback edition 1971
Printed in the United States of America

Acknowledgments

Acknowledgment is made to George Braziller, Inc. for permission to quote from the following works by Jean-Paul Sartre: *The Words*, translated from the French by Bernard Frechtman (English translation copyright © 1964 by George Braziller, Inc.); *Saint Genet*, translated from the French by Bernard Frechtman (English translation copyright © 1963 by George Braziller, Inc.); Introduction to *The Question* by Henri Alleg, translated from the French by John Calder (English translation copyright © 1958 by George Braziller, Inc.).

Acknowledgment is also made to Evergreen Review, Inc. for permission to quote from the article "Modern Theatre," translated by Richard Seaver, originally published in *Evergreen Review*, Vol. 4, No. 11 (Copyright © 1960 by Evergreen Review, Inc.).

Selections from the following articles, first published in *The Tulane Drama Review*, Vol. 5, No. 3 (Tll), March 1961 (© Copyright 1961 *The Tulane Drama Review*; © Copyright 1967 *The Drama Review*) are reprinted by permission, all rights reserved: "Beyond Bourgeois Theatre" by Jean-Paul Sartre; "Jean-Paul Sartre: Philosopher as Dramatist" by Michael Wreszin; "*Les Séquestrés d'Altona* of Jean-Paul Sartre" by Oreste Pucciani; "The Popular, the Absurd, and the *Entente Cordiale*" by Herbert Blau; and "An Interview with Jean-Paul Sartre" by Oreste Pucciani.

Quotations from the following sources are reprinted with the permission of the publishers:

Roland Barthes, "*Nekrassov* juge de sa critique," *Théâtre Populaire* XIV (Copyright © 1955 by L'Arche).

Bernard Dort, "*Les Séquestrés d'Altona* nous concernent tous," (interview with Jean-Paul Sartre), *Théâtre Populaire*, XXXVI (Copyright © 1959 by L'Arche).

"Jean-Paul Sartre nous parle de théâtre," *Théâtre Populaire*, XV (Copyright © 1955 by L'Arche).

Pierre-Henri Simon, *Théâtre & Destin* (Copyright © 1959 by Librairie Armand Colin).

Madeleine Chapsal, Interview with Jean-Paul Sartre in *Les Ecrivains en Personne* (Copyright © 1960 by Rene Julliard).

Denis Diderot, *The Paradox of Acting*, translated by Walter Herries Pollack (Copyright © 1957 by Hill & Wang).

Simone de Beauvoir, *The Prime of Life*, translated by Peter Green (Copyright © 1962 by World Publishing Co.).

Francis Jeanson, *Sartre par lui-même* (Copyright © 1955 by Editions du Seuil).

Gaëtan Picon, *Panorama de la nouvelle littérature française* (Copyright © 1960 by Editions Gallimard).

Jean-Paul Sartre, *Situations III* and *IV* (Copyright © 1949 and 1964 by Editions Gallimard).

Jean-Paul Sartre, *Le Diable et le bon Dieu* (Copyright © 1951 by Editions Gallimard).

Jean-Paul Sartre, "Departure and Return" in *Literary and Philosophical Essays*, translated by Annette Michelson (Copyright © 1955 by Rider and Company).

Jean-Paul Sartre, *What Is Literature?* translated by Bernard Frechtman (Copyright © 1949 by Philosophical Library).

Jean-Paul Sartre, *Being and Nothingness*, translated by Hazel Barnes (Copyright © 1956 by Philosophical Library).

Jean-Paul Sartre, "The Unprivileged Painter: Lapoujade" in *Essays in Aesthetics*, translated by Wade Baskin (Copyright © 1963 by Philosophical Library).

Jean-Paul Sartre, *No Exit*, translated by Stuart Gilbert (published in Great Britain as *In Camera*) (Copyright © 1947 by Alfred A. Knopf; copyright © 1946 by Hamish Hamilton).

Jean-Paul Sartre, *The Flies*, translated by Stuart Gilbert (Copyright © 1947 by Alfred A. Knopf; copyright © 1946 by Hamish Hamilton).

Jean-Paul Sartre, *Three Plays* (*The Victors, The Respectful Prostitute, Dirty Hands*), translated by Lionel Abel (British translation by Kitty Black) (Copyright © 1949 by Alfred A. Knopf; copyright © 1950 by Hamish Hamilton).

Jean-Paul Sartre, *The Condemned of Altona*, translated by Sylvia and George Leeson (published in Great Britain as *Loser Wins*) (Copyright © 1961 by Alfred A. Knopf; copyright © 1961 by Hamish Hamilton).

Jean-Paul Sartre, *The Reprieve*, translated by Eric Sutton (Copyright © 1947 by Alfred A. Knopf; copyright © 1948 by Hamish Hamilton).

Jean-Paul Sartre, *Troubled Sleep*, translated by Gerard Hopkins (published in Great Britain as *Iron in the Soul*) (Copyright © 1951 by Alfred A. Knopf; copyright © 1950 by Hamish Hamilton).

Jean-Paul Sartre, *Search for a Method*, translated by Hazel Barnes (published in Great Britain as *The Problem of Method*) (Copyright © 1963 by Alfred A. Knopf; copyright © 1964 by Methuen & Company).

Jean-Paul Sartre, *Nausea*, translated by Lloyd Alexander (Copyright © 1962 by Hamish Hamilton).

D.M.

Preface

A FEW WORDS about the organization of this book. To consider the plays in chronological order did not seem to me altogether satisfactory for two reasons. First, such a scheme would tell us less than might be expected about Sartre's development as a writer; his career as dramatist shows neither a growing mastery nor a decline in power but rather a series of successes and failures standing close together. Second, a chronological study would involve a good deal of repetition and backtracking in the steps of the argument; the play one should have in mind when trying to penetrate the locked doors of *The Condemned of Altona* (1959) is surely not *Nekrassov* (1955), its nearest neighbor chronologically, but *No Exit* (1944).

It seemed a better plan, therefore, to forgo chronological order in favor of one that springs from thematic continuity and technical similarities in the plays themselves. Sartre writes in his *Search for a Method:* "A life develops in spirals; it keeps passing by the same points but at different levels of integration and complexity." This statement finds a striking illustration in four of Sartre's major plays: *The Devil and the Good Lord* (1951) as it relates to *The Flies* (1943), and *The Condemned of Altona* as it relates to *No Exit.* In both cases, the later play goes back to the dominant theme of the earlier play, but at a more complex level. One of Sartre's fundamental aims as a playwright has been to forge dramatic action into myth. These two pairs of plays represent the two controlling myths in his theatre, dramatized with unequal success. Orestes and Goetz act out Sartre's myth of salvation; the three characters of *No Exit* and Franz in *The Condemned* give form to his myth of damnation.

Similarly, I have tried to group the remaining plays on the basis of intrinsic parallels. Both *The Victors* and *Dirty Hands* are plays in a realistic tradition; they dramatize different aspects of resistance movements. *The Respectful Prostitute, Nekrassov,* and *Kean* are comedies, principally about mystification. Nekrassov and Kean, mystifiers by profession, discover that they are in fact not *dupeurs* but dupes, manipulated by society, as Lizzie is in *The Respectful Prostitute,* into roles which do not permit them to exist as persons.

In all the plays it appears that Sartre, through his heroes, dramatizes his philosophy by recreating it in the form of acting. As he himself has put it:

Today, I think that philosophy is dramatic. It is no longer a question of contemplating the immobility of substances which are what they are, nor of finding rules for a succession of phenomena. It is a question of man—who is both an *agent* and an *actor*—who creates and plays his drama, living the contradiction of his situation to the point of breaking himself apart or solving his conflicts. A play (whether epic, like the work of Brecht, or dramatic) is today the most appropriate form to show man in *action*—that is, simply, man.[1]

I have relied extensively on Sartre's own writings, insofar as they elucidate what he is doing in the theatre. Very often, Sartre supplies effective arms both for and against himself; the trenchant perceptions of his nonfictional work—especially *Saint Genet,* his several volumes of *Situations* and, finally, *The Words*—serve to focus, more clearly than most outside commentary, the crucial problems of Sartre as a dramatist. At the same time, a close study of the plays reveals, perhaps more fully than any other single genre in which he writes, the moral and political complexities of Sartrean existentialism.

[1] Interview with Madeleine Chapsal, *Les Ecrivains en Personne,* p. 208.

PREFACE

Since this book is intended for an English-speaking audience, I have used translations whenever possible. Those that seemed to me inaccurate or misleading I have modified; they are indicated in the text by an asterisk (*). Titles given in their original French indicate works that, to my knowledge, have not been translated. Quotations from these works are, again, my own translations.

I should like to thank the many friends and scholars who have provided helpful suggestions and criticisms. I am grateful, first of all, to Mohamet Sahnoun for the conversations about Sartre that originally made me want to study his work. I am indebted to Professors Bédé, Roudiez, Shroder, Dodson, Keene, and especially to my adviser, the late Professor Justin O'Brien, of Columbia University. Alain Seznec and David Grossvogel of Cornell University also gave me their time and assistance. Special thanks are due my students at Cornell, whose questions and arguments offered me fresh insights and questions. A grant from the Fulbright Commission made possible a year of study in Paris, where I was able to interview Sartre, and where I had access to the theatre scrapbooks of the Collection Rondel at the Bibliothèque de l'Arsenal. (Quotations from articles in the Collection Rondel will be marked in the notes as [CR]). The Cornell Humanities Fund provided me with the financial support I needed to complete the project. Most of all I thank my husband, Dan, whose criticism and encouragement challenged me to what is best in this book.

Dorothy McCall

Contents

Introduction   1

CHAPTER ONE / ACTION AS SALVATION
The Flies   9
The Devil and the Good Lord   24

CHAPTER TWO / ACTION AND REALISM
The Victors   43
Dirty Hands   53

CHAPTER THREE / COMIC INTERLUDES
The Respectful Prostitute   79
Nekrassov   87
Kean   98

CHAPTER FOUR / ACTION AS DAMNATION
No Exit   110
The Condemned of Altona   127

Conclusion   152

*First Performances of the Plays
of Jean-Paul Sartre* 164

Notes 165

Selected Bibliography 179

Index 187

THE THEATRE OF JEAN-PAUL SARTRE

We can know everything about our attachments except their force, that is, their sincerity. Acts themselves cannot serve as a measuring-rod unless one has proved that they are not gestures, which is not always easy.

SARTRE, *The Words*

Introduction

S ARTRE has related the circumstances in which he wrote a play for the first time:

My first experience in the theatre was especially fortunate. When I was a prisoner in Germany in 1940, I wrote, staged, and acted in a Christmas play which, while pulling wool over the eyes of the German censor by means of simple symbols, was addressed to my fellow-prisoners. This drama, biblical in appearance only, was written and put on by a prisoner, was acted by prisoners, in scenery painted by prisoners; it was aimed exclusively at prisoners (so much so that I have never since then permitted it to be staged or even printed), and it addressed them of the subject of their concerns as prisoners. No doubt it was neither a good play nor well acted: the work of an amateur, the critics would say, a product of special circumstances. Nevertheless, on this occasion, as I addressed my comrades across the footlights, speaking to them of their state as prisoners, when I suddenly saw them so remarkably silent and attentive, I realized what theatre ought to be—a great collective, religious phenomenon.[1]

Simone de Beauvoir tells us that the apparent subject of that first play, *Bariona*, was the birth of Christ; actually, the dramatic action concerned the Roman occupation of Palestine.[2] With a Christmas story to appease the censors, Sartre was able to speak directly to his fellow prisoners, both Christians and nonbelievers, about resistance to their common enemy.

By 1940 Sartre had already published two of his best literary works: *Nausea* (1938) and the short stories collected under the title *The Wall* (1939). In addition to three other philosophical essays, he had almost completed *Being and Nothingness*, an ambitious phenomenological study that centers on the

1

problem of freedom. Yet, speaking many years later of his experience as a prisoner, he was able to say, "It was behind barbed wire that I understood what real freedom is." 3 The freedom in whose name Sartre first decided to write for the theatre was this "real freedom," a political rather than philosophical freedom, demanding acts in order to be realized. These two concepts of freedom are neither contradictory nor unrelated. Sartre has remarked: "One should not say that if man is free, his liberation no longer makes sense; on the contrary, this liberation would not be comprehensible if he were not free to begin with. Only a being free by essence can envisage freeing himself." 4 Sartre's experience that Christmas in a German prison camp, staging a play he had written for his fellow prisoners, was the occasion of a radical change both in his idea of freedom and in his idea of literature.

His beginnings as a playwright marked the emergence of his political commitment as well. Roquentin, completely detached from society, gives way to Orestes, who finds that his own liberation is intimately connected with the liberation of others. Drama became for Sartre his preferred means of expressing *une littérature engagée* committed to change both man's social condition and his conception of himself. A novel communicates with its readers as individuals, each in his solitude; a play in performance communicates directly with a group. During the war years, Sartre found in the theatre a way of speaking directly to an audience with whom he shared a common situation, the same anguish and the same hope.

Another aspect of theatre attracts Sartre: the need to make an immediate impression on the audience. In the theatre there is no possibility, as there is in a novel, to go back to certain scenes in order to understand them better. Sartre's plays abound in suspense, sudden reversals, and *coups de théâtre*. Contrasting the play and the novel, Sartre has noted:

A book recruits its public little by little. A play is necessarily 'theatrical' because the author knows he'll be applauded or whistled at
on the spot. It's like an examination with only one test, and no
re-exam. . . . A book can speak in hushed tones: drama and comedy have to raise their voices. Perhaps that's what interests
me about the theatre: this feat of skill or strength and this loud voice
and the risk of losing everything in one night.[5]

Theatre, then, is also a showdown—and Sartre clearly delights
in the game.

Since 1949, Sartre has ceased writing novels altogether. His
tetralogy *The Roads to Freedom* remains incomplete; it is
doubtful that the fourth tome, *La Dernière Chance*, will ever
appear in finished form.[6] He had wanted his tetralogy to end
on a positive note, with an account of the Resistance. Speaking
in 1959 of the Resistance, he explained his dilemma: "Then the
choice was easy—even if it later took a lot of strength and courage to keep to it. . . . I can't express the ambiguities of our
time in a novel set in 1943. And, on the other hand, this unfin-
ished work weighs on me: it's difficult for me to begin another
before I've finished this one." [7] There are more general reasons
as well. Robert Champigny has contrasted the novel and the
theatre as they relate to Sartre's purposes: "The novel stands
midway between the theatre and poetry. It mixes men and
things, dialogues and description. It is on the stage that the
interhuman aspect of morals can be revealed most clearly, for
the stage is a *huis clos*. On the stage, things are only props." [8] In
Sartre's novels, especially *Nausea* and *The Age of Reason*, the
natural world of substance dominates. His protagonists tend to
be more passive than heroic, exceptional only in their lucidity.
Bogged down in introspection, they are incapable of action.
Both Roquentin and Mathieu dissipate their energies in an
unsuccessful attempt to transcend—in thought—*le mou, le
douceâtre, le visqueux*, the incipient solidity which threatens
to overwhelm them.

Sartre's dramatic heroes attempt to transcend these obsessions by action. They are defined by change, usually in relation to one irrevocable act. Men change the world and are themselves changed by the act of changing it. If man has no nature, only a history, it makes sense to dramatize human conflicts in connection with the changing social realities upon which they depend. In the theatre, Sartre studies man as the inventor of acts that decide what he is. His plays present characters performing acts that redefine the meaning of both the actor and the action itself.

Against a static theatre of *caractères* with its image of man as eternally the same, Sartre's plays present the image of man as a being constantly in the process of becoming, because he is what he does. More than a half-century before Sartre's beginnings in the theatre, Strindberg, in his foreword to *Miss Julie*, voiced a similar opposition to *caractères* in the theatre:

In regard to the drawing of the characters, I have made my people somewhat "characterless" for the following reasons. In the course of time the word character has assumed manifold meanings. It must have originally signified the dominating trait of the soul complex, and this was confused with temperament. Later it became the middle-class term for the automaton, one whose nature had become fixed or who had adapted himself to a particular role in life. In fact a person who had ceased to grow was called a character, while one continuing to develop . . . was called characterless, in a derogatory sense, of course, because he was so hard to catch, classify, and keep track of. This middle-class conception of the immobility of the soul was transferred to the stage where the middle class has always ruled.[9]

Miss Julie and Jean evolve constantly in Strindberg's play. Their possibilities of character are expressed by their possibilities and ultimate realization of action. Not until the end of the last scene are they finally defined. Nor can we separate them from the transitional social conditions at a particular moment in history that make their relationship comprehensible.

For Sartre, to act is to change, to bring into being something that does not yet exist. What the Sartrean hero tries to bring into being is often himself. He is fascinated with the irremediable act, a choice that by committing him absolutely will paradoxically free him of his sense of weightlessness and make him into what he has done. At the same time, he tries to find in action a means of escaping from isolation by creating out of his act a magical bond between himself and other men.

What constitutes for Sartre genuine action? Serge Doubrovsky has attempted to define Sartre's position:

Only an act with a precise historical meaning becomes a genuine action, because it can be fully assumed by other people, thus ensuring a continuation of meaning beyond death and an actual transformation of the natural and human world. There can be survival through a common direction of projects. In Sartrean terms, our being-for-others, provided it is not used as a device to seek *individual* salvation (in which case we end up in a vicious circle, and the famous phrase in *No Exit*, "Hell is other people," becomes true), can alone escape the absurdity of death.[10]

In the plays, genuine action—action as a means of changing the world—becomes lost in a maze of reflections. With the exception of Hoederer, the acts performed by Sartre's dramatic heroes are first of all attempts to realize a certain desired image; that is, to become absolute objects for themselves and for others.

Sartre uses the ambiguity inherent in theatre—both real event and imaginary representation—as a dominating theme of his plays. Since for Sartre man is what he does, the crux of the typical Sartrean plot concerns the individual in an extreme situation, forced to make a choice of action which calls his whole existence into question. At the same time, since we are in the theatre, these acts are inevitably gestures, performed by actors for an audience. Sartre often dramatizes this ambiguity by means of protagonists who themselves are playing roles, assigned to them by real or imagined spectators. Iris Murdoch makes the important point that "Sartre is interested in man not so much as a 'rational' being but as a 'reflective' being: self-picturing, self-deceiving, and acutely aware of the regard of others." [11] His characters act in order to appropriate or to reject a particular image of themselves that they find in the eyes of others. As a result, they and their acts are constantly threatened with unreality, against which they chose to act in the first place.

The question of act or gesture appears as a *leitmotif* of *The Words*. Sartre modulates his theme by a constant reference to theatrical vocabulary:

I was a fake child . . . I could feel my acts changing into gestures. Play-acting robbed me of the world and of human beings. I saw only roles and props. . . . Worst of all, I suspected the adults of faking. . . . I was prepared to grant—if only I had been old enough to understand them—all the reactionary maxims that an old liberal taught me by his behavior: that Truth and Fable are one and the same, that one must feign passion in order to feel it, that human life is a ceremony. I had been convinced that we were created for the purpose of laughing at the act we put on for each other. I accepted the act, but I required that I be the main character. But when lightning struck and left me blasted, I realized that I had a "false major role," that though I had lines to speak and was often on stage, I had no scene "of my own," in short, that I was giving the grown-ups their cues.[12]

Much of the discussion about *The Words* has focused on the false notion that it contradicts Sartre's position on committed literature. Rather, *The Words*, pursuing the theme of gesture and act, makes explicit Sartre's questioning of literature as action, implicit in all his plays.

In a critique of bourgeois theatre given as a lecture at the Sorbonne in 1960, Sartre contended:

The theatre being an image, gestures are the image of action, and dramatic action is the action of characters. . . . Action, in the true sense of the word, is that of the character; there are no images in the theatre but the image of the act, and if one seeks the definition of theatre, one must ask what an act is, because the theatre can represent nothing but the act.[13]

This statement is crucial to an understanding of what Sartre is trying to do in the theatre. The word "gesture" as Sartre uses it means what an actor in the theatre does; an act becomes a gesture when it is committed not in order to accomplish a particular objective, but rather, in order to be seen and consecrated as image. The relation between an act and its image is central in Sartre's thought and finds its most appropriate projection on the stage. In this way, theatre represents for Sartre both a platform for social action and, at the same time, the place to play out his fascination with the sensational lie involved in dramatic performance.

The Flies

> I tell thee that man is tormented by no greater
> anxiety than to find someone quickly to whom he
> can hand over that gift of freedom with which the
> ill-fated creature is born.
>
> DOSTOEVSKY, *The Brothers Karamazov*

> Et par le pouvoir d'un mot
> Je recommence ma vie
> Je suis né pour te connaître
> Pour te nommer
>
> Liberté   ELUARD, *Poésie et Vérité*

IN HIS FIRST publicly performed play, *The Flies*, Sartre seeks
to transform the ancient myth of Orestes from a tragedy
of fatality into a tragedy of freedom. Although Orestes is presented as a free man at the very beginning of the play, the
meaning of his freedom changes entirely in the course of the
action. When he arrives in Argos, Orestes feels himself a
stranger, exiled from his past and from his city, defined by nothing but his tutor's "smiling skepticism." His relativism has
taught him "the infinite diversity of men's opinions"; his eman-
cipated mind has left him free from involvement, committed to
nothing. He celebrates his freedom with bitterness: "I'm free,
thank God. Ah! how free I am. And what a superb absence my
soul is"* (Act I). Like the intellectual Mathieu of *The Age of
Reason* and *The Reprieve*, his fear of losing his freedom has
prevented him from using it. As a consequence, he is detached
from others and hardly exists for himself.

9

It is after the ceremony of national repentance in Act II that a change takes place in Orestes. Unable to decide whether to leave or stay, disavowed by Electra who has no use for a *belle âme*, Orestes invokes Zeus for counsel. Jupiter, who has been following Orestes' movements since his arrival in Argos, is quick to answer.1 He utters a few words of magic gibberish and light blazes around a stone. The scene is central to an understanding of Sartre's idea of freedom in *The Flies*:

JUPITER [*aside*]: Ah, that's where I can help you, my friend. Abraxes, abraxes, tsou, tsou.
[*Light flashes out around the stone.*]
ELECTRA [*laughing*]: Splendid! It's raining miracles today! See what comes of being a pious young man and asking counsel of the gods! [*She is convulsed with laughter and can hardly get the words out.*] Oh, noble youth, Philebus, darling of the gods! "Show me a sign," you asked. "Show me a sign." Well, now you've had your sign—a blaze of light around that precious, sacred stone of theirs. So off you go to Corinth! Off you go!
ORESTES [*staring at the stone*]: So that is the Good. Be submissive, very still. Always say "Excuse me," and "Thank you." That's what's wanted. [*He stares at the stone in silence for some moments.*] The Good. Their Good. [*Another silence.*] Electra!
ELECTRA: Hurry up and go. Don't disappoint your fatherly old friend, who has bent down from Olympus to enlighten you. [*She stops abruptly, stupefied.*] What has come over you?
ORESTES [*slowly, in a changed voice*]: There is another way.*
(II, i)

Jupiter's Good is represented by a stone blazing with light. That surrounding light gives the stone a quality of divine revelation. In *The Reprieve* Sartre again uses the image of stone; it becomes a paradigm of the object: solid, complete within itself, no more or less than what it appears to be. Mathieu, standing on the Pont Neuf,

. . . reached out his hands and slid them slowly over the stone parapet, it was wrinkled and furrowed, like a petrified sponge, and still warm from the afternoon sun. There it lay, vast and massive, enclosing in itself the crushed silence, the compressed shadows that are the inside of objects. There it lay: a plenitude. He longed to clutch to that stone and melt into it, to fill himself with its opaqueness and repose. But it could not help him: it was outside, and forever.[2]

Man, always outside himself in time and space, lacks the plenitude of the stone. His consciousness exiles him from the natural world whose laws are not his own. If Good, like Jupiter's stone, is fullness of being, then whatever is, is right; value becomes identical with fact, what is and what should be can no longer be differentiated. In practical terms, Jupiter's sign tells Orestes: accept, submit. Do not try to change anything.

It is significant that the alias by which Orestes chose to be known in Argos was Philebus. In the Platonic dialogue, *Philebus,* Socrates leads his questioner to the revelation of the highest Good. The dialogue ends with Socrates' libations to the savior Zeus. As Robert Champigny points out, Sartre's Jupiter reveals the Good to Orestes in order to confirm him in the role of Philebus.[3] But, M. Champigny continues, the result is exactly contrary to his purpose. When Orestes asks, "But what was it—what was it that died just now?" Electra unwittingly answers as she calls to him, "Philebus—" (II, i).

What has happened at this moment in the play is a conversion in the character of Orestes. Sartre transforms what could be a gradual development into a sudden upheaval in which Orestes becomes radically different. In a strictly philosophical sense, the moment of conversion has no special importance. If man *is* free and not determined, he cannot be more or less free at any given moment. But from Sartre's point of view of character as an original choice of one's being, the phenomenon of conversion provides the most striking manifestation of man's freedom. Sartre describes such conversions in a single passage of *Being and Nothingness,* allowing himself a tone of excitement unique in that book:

One may recall the *instant* at which Gide's Philoctetes casts off his hate, his fundamental project, his reason for being, and his being. One may recall the *instant* when Raskolnikoff decides to give himself up. These extraordinary and marvelous instants when the prior project collapses into the past in the light of a new project which rises on its ruins and which as yet exists only in outline, in which humiliation, anguish, joy, hope are delicately blended, in which we let go in order to grasp and grasp in order to let go—these have often appeared to furnish the clearest and most moving image of our freedom.[4]

Sartre's plays, and especially *The Flies*, are generally considered to be vulgarizations of his previously elaborated philosophical positions. This assumption is misleading. *The Flies* is the first work in which Sartre presents what can be taken as an ethics of freedom. *Being and Nothingness* concerns not ethics but ontology, freedom not as value but as a structure of Being, that essential freedom which makes it possible and meaningful for man existentially to *make himself* free. In a footnote to the chapter of *Being and Nothingness*, "Concrete Relations with Others," Sartre indicates that his description of human reality does not exclude "the possibility of an ethics of deliverance and salvation." But, he continues, "this can be achieved only after a radical conversion." [5] Such a radical conversion takes place, as we have seen, in Act II of *The Flies*; it involves a complete transformation in Orestes' understanding and use of his freedom. In committing murder, Orestes overthrows the moral and religious laws established by Jupiter. He kills Aegistheus and Clytemnestra in the name of his own liberation and that of the people of Argos. He has discovered that there are no *a priori* values, and that he must therefore bear the anguish of full responsibility for inventing values by his acts. Against Jupiter, Orestes will reveal to the people of Argos their freedom, for "human life begins on the far side of despair" (Act III).

Clearly, Sartre intends Orestes to convey the idea that "existentialism is a humanism." The ethics of freedom embodied by Orestes involves a humanism that in certain historical situations must express itself in the form of violence. However, there is another aspect to Orestes which confuses his role as heroic liberator and points not to a dramatic richness in the character but to a confusion in Sartre's conception of him. Why does Orestes decide to leave Argos at the end of the play? Part of the reason is that Jupiter wants him to stay and to become ruler of Argos in place of the murdered Aegistheus. Here, as in committing the murder itself, Orestes' choice is defined in exact opposition to Jupiter's will. He says to the people of Argos: "I shall not sit on my victim's throne or take the scepter in my blood-stained hands. A god offered it to me, and I said no." On the other hand, he claims he has killed Aegistheus to liberate the people from their tyrant: "It was for your sake that I killed. For your sake" (Act III). Orestes has freed the people from Aegistheus, but nothing indicates that he has freed them from the slave mentality which made Aegistheus' tyranny possible. The crowd that shouts at Orestes: "Murderer! Butcher! Blasphemer! We'll tear you limb from limb" clearly does not claim Orestes' revolt against Jupiter as its own. By some mysterious logic, Orestes seems to believe that by liberating himself, he is also liberating "his" people. This hope is founded on what Francis Jeanson calls "a conception of the *prise de conscience* as an epidemic . . . contagion by example." 6

At no point after Orestes' conversion does he hesitate or recoil from his decision to murder Aegistheus and Clytemnestra. In his fascination with the dark destiny he knows will be his, he resembles more a romantic *force qui va*, gloriously doomed, than a *liberté en situation*. He acts, not with the fear and trembling of an individual who recognizes the risk inherent in every commitment, but with a kind of exalted joy. In his book *The Emotions*, Sartre describes "joy-emotion" (which he is careful to distinguish from "joy-feeling") as follows:

Joy is a magical behavior which tends by incantation to realize the possession of the desired object as instantaneous totality. . . . By means of [incantations] the object, which one could really possess only by prudent and, in spite of everything, difficult behavior, is possessed at one swoop symbolically.[7]

Of course freedom is not an object, a substance; this is precisely the problem.

The impression of Orestes' act as a possession of freedom through magic is reinforced by the special function of imagery of weight in *The Flies*. When Orestes first arrives in Argos he complains to his tutor of his weightlessness, his sense of walking "on air" (Act I); he envies "the dense passions of the living"* (II, i). Immediately following his conversion, he decides that his act will be "a very heavy crime"* (II, i). Through murder, the most irreparable form of action, Orestes hopes to give himself instantaneously the weight of reality that he has previously been unable to achieve. After killing Aegistheus and Clytemnestra he calls his crime a "precious load" (Act III) and says to Electra, "The heavier it is to carry, the better pleased I shall be; for that burden is my freedom" (II, ii). Orestes wants his crime magically to *be* his freedom, as if freedom were a substance which he could incorporate into himself and thus both embody and consecrate himself-as-freedom.

Orestes plays both an active and a passive role in the symbolic possession of his freedom. In stabbing Aegistheus and Clytemnestra to death, the new freedom he discovers is one which descends upon him: "I am free, Electra. Freedom has crashed down on me—like a thunderbolt" (II, ii). He expresses himself in similar language when he confronts Jupiter: "Suddenly, freedom crashed down on me and overcame me"* (Act III).[8] In an interview he gave to the French review *Théâtre Populaire* in 1955, Sartre himself criticizes this cataclysmic concept of freedom: ". . . the demystifying freedom which effective theatre must show us is essentially limited, defined. It cannot burst forth like an explosion." [9]

THREE YEARS after *Bariona, The Flies* attempted to establish
a community of thought and action with a much larger group
of prisoners: the French people. Both plays are *pièces de cir-
constance* written for a particular moment of history as ex-
hortations to resist oppression. When Sartre wrote *The Flies,*
the play had resonances that are lost to a spectator or reader
today. In 1943, the French were suffocating under Nazi occupation and the cult of *mea culpa* that Hitler's collaborators tried
systematically to instill in them.10 Sartre writes in *What Is
Literature?:*

> People of a same period and collectivity, who have lived through
> the same events, who have raised or avoided the same questions,
> have the same taste in their mouth; they have the same complicity,
> and there are the same corpses among them.11

This was especially true during the Occupation. The audience
of *The Flies* in 1943 was less interested in the philosophical
problems of the play than in its clear political meaning: satire
of the Vichy puppets and praise of the Resistance. Mme. Béatrix Dussane comments in her *Notes de théâtre:* "The name
of Sartre, like the name of Camus, drew a great many people
together, often through the simple solidarity of non-conformism.
. . . People arranged to meet at their plays as others had earlier
at the funerals of Armand Carrel or General Lamarque: they
knew how many they were by their applause." 12 The audience's conspiracy with *The Flies* gave extraordinary power to
certain lines, as for instance the confession Jupiter makes to
Aegistheus: "Once freedom has burst into a man's heart, the
gods are powerless against that man"* (II, ii). Sartre intends
Jupiter's words for those Frenchmen who believed Hitler *must*
be victorious and that therefore to bend to his will was to submit to necessity.

Within the context of the Occupation, *The Flies* can be read on one level as a kind of allegorical *pièce à clef* in which Aegistheus is the German invader, Clytemnestra the French collaborator, and Orestes the resistant. Jupiter stands for the "moral" commandments that the Nazis and their collaborators sought to impose on the French people as absolute law. Electra represents those who rebelled against the Vichy mentality but lacked the will to translate their rebellion into action.

While *The Flies* speaks specifically to the situation of the resistants during the Occupation, it is based on a myth consecrated by tradition. As Simone de Beauvoir remarks in *The Prime of Life*, Sartre needed a plot "both technically unobjectionable and transparent in its implications." [13] The Orestes myth filled both these requirements. Harry Slochower contends that Orestes' murder of Clytemnestra in *The Flies* is unmotivated; he remarks that in Aeschylus' play Orestes is motivated by obedience to Apollo, in O'Neill's by incest, and in Giraudoux's by Electra's fanaticism. There are no such compelling reasons for Sartre's Orestes to murder his mother. "The sole legitimacy for Orestes' murder is the tradition of the legend itself. That is, in this 'free' Existentialist act, Sartre's hero acts most like an unfree man, enslaved by the mere ritual of the old myth." [14]

Although it is true that for Sartre's Orestes—in contrast, one should add, to his Electra—the murder of Clytemnestra is not radically different from the murder of Aegistheus, it does not follow that Orestes is simply "enslaved by the mere ritual of the old myth." When we refer to the political context of the Occupation in which Sartre was writing, Orestes' murder of his mother becomes more comprehensible. By making the unrepentant matricide Orestes his hero, Sartre is clearly upholding those terrorists and saboteurs who killed not only German Nazis but also Nazi Frenchmen. [15]

It is not surprising, then, that Sartre reverses the classical motivation for Orestes' murder of Aegistheus and Clytemnestra. The Orestes of Aeschylus, Sophocles, and Euripides, however they differ in other respects, all murder in obedience to the god Apollo, who has commanded that they avenge the murder of Agamemnon. Sartre's Orestes never speaks of avenging his father's death. Rather than obey the gods, his primary purpose is to disobey them. Since Jupiter wants him not to interfere with the status quo, Orestes will defy him by the most extreme means possible, by the murder of his secular representative, Aegistheus, and Aegistheus' accomplice, Clytemnestra. His goal is to destroy the order that Jupiter has consecrated.

The actual killing of Aegistheus and Clytemnestra, foreordained by the legend's tradition, is of secondary importance in Sartre's play. Aegistheus, although warned by Jupiter of Orestes' intention, does not even try to defend himself when Orestes enters, challenges him, and then assassinates him. Since he is no more than an instrument of Jupiter, Aegistheus hardly counts as Orestes' antagonist. The central question in the plot of *The Flies* is not whether Orestes will murder Aegistheus but how he will bear his act: will he take full responsibility for it, or will he abdicate his responsibility and disavow what he has done? The real murder of Aegistheus and Clytemnestra is meaningful only because of the symbolic murder of Jupiter that follows it.

Jupiter and his image shadow Orestes from the outset of the play. The huge statue of Jupiter "god of flies and death," with "white eyes and blood-smeared cheeks" dominates the set of Act I and stands over the *persona* Jupiter as he explains to Orestes the history of Argos and tries to persuade him to leave the city. In Act II, Jupiter watches the ceremony of the dead and stops Electra with a convenient miracle—a rock rolls against the cavern entrance—when her dance and impassioned words threaten to let things get out of hand. Hidden, Jupiter observes Orestes' conversion and tries to prevent Aegistheus' murder.

Jupiter is both a terrible god and the parody of a terrible god. His power over nature is real and absolute but his power over man exists only insofar as men, through fear, will submit to him. Like Dostoyevsky's Grand Inquisitor, he rules by those three forces that by themselves can hold men captive: miracle, mystery, and authority. If Jupiter has succeeded in maintaining his tyranny over the people of Argos, it is not through omnipotence but through mystification. The awful mask of Jupiter's statue conceals nothing more than a cunning magician whose miracles are about as impressive as parlor tricks. What Jupiter reveals to Aegistheus prepares us for Orestes' final victory: "The painful secret of gods and kings: that men are free. Yes, Aegistheus they are free. But your subjects do not know it, and you do"* (II, ii).

Electra's revolt against Jupiter serves as a foil to that of Orestes. She plays her self-assigned role of tragic heroine with theatrical passion, but cannot make the leap from acting to action. Her invective against the statue of Jupiter and even her dance in defiance of Aegistheus remain gestures. In fact, she needs the enemies she claims to hate; it is their tyranny that makes her ceremony of rebellion possible. Although she dares to defy her enemies, she cannot bear to see them overthrown. Since she lives only for her dream of revenge, that dream must remain virtual, on the point of being realized. When Orestes actually kills Aegistheus and Clytemnestra, realizing her dream in fact, she loses her dream and her *raison d'être* with it. "Where now have I seen dead eyes like those?" (Act III), Orestes asks her. By the end of the play Electra has taken the place of the woman she wanted destroyed: she has become her mother's image.

In killing Aegistheus and defying Jupiter, Orestes breaks the corrupt moral order founded on their alliance. M. Champigny, usually one of the most acute of Sartre's critics, is mistaken, it would seem, when he contends that in *The Flies* it is Electra and not Orestes who illustrates the stage of revolt. "Since at the start," he says, "Orestes does not 'belong,' how could he be a rebel." 16 It is true that Orestes, unlike his sister, is a stranger in the city of Argos. But until his conversion he does "belong" to Jupiter. This is made clear by the fact that in his moment of crisis it is to Jupiter that he turns for help, imploring some sign which will show him right from wrong, with the clear intention of obeying Jupiter's will. In saying no, it is against Jupiter that his revolt asserts itself. While Electra disavows her revolt and submits to Jupiter once the crime is committed, Orestes vindicates his revolt, refusing Jupiter's demand that he repent for what he has done.

The showdown between Jupiter on the one hand and Orestes and Electra on the other climaxes both the plot and the argument of *The Flies*. Dramatically, it is the most effective scene of the play. An observation by Strindberg is precisely applicable to this scene in *The Flies*:

One who has had the job of reading plays which are submitted to a theatrical director soon observes that every play seems to have been written for the sake of a single scene, and that all the author's creative joy centered around this scene which sustained him during the terrible pains which exposition, presentation, entanglement, disentanglement, *peripeteia*, and catastrophe caused him.17

We know that something fundamental is at stake here: either Jupiter or Orestes, god or man, must emerge diminished.

Jupiter's confrontation with Orestes and Electra after the murder is presented as a contest in which Jupiter initially appears in the role of god the father-figure scolding his wayward children. With well-played pity he offers them rest and protection in exchange for a little repentance. If the scene is a metaphysical duel, as many critics have suggested, it is also a scene in which Jupiter tries to spellbind both Electra and Orestes. Electra, eager to hide from what she has done, succumbs with relief to Jupiter's suave coaxing; she accepts Jupiter's version of her crime, denying she ever willed it. For Orestes, Jupiter changes his technique from condescending pity to threat. Here Sartre uses the device of a microphone to enable Jupiter to inflate himself one last time into the terrible God of Creation. "You are not in your own home, intruder," says Jupiter to Orestes. But it is precisely because man is exiled from nature and outside its laws that his freedom is even conceivable. In claiming his act as his own and refusing to repent for it, Orestes makes Jupiter's power over nature irrelevant to him. When Orestes continues to defy Jupiter after the god's grandiloquent performance, Jupiter emerges "tired and dejected; he now speaks in his normal voice" (Act III). By his successful resistance to Jupiter's mystification, Orestes reduces his opponent to an equal, who can fail as well as triumph. Jupiter does not again appear on stage after this scene.

The role of Jupiter in the Occupation production of *The Flies* was played by Charles Dullin, who also directed the play; his interpretation, emphasizing the satiric aspect of the role, presented Jupiter as a kind of cunning Mephistopheles who tries to tempt Orestes and Electra to make a deal wth him.[18] Electra accepts because Jupiter has tricked her into believing his power is absolute. Orestes denies Jupiter's omnipotence and refuses any contract with him. Electra's conduct here is not different from that of many collaborators during the war who thought against Hitler and acted, in effect, for him. After the crime, Orestes repeatedly tells Electra that she resembles Clytemnestra. In one respect, the differences between them are more of degree than of kind. Sartre explains in his "Qu'est-ce qu'un collaborateur?" that many Frenchmen who collaborated during the war did so out of a false conception of realism. Accepting as fact that Hitler and Nazi philosophy would necessarily triumph, they concluded that they had to bow to what would be and approve it as what should be as well.19

Sartre also uses the character of Jupiter to attack those Pétainistes of the Catholic hierarchy who supported Vichy's line that France's defeat in 1940 was willed by God and justified by the sins of the French people. R.-M. Albérès complains that in *The Flies* the "political satire was unfortunately mingled with equal parts of religious satire." 20 Since Jupiter and Aegistheus are allies, this double satire would seem entirely justified. The two monarchs share a "terrible and divine" passion for order. Both are no more than their images: Aegistheus is the image of Jupiter who is the image of his own statue. Aegistheus, like Jupiter, depends for his power on rituals which makes his image fearful in the eyes of others.

Like the plague in Camus' novel of that name, Sartre's symbol of the flies evokes the oppressive atmosphere of the Occupation years. However, Camus' plague is a scourge of nature that represents an evil inherent in the universe: it suddenly erupts in the city of Oran in 1941, and disappears at the end of the novel in the same mysterious way. Sartre's flies have a more specifically political meaning. Jupiter has sent the flies to prey on the people of Argos after Aegistheus' murder of Agamemnon fifteen years before. They symbolize the cult of repentance Aegistheus has instituted to strengthen the "moral order" of his tyranny. After Orestes' crime, the flies grow into the Furies who fling themselves after Orestes when he leaves the city of Argos.21

In his essay "Paris sous l'Occupation," Sartre describes the surrender to shame and remorse which Vichy solicited from the French people:

The Occupation was not only the constant presence of the conquerors in our cities: it was also, on all the walls and in the newspapers, the filthy image that they wanted to give us of ourselves. The collaborators started by calling on our good faith. "We are

defeated," they said. "Let's show that we are good losers and recognize our faults." And right afterwards: "We should admit that
the Frenchman is light-headed, thoughtless, boastful, and selfish,
that he understands nothing about other countries, and that the
war found our country in complete decay." Humorous posters
ridiculed our last hopes.[22]

Aegistheus' ceremony of national repentance expresses in the
form of ritual a policy analogous to that of Vichy. With lucid
cynicism, Aegistheus plays upon the *mauvaise foi* of the people
of Argos who are only too eager to deceive themselves by any
means offered to them. To make the people forget that it is he
who killed Agamemnon, he convinces them that he is the
spokesman for the dead, seeing what they see when yearly they
rise from their graves to watch the living. Their terror of being
looked at prevents the people of Argos from seeing the man
Aegistheus who killed Agamemnon. Instead they see only the
image of Aegistheus' eyes looking down upon them and judging
them.

Throughout the play, Sartre does not hesitate to mingle
Greek mythology with Christian doctrine. As Pierre-Henri
Simon has observed, "Sartre's Orestes is exactly the Anti-Christ:
he who opposes to Christian redemption another kind of redemption, saving men because he frees them not from sin but
from the fear of sin—in short, because he relegates God to
nothingness." [23] Orestes' language after the conversion scene
leaves no doubt as to Sartre's intention in this respect:

ORESTES: Listen! All those people quaking with fear in their dark
    rooms, with their dear departed round them—supposing I take
    over all their crimes. Supposing I set out to win the name of
    "guilt-stealer," and house in myself all their remorse. . . .
ELECTRA: So you wish to atone for us?
ORESTES: To atone? No. I said I'd house your penitence, but I
    did *not* say what I'd do with all those cackling fowls; maybe
    I'll wring their necks.   (II, i)

In a sense *The Flies* is what Jacques Guicharnaud calls "a
sumptuous metaphor intended to show men that responsibility

is not synonymous with guilt." 24 By clinging to the official dogma of an original sinlike guilt that all share equally, the people of Argos evade their specific individual responsibility. Since they saw what Aegistheus and Clytemnestra were planning and chose to remain silent, secretly enjoying the thought of a spectacle of violence which would relieve their boredom, they are responsible as passive accomplices in the murder of Agamemnon. But it is Aegistheus and Clytemnestra who alone murdered Agamemnon and bear the responsibility for committing that act. Aegistheus' cult of *mea culpa* skillfully obscures these distinctions. Orestes says: "A crime that its doer disowns becomes ownerless—no man's crime; that's how you see it, isn't it? More like an accident than a crime" (Act III). In this context, Orestes' act of revolt must be a crime for which he assumes total responsibility.

Like Anouilh's Antigone, Orestes is symbol of refusal. When Creon tries to explain to Antigone the necessities of his position, she declares: "I am not here to understand. I am here to say no to you, and die." Orestes' act of murder and Antigone's chosen martyrdom do not attempt to go beyond negation to create a new order. The role of both is to express the anarchist's "no" to an order judged unacceptable. Antigone is one in a long line of Anouilh heroines who chooses to die rather than to compromise an ideal. Produced in 1944, *Antigone* was the most successful play of the Occupation years. In contrast to Sartre, however, Anouilh's intentions were not political. Sartre in *The Flies* is directly attacking Vichy's cult of remorse which was infecting the French people. Orestes' "no," therefore, can only be an act of violence against those who perpetrated that cult. Except for the Communists, the Resistance was a movement not of revolution but of revolt. It had no intention of taking power after the war; its single goal was to liberate France from the occupying Nazi forces.

In murdering Aegistheus and overthrowing the oppressive order established by Jupiter, Orestes dramatizes in its most extreme form the power of freedom against tyranny. Sartre wrote his first play as a call to revolt; the freedom which inspires that revolt is meant as a passionate imperative. *The Flies* remains indispensable to any understanding of what Sartre is about. Francis Jeanson is accurate when he says of this first public play that "Sartre's work in its entirety can be considered, without too much exaggeration, as commenting, criticizing and going beyond the conception of freedom proposed in *The Flies*." 25

The Devil and the Good Lord

Now, gods, stand up for bastards!
SHAKESPEARE, *King Lear*

Tout aventurier est né d'un mythomane.
MALRAUX, *La Voie royale*

The *Devil and the Good Lord* is Sartre's most ambitious play. Goetz, the central character, defines himself only in relation to the Divine; other men have no reality for him except as pawns in his contest with God. In *Saint Genet*—which closely parallels *The Devil and the Good Lord*—Sartre writes of Genet's characters:

[They] are not first defined by the relations they maintain with their fellows but by the place they occupy in Creation. Before being human and social, the persons and events have a religious dimension: they have dealings with the All. If Divine and Darling suddenly became conscious of themselves and their solitude, they could say, with the mystics, "God, the world and I." 26

Similarly, Goetz proclaims: "There is only God, the phantoms, and myself" (I, iii). Like Genet's characters, Goetz plays a role with God as his audience; like them he is a victim of his self-assigned role. In such a context "the world" and "phantoms" mean the same thing: both refer to an insubstantial appearance. Since the world is unreal, Goetz cannot *do* anything; even his crimes are not acts but rituals. God functions for him as a kind of supreme spectator; the look of God freezes him into an object and confirms the reality of his existence which he cannot feel from within himself.

In *The Reprieve*, Daniel's letter after his religious conversion involves this same kind of obsession:

God sees me, Mathieu; I feel it and I know it. . . . I know at last that I am. I adapt for my own use, and to your disgust, your prophet's foolish wicked words: "I think, therefore I am," which used to trouble me so sorely, for the more I thought, the less I seemed to be; and I say: "I am seen, therefore I am." I need no longer bear the responsibility of my turbid and disintegrating self: he who sees me causes me to be; I am as he sees me. . . . At last I am transmuted into myself. Hated, despised, sustained, a presence supports me to continue thus forever. I am infinite and infinitely guilty. But I *am*, Mathieu, I am.[27]

Daniel is a coward and a homosexual, Genet a homosexual and a thief; Goetz is illegitimate: "my mother gave herself to a no-account, and I am made of two halves which do not fit together" (I, ii). All three—Daniel, Goetz, and Genet—represent in extreme form what Jeanson calls "our common and original bastardy," the alienation between the self as we experience it from within and the self as it is seen and judged by others. All three are outside society, branded guilty by its laws. Like Genet, Goetz wills to become what the judgment of others has made of him; named a bastard and an evildoer, he transforms that condemnation into a free choice.

Goetz's revolt does not imply, however, an attempt to change the social order that makes him suffer. On the contrary, he needs to maintain that order intact so that he can continue to rebel against it. When Nasty, leader of the peasants, urges

Goetz to use his military abilities for the peasant cause, to take the city of Worms, give it to the poor, and raise a peasant army, Goetz is stupefied at the suggestion. He has no desire to make his destructiveness useful; his purpose is precisely to serve no one. In his limitless pride, he demands to be seen and judged not by other men, but by God alone: God is the only enemy he will recognize. He carries his choice of evil to its logical extreme, that of evil not as a means to accomplish any other end, but rather as an end in itself, a theological absolute. Since God represents the principle of good, Goetz chooses evil as the only role which will allow him to be unique, an opposition to God on His own terms. "The devil is pure because he wants only Evil," writes Jacques Maritain.28 Like that of Satan, Goetz's claim to be an "unalloyed monster," is a defiance of God; it is also an admission of his complete dependence on God for his own reality. In fact, Goetz is the ape of God, *simia dei;* his demonics need God's order of good as their first truth. Goetz destroys in order to be an object of pure evil in the eyes of the Lord; each crime is an incantatory dance which bestows upon him his sacred identity. His crimes are meaningless without the principle of God to make his evil metaphysical—the absolute evil of the Devil.

In the first scene between Goetz and Heinrich, each sees in the other his own image. Heinrich, too, is a bastard: "Hail, little brother! Welcome to bastardy! You, too, are a bastard. To engender you, the clergy coupled with Misery; what joyless fornication" (I, ii). Goetz does evil by choice; he betrays his brother Conrad because treason seems to him the highest form of evil: it demands an initiation into the secrets of its intended victim before the betrayal can be successful. Heinrich does evil out of his helplessness to do anything else. Belonging to two hostile worlds and loyal to both, Heinrich must betray one of them with every act he commits. The Bishop reviles him as a "priest apostate"; Nasty sees in him the most dangerous of all the priests. His life is a contradiction. As a priest whose interests, insofar as he is part of the temporal Church, are opposed to Nasty's heresies, Heinrich accepts the sufferings of the poor. As a man who lives with the poor, he is unable to justify their sufferings, although he needs to believe that all is good. Completely mystified, he takes refuge in Tertullian: "I believe because it is absurd!" (I, i).29 Picking up the Archbishop's key to the underground passage into Worms, Heinrich must choose whether or not to deliver that key to Goetz; he must choose between the lives of two hundred priests or twenty thousand men. In *Saint Genet* Sartre quotes the words of T. E. Lawrence: "And then madness was very near, as I believe it would be near the man who could see things through the veils at once of two customs, two educations, two environments." Sartre adds: "Such is the case of the traitor." 30 To escape from this madness, Heinrich invents a Devil in whom he only partially believes. The Devil dictates Heinrich's conduct and is responsible for what he does. His appearance in Heinrich's mind becomes increasingly frequent and more real as the play progresses. When Goetz wants to know if he resembles the Devil of Heinrich's vision, Heinrich mocks him: "You, my poor man? You are the jester" (I, ii).

Heinrich's impotence to do anything but evil challenges Goetz's uniqueness as the incarnation of evil, the single opponent of God's good. Genet writes of himself in *The Thief's Journal*: "[I thought] that the domains of Evil were less frequented than those of Good and that I would be alone there. . . . My taste for solitude incited me to seek out the most virgin lands." 31 Goetz is concerned with the same kind of aloneness, the same uniqueness. Frederick Lumley contends that "it seems singularly false that Goetz cannot succeed in evil." 32 True, Goetz succeeds with no difficulty whatever in betraying his allies and leading his troops to massacres. His failure lies elsewhere. If anyone can do evil, Goetz's posture before God loses its metaphysical privilege. Goetz's metamorphosis, then, is simple. Heinrich tells him that men are evil, that good is impossible on this earth. Therefore, Goetz decides to do good: "I was a criminal—I will reform. I turn my coat and wager I can be a saint" (I, iii). When Heinrich points out that Goetz loses in advance if he does good to win a bet, Goetz decides to gamble his conversion on a throw of dice so that God will bear full responsibility for the outcome: "I want to drive the Lord into a corner" (I, iii).33 If Goetz wins, he will burn down the entire city of Worms. If he loses, he will do God's will and choose good. Although he throws the dice with the prostitute Catherine, his real partner is God. But it is all an act; a few moments later we learn from Catherine that Goetz has cheated in order to lose.

Goetz's pact with Heinrich is not unlike Faust's pact with Mephistopheles. In Marlowe's *Doctor Faustus*, Mephistopheles first enters Faustus's chamber as a Devil, but Faustus demands:

> I charge thee to return and change thy shape;
> Thou art too ugly to attend on me.
> Go, and return an old Franciscan friar;
> That holy shape becomes a devil best.   (I, iii)

The false priest Heinrich tempts Goetz by an absolute good that, as we see in Act III, is merely another form of evil. As in *Doctor Faustus*, the Hell which Heinrich sees for Goetz is no different from this earth. Compare:

GOETZ: Ah yes, we still have Hell. Well, it will be a change.
HEINRICH: It won't be any change for you; you are there already.
          (III, x)

FAUSTUS: How comes it then that thou art out of hell?
MEPHISTOPHELES: Why this is hell, nor am I out of it!
          (I, iii)

The pact between Heinrich and Goetz, like that between the false friar Mephistopheles and Faustus, involves a fixed period of time, after which Goetz will be judged for what he has done: "I'll follow you, yes, I'll follow, step by step, night and day," Heinrich warns him. "You can rest assured that in a year and a day, wherever you may be, I shall meet you at the appointed time and place" (I, iii). During that time Goetz will be possessed by Heinrich and what Heinrich represents no less than Faustus was possessed by Mephistopheles.

Goetz's switch from evil to good involves no radical change; God remains the only partner he consents to recognize. Inverting his first role, he simply becomes the other half of the "eternal couple of the criminal and the saint." The change is possible because Goetz's evil is not presented as his nature, nor as a character which he passively accepts. Goetz does evil by choice; he plays the role of evil as a means of realizing himself as an absolute object. When this attempt proves itself a failure, he chooses good. His morality is still what Sartre has called "inhumanism"; he still puts the world in parentheses and refuses to recognize other people as real. His new humility is merely his former pride turned on its head. In giving his lands to the poor for the creation of a City of the Sun, Goetz wants to establish love at once, through magic. He rejects Nasty's plea that he keep his lands and use them as a meeting place from which the peasants can prepare their revolution. Goetz's concern is not for the effectiveness of his gift in helping the peasants, but for his own salvation: "Then what will become of me, if you take away my means of doing Good?" (II, iv).34

All his seeming actions, in good as in evil, are no more than gestures. For Sartre, the intimate substance of a gesture is the look of other people; it is that look which gives the gesture its reality. Sartre presents this idea in its most spectacular form in the stigmata scene of *The Devil and the Good Lord*. When God does not send a miracle to save the soul of the dying Catherine, haunted by demons, Goetz climbs into the altar of the church and inflicts upon himself the wounds of Christ.35 Having failed as a man, Goetz transforms himself into a holy object, to incarnate himself and to possess his audience. Since he has been unable to gain the love of the peasants in his own person, he will force their love through a false miracle, by appropriating symbolically the person of Christ. The fascination of the crowd makes Goetz's stolen symbol a sacrament. His successful performance gives him the power he needs to play the role of prophet and patron saint for his model community.

The genuine goodness of Hilda, who lives with the peasants and is loved and trusted by them, emphasizes Goetz's fraudulent saintliness. Hilda is, in Sartre's terms, "pure reciprocity": there is no charity in her love; she needs the peasants as much as they need her. Although she was rich and chose to give up her wealth, she does not now work for the peasants but, rather, with them. Their cause has become her cause. Maurice Cranston calls Hilda a "saintly Christian." [36] This is precisely what she is not. She is the only character in the play—until Goetz's conversion—who does not define herself in relation to God, whose passions and will are entirely of this world. For Hilda others are ends and not means; it is for this reason that she forbids Goetz to lead the peasants in battle when he asks her advice. Thus, it is she as well as Goetz who bears responsibility when the entire City of the Sun is massacred because the peasants refuse to fight.

The story of Goetz's City of the Sun functions as a kind of parable within the play, enforcing a clear moral lesson. For Sartre, as for Brecht in the *Good Woman of Setzuan*, traditional Christian virtue is ineffectual in a world governed by violence and social injustice. Goetz's utopian island of brotherhood can only mystify those who are supposed to profit from it. There is no way for the peasants to put into practice the universal love which is taught them as an abstract principle. The artificial happiness created by Goetz in his city isolates the peasants, blinds them to the realities of their situation, turns them away from socially meaningful action, and makes their ultimate destruction inevitable.

The action of the play reaches its climax in the final confrontation between Goetz and Heinrich. As in the scene between Orestes and Jupiter in *The Flies,* only one of the antagonists can emerge victorious from the struggle; the other must be irrevocably defeated. The confrontation between Goetz and Heinrich takes the form of a trial. A year and a day has passed: Goetz's time is up and Heinrich is there to judge him. Goetz is more than eager to begin the indictment against himself; he has already lost his trial in his own mind but needs Heinrich in order to externalize his guilt. When Heinrich, stupefied by Goetz's unexpected attitude, gropes for the accusations he has so often rehearsed, Goetz acts as his prompter and gives Heinrich the lines for his own indictment. Step by step they establish that God is indifferent to what Goetz does, that Goetz himself decided on evil and on good. But Goetz goes further than Heinrich will follow him. If God exists, reasons Goetz, man is nothing; if man exists, God is nothing. Goetz finally announces his conclusion: "Heinrich, I am going to tell you a colossal joke: God doesn't exist" (III, x). If what Goetz says is true, Heinrich can no longer find refuge in the certainty of God's damnation; he must confront the judgment of other men, his equals. Rather than face what he has spent his life trying not to see, Heinrich tries to strangle Goetz to death. Goetz wins the struggle and kills him.

When Orestes defiantly vindicates his murder of Aegistheus and Clytemnestra, he symbolically kills Jupiter as well. When Goetz stabs Heinrich, he kills at the same time the symbol of his possession by the absolute. In both plays freedom asserts itself as independence from a divine order. Goetz's partner was God; Heinrich's constant companion was the Devil. In the world of the play, this difference is not so great as it might appear: the Devil and the good Lord, like Genet's criminal and saint, are an eternal couple. Mr. Cranston claims that the main theme of *The Devil and the Good Lord* is "the conflict of Good and Evil." 37 But the fundamental relationship between them in this play is one of interdependence rather than conflict. Goetz's ultimate choice is not either God or the Devil, but either God and the Devil, or man. Goetz discovers that only with the destruction of both these absolute antagonists, God and the Devil, can he assume an active role in a real world. Killing Heinrich, the reductive mirror image of his servitude, Goetz kills himself—that part of himself which depended on an absolute to guarantee the reality of his own existence.

Sartre has insisted that it was not his purpose in writing *The Devil and the Good Lord* to demonstrate that God does not exist. He stopped believing in God when he was twelve years old, he has asserted, and "the problem of God interests me very little." 38 Robert Champigny makes the important point that "It is not the metaphysical problem of the existence of a divinity that concerns Sartre; it is the psychological and ethical implications of a hieratic way of thinking." 39 Sartre deals in this play not so much with God as with all absolutes—Good and Evil, God and the Devil, Heaven and Hell—as evasions from the finitude of existence.

Sartre intends *The Devil and the Good Lord* to be the story of a liberation. Jean Vilar, who played the part of Heinrich in the original production, said of *The Devil and the Good Lord:* "Jean-Paul Sartre has opened the 'huis-clos.' " 40 The play ends with a beginning. Goetz converts from theatrical role playing before God to authentic commitment, from gestures to be seen to acts to be done. Only after Goetz has asserted his autonomy does Hilda become real for him; he is then able to respond to her love: "You are myself. We shall be alone to-

gether" (III, xi). M. Champigny emphasizes the importance of
this formula in Sartre's thought:

Sartre stresses both solidarity and aloneness, for they imply each
other. It is through the subjectivity of others that our autonomous
subjectivity, our aloneness, is revealed to us. It is because Sartre
wants his philosophy to be a humanism, it is because he wants his
"myth" to be human—not animal, not divine—that he stresses
aloneness and solidarity, not communion.[41]

For Sartre freedom and solidarity are facts of human existence.
They are also the basis for judgments of value. It is in the individual's awareness of his freedom and his solidarity with other
men, in his will to assume responsibility for these facts and to
work toward their realization as practical realities, that moral
judgments are possible. In both *The Flies* and *The Devil and
the Good Lord* the hero's conversion involves precisely this kind
of awareness. "One becomes a revolutionary through an inner
revolution," Sartre writes.[42] Goetz's "inner revolution" is a
Sartrean form of the climactic recognition scene of classical
tragedy in which the tragic hero sees clearly the fatal flaw which
has led inevitably to his defeat.

Sartre, however, is more optimistic. Once Goetz recognizes the reasons for his failure, he is able to start again. Pierre
de Boisdeffre tells us that once God is dead for Goetz "everything is lost: Goetz reverts to his original nature." [43] First of
all, Goetz has no "original nature"; his evil was not a *caractère*
but a role. Second, Goetz's violence at the end of the play is
presented not as arbitrary destruction but as a necessary means
to achieve authentic ends. Earlier in the play Sartre shows,
through the character of Hilda, the failure in a political context
of Kant's ethic that men must always be treated as ends and not
as means. Sartre would accept Merleau-Ponty's judgment in
Humanisme et Terreur that

To treat one's fellow man as an end and not a means is a com-
mandment which is inapplicable in any concrete politics—even if

one has chosen as a supreme purpose the realization of a society
in which this law will become a reality. . . . Politics is by essence
immoral.[44]

Joan Dark, the little Salvation Army girl of Brecht's *Saint Joan
of the Stockyards* tries to relieve suffering by Christian kindness.
But in the hour of her death she comes to the conclusion:

> For only violence helps, where violence reigns
> And only men can help where there are men.   (XI)

This is exactly Goetz's conclusion at the end of *The Devil and
the Good Lord*. The morality of individual goodness—that of
Hilda, that of Joan Dark—is impotent as a means of changing
the world to make it more just. As Sartre writes in his introduction to Frantz Fanon's *The Wretched of the Earth*:

> Try to understand this at any rate: if violence began this very
> evening and if exploitation and oppression had never existed on
> the earth, perhaps the slogans of non-violence might end the
> quarrel. But if the whole regime, even your non-violent ideas, are
> conditioned by a thousand-year-old oppression, your passivity serves
> only to place you in the ranks of the oppressors.[45]

Nor can man depend on any divine order to right the wrongs of
the universe: he is alone with other men, fallible as he is. Joan
Dark is defeated at the end of the play; Goetz is allowed to use
what he has learned. Having overcome his obsession with the
absolute, he is able to take the place that has been waiting for
him as leader of the peasant army.

A t the end of *Being and Nothingness* (1943) Sartre an-
nounced that he would devote a forthcoming work to the
moral questions raised by his philosophy of freedom. This work
has still not appeared. In 1945 Sartre delivered a lecture to the
Club Maintenant which was later published as *Existentialism
and Humanism*. The lecture was intended as an answer to
Christian and Marxist critics of existentialism; it is hardly a sys-

tematic study of the problem of ethics. Sartre himself has since dismissed it as hastily written and inaccurate. Any remaining possibility that Sartre might still be thinking of an existentialist ethics was dispelled in 1960 with the publication of the first tome of his Marxist study, *Critique de la raison dialectique*. Sartre has been obsessed with "the moral problem" since 1940; yet he has abandoned definitively the project of resolving this question on the level of the individual.46 He gives an explanation of his position in a footnote to *Saint Genet:*

Any Ethic which does not explicitly profess that it is *impossible today* contributes to the bamboozling and alienation of men. The ethical "problem" arises from the fact that Ethics is *for us* inevitable and at the same time impossible. Action must give itself ethical norms in this climate of nontranscendable impossibility. It is from this outlook that, for example, we must view the problem of violence or that of the relationship between ends and means. To a mind that experienced this agony and that was at the same time forced to will and to decide, all high-minded rebellion, all outcries of refusal, all virtuous indignation would seem a kind of outworn rhetoric.47

As a philosopher, Sartre refuses to claim that he can transcend the moral contradictions of political action in some ideal synthesis where opposing moral exigencies resolve themselves.

What Sartre cannot do, his heroes can. Both Orestes and Goetz depend for their identity on the collectivity they have chosen to make their own, although they remain outside it. Conversely—and more spectacularly—the collectivity depends for its destiny upon them. Goethe's sixteenth-century outlaw hero, Goetz von Berlichingen, puts to rout single-handed an entire detachment of men. In other words, he is indispensable. So, too, are Sartre's heroes. Their practical freedom is unlimited: they act and are not acted upon. Only Orestes can free the people of Argos from the tyranny of Aegistheus; Goetz alone can successfully lead the peasants of Worms in the war against their oppressors. Once they have passed through a purifying conversion from which they emerge beyond the categories of good and evil, they see their tasks clearly: Orestes must kill the tyrant Aegistheus; Goetz must take his place as head of the army. The past and its unreality is washed away in purifying blood.

Notwithstanding the philosophical machinery of the two plays, Orestes' and Goetz's spectacular heroism recalls the childhood fantasies Sartre describes in *The Words:*

> I became a hero. I cast off my charms. It was no longer a matter of pleasing, but of impressing. . . . Sated with gestures and attitudes, I performed real acts in my reveries. I invented a difficult and mortal universe, that of Cri-Cri, of The Stunner, of Paul d'Ivoi. Instead of work and need, about which I knew nothing, I introduced danger. . . . I thrust [young ladies] into such great perils that nobody could have rescued them unless he were I. When the janissaries brandished their curved scimitars, a moan went through the desert and the rocks said to the sand: "Someone's missing here. It's Sartre." [48]

Unfortunately, the melodramatic heroics Sartre plays out in his two epic-scale plays lack the saving irony of *The Words.* To be sure, *The Devil and the Good Lord* is not simply a repeat performance of *The Flies.* A comparison of their respective dénouements affords a measure of the change in Sartre's political thinking between 1943 and 1951. Orestes gives a theatrical speech telling the people of Argos they are free—and then nobly departs; Goetz stays with the peasants and accepts the responsibility of being their leader.

But this choice is not altogether clear in its implications. Like Orestes, Goetz is meant to serve as an example. The audience is supposed to identify with him, to learn from his mistakes and from his final heroic decision. In *Force of Circumstance* Simone de Beauvoir tells us that Goetz is "the perfect embodiment of the man of action as Sartre conceived him." In the same passage about *The Devil and the Good Lord* Mme. de Beauvoir quotes an unpublished note of Sartre: " 'I made

Goetz do what I was unable to do.' " 49 These disclosures raise an obvious question. While Orestes' act in *The Flies* was clearly applicable to the Resistance, it is difficult to see how Goetz as "the man of action" is relevant to postwar France in any concrete way. As Elsa Triolet pointed out when the play first opened, there is little in common between the situation of the peasants in *The Devil and the Good Lord* and that of the French proletariat in 1951.

Both *The Flies* and *The Devil and the Good Lord* are dramas of huge dimensions, far removed in time, staged with elaborate sets and costumes, and involving large numbers of characters who represent an entire collectivity. *The Devil and the Good Lord* has eleven tableaux which cover a year and a day in time; in performance it lasts over four hours. We are told on the program that staging the play required 104 technicians, 10 different sets, 35 actors and 90 costumes. This spectacular aspect does not succeed in disguising the fact that, like *The Flies*, it is essentially a thesis play. Brecht's achievement in the drama has brilliantly demonstrated that didacticism, even in its most explicit form, does not necessarily lessen the dramatic effectiveness of a play. We have seen earlier that Brecht's message in *Saint Joan of the Stockyards* is similar to that in *The Devil and the Good Lord*. But Brecht's didacticism is fundamentally different from that of Sartre. Brecht intends to teach a lesson; it is part of his theory of what the drama ought to do. With that goal clearly established, he was able to create a new form which could function as a means of conveying his message in theatrical terms.

Sartre claims he has no such intention. During the rehearsals for *The Devil and the Good Lord* in Paris, he told a reporter: "When I write for the theatre, it's not to resolve a problem, it's to present it." 50 Nevertheless, the play as it stands does not only ask questions; it gives answers. Goetz is Evil; then

he undergoes a false conversion and is Good; then he undergoes
a true conversion from the morals of being to the morals of
doing and becomes a man among men. The play reads like a
kind of atheist allegory in which Goetz, tempted by God or
Being, lives in "sin" until he sees the truth, rejects all absolutes,
and is saved.

In spite of the horrors committed by Goetz, his worst acts
are transformed by their motive into ceremonial gestures, a per-
petual black mass to make God suffer: "God sees me, priest. He
knows I killed my brother and His heart bleeds" (I, ii). The
evil with which Sartre is concerned in this play has no relation
to the evil of which he has been able to speak so powerfully during and since the Occupation. It is a theological principle, by
definition impossible to realize. Sartre explains his concept of
"pure" evil in *Saint Genet:* "If he does not abhor Evil, if he
does it out of passion, then, as Genet himself says, Evil becomes
a Good. In actual fact, the person who *loves* blood and rape,
like the butcher of Hamburg, is a criminal lunatic but not a
true evildoer." [51] The only "true evildoer," then, is Satan; no
merely human creature is capable of pure evil. Even Faust, who
sells his soul to the Devil, does not do evil for its own sake: he
wants gold, women, power. It is because he is the Devil that
Satan, through Faust, can be evil.

In another sense, too, Goetz's evil does not count as real.
He pays no price for what he has done; his acts carry no consequences that limit his future possibilities. With Goetz's conversion, his past evil is erased. Sartre writes of such conversions in
The Words:

I subordinated the past to the present and the present to the
future; I transformed a quiet evolutionism into a revolutionary and
discontinuous catastrophism. A few years ago, someone pointed
out to me that the characters in my plays and novels make their
decisions abruptly and in a state of crisis, that, for example, in
The Flies, a moment is enough for Orestes to effect his conversion.

Of course! Because I create them in my own image; not as I am, no doubt, but as I wanted to be.[52]

Although Sartre speaks of "the characters in my plays," this kind of conversion actually occurs in only two of his plays: *The Flies* and *The Devil and the Good Lord*. These are his two spectacular plays; Orestes and Goetz are his two "heroic" heroes. In both cases, their conversions signify an absolute break with the past. Orestes' conversion, however, occurs early in the play. In *The Flies*, we know that Orestes was the product of his liberal education; "enlightened," but also rootless and without purpose. For Orestes, the past involves no clearly definable self—that is, in Sartre's terms, no irrevocable action. Consequently, the past does not count heavily in that play's dramatic economy. Just before Orestes' conversion, his self is so light as to be almost nonexistent. This is not true in *The Devil and the Good Lord*. Goetz's conversion occurs in Act III, scene x; at this point his past should carry a good deal of weight. Man *is*, for Sartre, to the extent that he *has done*. Goetz has done many things, all of them with disastrous outcome. But the crimes of Goetz-Evil and the catastrophic mistakes of Goetz-Good never have any weight in themselves; they are simply lessons for Goetz and for the audience. With each metamorphosis Goetz is able to start again *tabula rasa*.

In *Saint Genet*, published a year before *The Devil and the Good Lord*, Sartre analyzes Genet's successive metamorphoses from criminal, to esthete, to poet. A study of the two works shows striking resemblances between Goetz and Sartre's Genet. Simone de Beauvoir has enumerated some of the themes common to both works: "the same themes are to be found in both —Good, Evil, holiness, alienation, the demonic—and Goetz, like Genet, is a bastard, bastardy being a symbol of the vital contradiction Sartre had experienced between his bourgeois birth and his intellectual choice." [53] Like Goetz, Genet lives in a world of appearances in which all his acts are gestures, performed not to attain a particular objective, but to be seen by some absolute Other, whose look can sanctify what he *is* and at the same time make him real. As Sartre carefully emphasizes, Genet's decision to write does not magically annihilate Genet the criminal-saint, trapped in his obsessions.

"Genius," Sartre writes in his conclusion to *Saint Genet*, "is not a gift but the way out that one invents in desperate cases." 54 Genet invents a universe of words as his only means of harnessing obsessions that threaten to crush him. Such complexity is lacking in Goetz's transformation at the end of *The Devil and the Good Lord*. In his final encounter with Heinrich, Goetz suddenly realizes that all his buffoonery has been in vain, that he cannot *be* anything in the eyes of God because there is no God for him to be for. Sartre would have us believe that this discovery makes of Goetz a completely changed man. This is difficult to believe, even on the basis of Sartre's own theories. His analysis of Genet draws extensively from Freud as well as from Marx; the conditions that define the situation within which Genet makes his choices are psychological as well as social. Sartre emphasizes the continuity underlying even the most radical of Genet's transformations. There is no such continuity in Goetz's conversion. Except for his unique ability as "the finest captain in all Germany," Goetz's past does not even impinge upon his brand-new present.

Sartre intensifies our disbelief in Goetz's conversion by using language which never registers that conversion. For instance, Goetz (Good) says of the peasants: "The more they love me, the more I feel alone. I am their roof and I have no roof. I am their heaven and I have no heaven" (III, vii). Goetz (man among men) says to Nasty in the last speech of the play: "I shall make them hate me, because I know no other way of loving them. I shall give them orders, since I have no other way of obeying. I shall remain alone with this empty sky over my

head, since I have no other way of being among men" (III, xi).
Both speeches display the same grandiloquence and the same
repetition of abstract paradoxes. In *The Devil and the Good
Lord* Sartre fails to create a language capable of embodying his
hero's stated transformation. "There is no hero," Malraux has
written, "without an audience." 55 In spite of his speeches to
the contrary, Goetz's rhetoric indicates that he is still performing for an audience; he remains a hero in this sense even at the
end of the play.

The character in the *The Devil and the Good Lord* with
the potential stature for a genuine opposition to Goetz is Nasty.
Nasty is a militant entirely committed to the revolutionary
cause of the peasants. Unlike Goetz and Heinrich, he has no
self that interferes with what he decides he must do to attain
his ends; his personality is indistinguishable from his actions.
His interest in Goetz is a practical one: he cares only whether
Goetz can be useful to the peasant cause. Pierre-Henri Simon
sees the conflict between Nasty and Goetz as a central conflict
within Sartre himself:

[Nasty], exactly defined and opposed to the mystique of anarchy,
represents the method of the marxist-leninist revolution with its
rigorous discipline and its drive to remake the State. Between these
two ways Sartre continues to hesitate, and this game of back and
forth which he plays with the Communist party is the sign of a
secret and intimate contradiction between a nature which demands
the fullness of its autonomy, and an informed reason which cannot
ignore the fact that individualism does not suffice to emancipate
the individual.56

Nasty is the undisputed leader of the peasants; his voice speaks
with full authority for their cause. Without Goetz's support,
however, he seems to be powerless. Goetz has betrayed his own
brother Conrad and has chosen at three different times to op-
pose Nasty instead of fighting with him; Goetz's impostures are
responsible for the outbreak of open rebellion by the peasants
before they have a chance to win and for the death of the entire
City of the Sun because Goetz has taught them not to fight. In

spite of all this, Nasty continues to depend entirely on Goetz
for the success of his revolution. At the end of the play Goetz's
presence alone gives the peasants a chance to win their struggle.
"Speech," Elizabeth Bowen has written, "is what the characters
do to each other." Nasty's words never "do" anything; they
make not even a dent in Goetz's armor of illusion. Ideas in this
play do not arise from the confrontation of two wills in conflict; they exist as packaged goods compartmentalized within
each character.

Like *The Flies, The Devil and the Good Lord* can too easily be taken as a theatrical summary of Sartrean thought.[57] In
1943 the rebel Orestes kills Aegistheus, thus saying no to tyranny and at the same time destroying the alliance between god
and king. In 1951 the revolutionary Goetz, rejecting God and
all other absolutes, discovers his fellow man and takes command
of the peasant army. In both *The Flies* and *The Devil and the
Good Lord* the dénouement involves not only the hero's liberation, but also his salvation. Goetz at the end of the play is like
Faust saved instead of damned. Once he has seen the truth, he
is able to take back his pact with the Devil and the Good Lord.

Referring specifically to the ending of *The Devil and the
Good Lord,* Sartre asserted in 1964: "there is no existentialist
ethics; there are only valid choices." [58] This statement implies
that Goetz's final decision is one valid choice among others;
that as general of the peasant army he is serving a useful and
legitimate function. But the dramatic action of the play claims
much more. The entire play is waiting for Goetz. Nasty tells
him: "For a year and a day, your place has been waiting for you.
Take it. You shall command the army" (III, xi). Only Goetz,
it seems, can lead the peasants, can change the course of the
war, can give the revolution its chance. To paraphrase *The
Words:* Someone is missing here. It's Goetz.

The Victors

> Il était résolu à ne pas entendre les insultes, à sup-
> porter tout ce qui pourrait être supporté; l'important
> était de sortir de là, de reprendre la lutte. Pourtant,
> il ressentait jusqu'à l'envie de vomir l'humiliation
> que ressent tout homme devant un homme dont il
> dépend: impuissant contre cette immonde ombre à
> fouet—dépouillé de lui-même.
>
> MALRAUX, *La Condition humaine*

Although the theme of *The Victors* is heroism, the play
has no hero. There is no spectacular, exemplary individual
like Orestes in *The Flies* or Goetz in *The Devil and the Good
Lord*. Orestes and Goetz can rebel triumphantly against an oppressive order; they have the power to act, to change the world
in which they find themselves. The five Resistance fighters in
The Victors have no such power; things happen to them but
they cannot make things happen. Evil in this play is not a
metaphysical or theological idea as it is in *The Devil and the
Good Lord*. The emphasis is on an extreme situation: torture.
Sartre writes in *What Is Literature?*:

It is neither our fault nor our merit if we lived in a time when
torture was a daily fact. Chateaubriant, Oradour, the Rue des
Saussaies, Tulle, Dachau, and Auschwitz have all demonstrated to
us that Evil is not an appearance, that knowing its cause does not
dispel it. . . . Therefore, in spite of ourselves, we came to this
conclusion, which will seem shocking to lofty souls: Evil cannot be
redeemed.[1]

Simone de Beauvoir describes the state of mind in which Sartre
wrote *The Victors*: "He had thought a great deal about torture
for four whole years; alone, and among friends, we asked our-

43

selves: Am I sure I would not talk? How do you manage to hold on? All these thoughts that haunted him he threw into his play."*2

Each of Sartre's Resistance fighters in *The Victors* is an exploration of one possible answer to the question: If they tortured me, what would I do? The *maquisards* are trapped in a closed situation in which action is no longer available to them. There is only suffering; all they can choose is the meaning of that suffering. They are defined not as personalities but in relation to their ordeal: to the threat of torture and to torture itself. In this situation, the problem of freedom is posed in a radical form. Each man must choose the attitude with which he will confront his torturers. Even under torture he is free since he must *decide* the exact moment he can no longer stand the pain, and what he will do at that moment. Henri screams. Sorbier escapes from his torturers and kills himself. Canoris, the militant Communist, is able to bear the pain in silence.

Canoris is the most dedicated of the Resistance fighters, but not the most interesting. Like Brunet in the first two volumes of *The Roads to Freedom,* he has no self which creates conflicts and fears to encumber his decisions. What will be useful to the cause is all that counts for him; the rest has no importance. He fits precisely the portrait of the militant whom Sartre, in one of his best essays, opposes to the adventurer, to men like T. E. Lawrence and the heroes of Malraux:

[The militant] has neither depth nor secrets. Even the most humble complex is refused him: he is constituted in his own eyes by strictly objective facts; he is explained by his class, by his time. He sees himself from within as he is seen from without. . . . It is for convenience that he does not speak of himself in the third person.3

Canoris does not fear what he will do or say under torture; nor is he concerned about the private meaning of his ordeal. He does not have to question his motive in the killing of François;

it is entirely pure. When the torturers offer their victims life in return for information, Canoris is the only one who does not hesitate to appear a coward. The officers' look of triumph cannot touch him any more than their torture—nothing is relevant except the consequences of his decisions for the Resistance cause.

The intellectual Henri is the most Sartrean character of the play. Canoris's admonition to Henri sounds like Sartre speaking to Sartre: "You're too concerned with yourself, Henri; you want to redeem your life . . . Hell, what you need to do is work, and you'll be saving your life into the bargain" (Act IV). Henri must know *why* he will die and cannot accept Canoris's answers. Like Roquentin and Mathieu, he is preoccupied with meaning. He thinks of his life as an error and feels himself *de trop* in the world: "No, I'm not missed anywhere, I haven't left any vacancy. The subways are jammed, the restaurants are packed, heads are full to bursting with petty cares. I've slipped out of the world and it has remained full. Like an egg. So it must be that I was not indispensable" (Act I). When Jean is unexpectedly ushered into the attic, Henri greets him "almost joyfully." Before Jean's arrival his torture was simply horrible pain; now something is at stake—he can believe that his suffering and death will have a purpose. It is Henri who decides that François must die and kills him, with the consent of the others. Objectively, François's death is necessary for the Resistance cause. Subjectively, Henri's motives are suspect. If François lived and denounced Jean as their leader, Henri's suffering would again have become useless, his death would again fall into absurdity.

Sorbier's obsession is not with the meaning of his death but with pain. The response he will make to torture represents for him a definitive form of self-knowledge. He is aware that he has "the nerves of a virgin"; after his first session of torture he knows also that his will cannot overrule his body, that he will talk if he has something to say. He has failed his test and pronounces on himself the verdict of coward. The scene in which Sorbier leaps out of the window to his death proclaims his final victory over his torturers and over his self-verdict.

The greatest change of character occurs in Lucie. At the beginning of the play she concentrates all her energy on remembering Jean and their love. The fact that Jean is still alive and thinking of her is sufficient to make her own situation bearable. Before the session with the torturers she is able to promise him that whatever they do to her "You'll see nothing in my eyes but love" (Act I). The three officers rape her. When she returns to the attic unable to look at anyone, her love for Jean is dead. It had lived on the promise of the future; now her future holds only death. Lucie's tenderness cannot survive her passion to shame her tormentors. Jean, a "vivant," is now superfluous to her world, outside the close solidarity of the prisoners. The lovers no longer have anything in common.

Lucie's fifteen-year-old brother François is the weakest link of the chain. We know that the others were at least aware when they joined the Resistance that they might be tortured and killed. François merely followed his older sister and did what he was told to do for the movement. His panic at the torture that awaits him is like that of a trapped wild animal. Pride and principle are equally meaningless to him; he wants only to live. He does not care about betraying Jean as long as he himself can survive. In his eyes, any kind of life is better than none. As the play progresses, it becomes increasingly clear that François will talk under torture; he says so himself. If he talks, he will cause the death of their leader Jean and all his men. He must be killed to save sixty-one lives. On the other hand, he is only a boy who had no idea what his commitment to the Resistance might involve: he is innocent. His death is both necessary and absolutely unjust. The murder of François, like the failure of Hilda's nonviolence in *The Devil and the Good Lord*, contests Kant's categorical imperative, making of it an abstraction that cannot be realized in an extreme situation in which there can be a choice only between two great wrongs.

Each of the prisoners in *The Victors* acts as a foil to the others. The central conflict, however, is not among individuals but between groups: the five Resistance fighters against their Nazi torturers. The torturer's first aim is not to get information but to make his victim contemptible. A role has been assigned to the victim: that of a human animal, a bundle of terrified flesh. The torturer's pleasure is in forcing the victim to play that role, to surrender his dignity and freely identify himself with his tortured body. In this enterprise of humiliation, the torturer demands that his victim become his accomplice, that he designate himself, by his confession, as something less than a man. After Pellerin and Clochet have been unable to force Henri to speak, Landrieu says: "He'll have to talk. He's a coward, he must be a coward" (Act II). And after all have succeeded in remaining silent: "I tell you they will talk. They're animals, you just have to know how to handle them" (Act IV). Landrieu needs to believe in the baseness of his victims to blind himself to his own bestiality. It is for this reason that Sartre calls torture "one consciousness and another in a fight to the death." 4

Sartre called his introduction to Henri Alleg's account of his torture in the Algerian war "A Victory." Torture excludes the choice of being merely human; the victim who successfully resists his torturers, who refuses to become an abject traitor, must show a will and courage beyond what we can call human. Sartre writes:

But in the case of torture, that strange contest of will, the ends seem to be radically different: the torturer pits himself against the tortured for his "manhood" and the duel is fought as if it were not possible for both sides to belong to the human race. . . . He who gives way under questioning is not only forced to talk: a new status has been forced on him, that of a sub-man.* 5

For the victims as well as the torturers in *The Victors* the particular stake—that of the information to be given or withheld—fades into the background. Once the *maquisards* have undergone the torture, when they know what it is, no principle or cause still has meaning for them. Except for Canoris, the only Resistance fighter who does not change in the course of the action, they have only one purpose left: the frenzied will to triumph over their adversaries.

Michael Wreszin calls *The Victors* "a case study of the morality of heroism": "It deals with the motives and consequences of the heroic act, drawing the fine distinction between heroism and heroics—the former based upon 'authenticity' and objective reason arrived at subjectively; the latter based upon pride and fundamental insincerity or self-deception." 6 Certainly the initial refusal of Henri and Lucie to save their lives by sending the officers on a false mission is based solely on pride. Although they would only appear to betray, neither can bear the humiliation of seeing that flash of triumph in the eyes of their tormentors. But there is no "insincerity or self-deception" involved in that pride. Henri says to Jean earlier in the play: "The important thing is to win. . . . There are two teams: one wants to make the other talk. [*He laughs.*] It's ridiculous, but it's all we have left. If we talk, we lose everything. They have run up a few points because I screamed, but on the whole we're not in such a bad position" (Act III). Even their physical suffering is no longer as real as the contest, the necessity of winning this hideous game. Thus Lucie can say to Jean of her tormentors: "I feel nearer to them than to you" (Act III). In spite of Lucie's former love for him, Jean is now only a spectator; he is outside the game. It is with her torturers that Lucie must fight this game, and win or lose. When Sartre was writing

The Victors in 1945, he said in an interview: "I will try to show how heroism is total." 7 Heroism, the determination to overcome the enemy at any cost, becomes in the play a total entity of passion and will, from which any other feelings or attitudes must derive as secondary truths.

The ending of *The Victors* is comparable to that of Sartre's short story "The Wall," which takes place during the Spanish Civil War. Captured by Franco's soldiers, Pablo spends the night with other prisoners, each of them awaiting death. The next morning he is told that his life will be spared if he reveals the hiding place of his friend Ramon Gris:

I would rather die than give up Gris. Why? I didn't care about Ramon Gris any more. My friendship for him had died a little while before dawn at the same time as my love for Concha, at the same time as my desire to live. . . . I knew he was more useful than I to the cause of Spain but I thought to hell with Spain and anarchy; nothing was important. Yet I was there, I could save my skin and give up Gris and I refused to do it. I found that somehow comic; it was obstinacy. I thought, "I must be stubborn!" And a droll sort of gaiety spread over me.[8]

Sartre explores this "obstinacy"—the simple but all-powerful desire to get the better of the enemy—in both the play and the story. Pablo sends the officers on a wild-goose chase to the cemetery with the intention of saving Ramon Gris. Canoris, Henri, and Lucie send the officers on a wild-goose chase with the intention of saving their own lives. Neither intention is realized. By a grotesque coincidence, Gris is actually in the cemetery and is shot by the officers. Similarly, the Resistance fighters in *The Victors*, after reluctantly allowing themselves to appear cowardly so they can continue to serve the movement, are shot anyway. Joseph McMahon complains that the play is "cruel and uselessly rigid in its suggestion that the three *maquisards*, who in the end are duped, are thereby snatched from the sort of stalwart virtue they can legitimately lay claim to." 9 The suggestion is his, not Sartre's. The Resistance fighters are not deprived of any virtue, stalwart or otherwise, because they give a false confession and are killed nevertheless. The fact remains that they did not speak, that they won their battle.

Sartre himself has been hard on *The Victors*. In 1960 he said to an interviewer from *L'Express*: ". . . as for *The Victors*, I simply think that it is an unsuccessful play." 10 Sartre ignores in this play the idea of drama he proclaimed in his famous speech, "Forgers of Myth," in 1946: "Since it is their aim to forge myths, to project for the audience an enlarged and enhanced image of its own sufferings, our playwrights turn their backs on the constant preoccupation of the realists, which is to reduce as far as possible the distance which separates the spectator from the spectacle." 11 "Our playwrights" refers primarily to himself, Camus, and Anouilh; to the plays *The Flies*, *No Exit*, *Caligula*, *Cross Purposes*, and *Antigone*. In *The Victors*, Sartre rejects the mythical superstructure he used earlier in *The Flies* and, in a very different sense that will be discussed later, in *No Exit*. He allows his audience no distance in time or space that could mitigate the atrocity in his subject. Written early in 1946, the play dramatizes horrors which had ended little more than a year earlier. The subject of Sartre's other realistic play of the Resistance years, *Dirty Hands*, depends for its effect on the intimate daily relationship between its two main characters, Hugo and Hoederer. The play could not work if there were any distance between them and the spectator. We must not only observe their actions as witnesses, but also identify with them as participants in their experience.

What helps Sartre in *Dirty Hands* greatly hinders him in *The Victors*. As Philip Thody puts it, "The 'willing suspension of disbelief' on the part of the audience collapses at the sight of one man pretending to torture another." 12 The play is full of

scenes which so shock the senses that the mind is no longer able
to function meaningfully. Its first production in Paris at the
Theatre Antoine in 1946 created a scandal. At the sight of the
maquisards being tortured, spectators screamed; a few fainted.
M. Jean Gandrey-Rety may be right when he says that those
who protested most violently were "those who for four years
showed themselves much less sensitive to the real tortures en-
dured by the Resistance fighters." [13] But many of the critics
who were generally sympathetic to the play nevertheless re-
proached Sartre for its Grand Guignol aspects: the torture, the
screams of Henri and Sorbier, the slow strangulation of François. Sartre now seems to be aware of this problem. In his essay
on Lapoujade, "The Unprivileged Painter," he writes about
one of Lapoujade's paintings:

Attempts to depict acts of violence, mutilated corpses and living
bodies racked, tortured, and burned have been sterile. By falling
back upon visual conventions, artists have given us the troubling
imitation of reality and have conditioned us to react as we normally
would—with horror, anger, and especially with the dull sympathy
that makes every man experience the wounds of other men as so
many mouths opening in his own flesh. This unbearable spectacle
puts the spectator to flight. A painting may then evidence ingen-
ious composition, correct proportions and harmony, but everything
is wasted if the spectator flees and fails to return. And if he should
come back, punctured eyes and infected wounds—everything—
would disintegrate and beauty would never again be reconstituted.
Total failure.* [14]

The sensational aspect of *The Victors* is intensified by
Sartre's characterization of the Vichy Militia. He makes only
the most summary attempt to create differences among Pellerin,
Clochet, and Landrieu. Thirteen years later, Sartre was able to
penetrate the consciousness of a particular torturer, forcing us
to enter into his madness and his self-horror. We see Franz of
The Condemned of Altona not only as a monster but also as
both a half-willing accomplice and a victim of the system that

gave him the legal right to torture. The torturers of *The Victors*, however, are presented entirely from the outside, almost as caricatures. In Brecht's *A Man's a Man*, it is essential for Bloody Five to emerge as a kind of political cartoon; Brecht sees his characters as existing on different levels of reality and writes his plays on that principle, using masks and other devices. But a play like *The Victors* has no room for caricature.

In the same *L'Express* interview quoted earlier, Sartre concluded his comments on *The Victors* with the remark: "It would have been better to make it a novel or a film." [15] The play is better read than staged; it cannot take any visual realization. As has been indicated, in certain respects, it is too realistic; in others, it is not realistic enough. The prisoners are in close proximity to their torturers; their principal goal is silence. Both practically and psychologically one would expect whispered fragments of conversation, evasions, difficulty in verbalizing what has happened to them. Yet they analyze rationally each issue as it confronts them; nothing is said that brings in its wake all the significance of what has remained unsaid.

One has to agree with Sartre that *The Victors* is less than successful. It fails for several reasons: the unsuitability of torture on the stage, the sketchy characterization of the torturers, the victims' failure to behave in such a way that the dramatic illusion is maintained. Its legitimate achievement is its presentation of the contest between torturer and tortured and its study of the fanatic pride that is part of heroism.

Dirty Hands

El fin justifica los medios.　　　　　　　　LOYOLA

La tragédie, maintenant, c'est la politique.

NAPOLÉON

ON ITS simplest level, *Dirty Hands* is effective as an exciting suspense drama. Although we know from the outset that Hugo does indeed kill Hoederer, tension remains strong throughout the play; there is a revolver in almost every scene, either hidden or aimed at someone. In form *Dirty Hands* meets the criteria of the nineteenth-century well-made play: lively action, frequent surprises and *coups de théâtre,* a dark secret hidden from most of the characters (Hugo's intention to assassinate Hoederer), and a scene of misunderstanding with drastic consequences (Hugo's belief that Jessica has become Hoederer's mistress). With each confrontation between Hugo and Hoederer we ask ourselves: Is he going to kill him this time?

When the play begins, Hugo has just been released from prison after serving his term for the assassination of Hoederer. The leaders of the Proletarian Party, having decided that Hugo is potentially dangerous, are out to kill him. Hugo seeks refuge with Olga, who wins a delay of three hours to hear his story and decide whether he is "salvageable" for the Party. The first and last scenes take place in early 1945, a few months before the Liberation. The rest of the play flashes back two years to the time Hugo first undertook the "confidential mission" to assassinate Hoederer. Sartre does not try to maintain the action within the inevitably partial perspective of Hugo's narration. The flashback that makes up most of the play dramatizes the events —including the two private meetings of Hoederer and Jessica— leading up to Hoederer's assassination. When Hugo has finished his story, Olga is willing to judge him "salvageable" because he does not know why he committed his act. But Hugo, learning of the change in the Party line, in desperation opens the door to his assassins and lets them kill him.

The play's plot makes for good melodrama, but it is, in Sartre's words, "a false melodrama" and a false *pièce de Boulevard* in the well-made play tradition.16 The play does away with the first detective-story question: Who killed Hoederer? and gives no real answer to the second question: Why did he do it? When the play opened, Sartre told the press that "The words of Saint Just gave me the theme of *Dirty Hands:* 'No one governs innocently.' Starting from that, I put on stage the conflict of a young, idealistic bourgeois with political necessities." 17 "It is the question of ends and means which is presented in *Dirty Hands.*" 18

Sartre's treatment of his political theme has made this play the most controversial of his works. Produced in 1948, it was attacked by the Communists and applauded by the conservatives. Pol Gaillard, the drama critic of *Les Lettres Françaises,* wrote bitterly: "It's Sartre who has dirty hands." Both Jessica and Hugo, he continues, are "mouthpieces of the author . . . in other words, pure, deranged existentialists." 19 Pierre de Boisdeffre, on the other hand, has praised the play as "a luminous anti-communist demonstration." 20 When Sartre attended the 1954 International Peace Congress in Vienna, *Dirty Hands* was in dress rehearsal there. Sartre held a special press conference in which he protested that its performance would tend to sharpen the tension between East and West. The play was originally written, he contended, not to attack communism but in order to show the conflict between two Resistance groups.21 Since that time, Sartre has not allowed *Dirty Hands* to be produced "since it is used as a weapon against me." 22 The play's political label remains. In 1964, when Sartre refused the Nobel Prize and newspapers were publishing summaries of his philosophical and literary achievements, *Dirty Hands* was often referred to simply as Sartre's anti-communist play.

The play's political position is a good deal more complex and more ambivalent than the "anti-communist" epithet suggests. Speaking of Hoederer, both Hugo and the militant Louis declare more than once: "Objectively, he is a traitor." Sartre is clearly referring here to Stalin's doctrine that opposition is betrayal of the revolution. In such a system the state takes on a theological character, appointing truth to itself and relegating all opposition to error. Louis makes claim to the same kind of omniscience. Hoederer opposes his views; Hoederer is therefore by definition a traitor. Philip Thody is right when he says that "Hoederer is the type of man who, if lucky, becomes a Tito or a Gomulka, but if unlucky a Nagy or a Trotsky." 23

Simone de Beauvoir tells us that the subject of *Dirty Hands* was suggested to Sartre by the assassination of Trotsky.24 Knowing that the Stalinists were planning to kill him, Trotsky lived in a fortified villa in Mexico. Like Hoederer, Trotsky was not given to the intense suspicion that could be expected under the circumstances; he preferred to trust those around him. Trotsky was affectionately referred to by his guards as the Old Man; Slick and George, too, call Hoederer "le Vieux." Ramon Mercader, Trotsky's future assassin, managed to introduce himself into the Trotsky household and eventually became a familiar figure there.

Isaac Don Levine's book, *The Mind of an Assassin*, annalyzes in great detail the psychology and politics of the man who killed Trotsky. Like Hugo in Sartre's play, Mercader hated his bourgeois father and the values he represented. Yet they both dressed elegantly, to the point of fastidiousness. "A dressing gown," Hoederer says to Hugo, "you're well set up. You took it with you when you left your father?" (Act II). Mercader seems to have been absolutely dedicated to Stalin's purposes, although to Trotsky he presented himself as uncertain of his own political ideas. He would write articles and present them to Trotsky for criticism. Hugo is just as dedicated to his Stalinist mentor, Louis. Trotsky showed a desire to win over Mercader, to make him a disciple of his cause. Similarly, Hoederer tries to win over Hugo. Mr. Levine writes that after the assassination, in prison, Mercader was asked on a written test: Were you right or wrong to kill Trotsky? "Mercader became very nervous and wrote the answer with great indecision and many ink blots: 'Yes, since if I had waited and allowed myself to be convinced by him . . .'" [25] Mercader did not finish his sentence. It seems clear that he acted partly out of a fear of being won over to the cause he was assigned to fight. The same kind of fear causes Hugo to say to Jessica before the assassination: "He didn't convince me. . . . But if he had convinced me, that would be one more reason to kill him, because that would prove that he's capable of convincing others" (Act V).

Although it is clearly anti-Stalinist, *Dirty Hands* is not an anti-communist play. Sartre's sympathy with heretical or independent communists is obvious in many of his essays. In a piece entitled "Faux Savants ou Faux Lièvres," prefacing a book about Tito, Sartre welcomes Tito's break with the Kominform as a rebellion whose success calls into question the principle of infallibility at the basis of Stalinist rule.[26] Sartre writes in that essay: "Mallarmé slips to the bottom of the sea, defeated and triumphant, but the functionary of a popular republic cannot play loser wins. Success is the criterion for truth." [27] By that

standard Hoederer, like Tito and unlike Trotsky, is ultimately
proven right, since at the end of the play it is his policy that is
being followed, according to the exact terms he had set up.

Dirty Hands is set in a country called Illyria, whose political situation closely resembles that of Hungary in 1944. The
German troops have been losing more and more ground; World
War II is almost over. Within a year, the approaching Russian
army will be in Illyria. Three Illyrian parties are contending for
power: the Prince's Fascist government which has collaborated
with the Axis forces, Karsky's nationalist party which represents
the conservative and liberal bourgeoisie, and the Proletarian
party of Louis and Hoederer. Hoederer wants to divide power
with Karsky and the Prince after the Russians come; he calculates that, as an occupying force, the Russians will inevitably be
unpopular, and that therefore his Proletarian Party will be better off as a minority in the government. Louis's faction rejects
such a pact, judging it against the interests of the Party. Hugo,
Louis's young disciple, regards the pact with horror as a corrup-
tion of the Party's purity: "I abandoned my family and my class
the day I understood what oppression was. Under no circumstances will I compromise with it"* (Act II). Louis sends
Hugo on a mission to become Hoederer's secretary, gain his
confidence, and then find an opportunity to assassinate him.

Both the title and the structure of the play lead us to
expect a confrontation with the problem of means and ends.
Sartre chose his title from a speech by Hoederer which defines
the opposition between "clean hands" and "dirty hands":

How you cling to your purity, young man! How afraid you are to
soil your hands! All right, stay pure! What good will it do? Why
did you join us? Purity is an idea for a yogi or a monk. You intel-
lectuals and bourgeois anarchists use it as a pretext for doing nothing. To do nothing, to remain motionless, arms at your sides,
wearing kid gloves. Well, I have dirty hands. Right up to the el-

bows. I've plunged them in filth and blood. But what do you hope? Do you think you can govern innocently?   (Act V)

Hoederer, as a man of action, must depend on well-timed maneuvers and compromises. For Hugo, questions of effectiveness are not of primary importance; he has joined the Party in the name of a certain idea of justice and it is that idea alone that counts and that must triumph.

Hugo is supposed to represent, then, the purity of ends. But does he really? From his pedestal in the realm of absolutes, he sees Hoederer's pragmatic humanism as dirty and corrupt. His own idealism, however, is self-deception. Although he cannot accept Hoederer's willingness to "lie to his comrades" when necessary, the use of violence gives Hugo no qualms whatever. When Hoederer informs him that, should parleys be broken off, hundreds of thousands of men will lose their lives, Hugo answers: "You can't make a revolution with flowers. If there's no other way . . . HOEDERER: Then? HUGO: Why then, so much the worse!" Hugo loves Justice because he is incapable of loving human beings; their life or death, as far as he is concerned, is an irrelevant problem. He has joined the Party not to liberate other men, but to escape from his own freedom into a strict discipline that will rid him of his hated self. The attempt has failed; he is still condemned to think, to make choices. Hoederer says to him: "You don't want to change the world, you want to blow it up." Behind Hugo's purity is the desire for an apocalypse that will explode the world and himself with it. In this he resembles Electra in Giraudoux's nonpolitical play of that name. But Electra's apocalyptic dream is realized. After Aegistheus' conversion, when the Corinthians are attacking Argos, Aegistheus begs Electra—who is entirely in his power— to let him save the city before he surrenders himself to her justice. Electra refuses: "One has the right to save one's country only if one's hands are clean" (Act II). At the end of the play, when the city goes up in flames, an old woman asks: "What do you call it when the city is in ruins, sacked and pillaged, and yet morning comes, and there is a freshness in the air? When the city is in flames, when all is lost, when the innocent are killing each other, and yet over in a corner in the morning light the guilty are dying?" The beggar answers: "It is called dawn" (Act II).

Hugo, however, has neither the stature nor the authority of Giraudoux's Electra. In the stage direction for Hugo's first entrance, Sartre describes him not as a young man but as a "grand garçon de 23 ans" (I, i). Throughout the play he shows himself to be an insecure adolescent thrown into the adult world, confronted with problems he cannot yet handle. We have the impression that his ideas come less from studying Marxist ideology than from parroting what he thinks are the ideas of Louis and Olga. Although almost all critics of *Dirty Hands* have referred to Hugo as a Hamlet-like character, the comparison does not take us very far, in spite of Hugo's long drunken tirade—"To be or not to be, eh? You see what I mean"—the worst speech in the play. Hamlet intellectually dominates every contest; Hugo always comes out a loser. He is bested by all the other characters—by Louis and Olga, by Hoederer, by Slick and George—even by Jessica, who shows herself to be much more alert than her husband. Hugo is supposed to be lucid, but actually his lucidity operates only on his own inadequacies; he has little understanding of the events in which he wants to play a role.

As a psychological study (a problem that will be discussed later), Hugo is complex and interesting—one of the most fully realized characters in Sartre's plays. As spokesman for the moral position, however, he carries no weight at all. We are given psychological problems parading as legitimate moral dilemmas.

Hugo does not have clean hands; nor, contrary to the implication of the play's title, does Hoederer have dirty hands. For Hoederer, in contrast to both Hugo and Louis's way of thinking, "one man more or less in the world is something that counts." He is willing in principle to use violence if necessary and to lie if necessary, but only under one condition: he must be convinced that no alternative means of achieving his objectives is possible. In fact, within the dramatic action of the play, Hoederer's hands are quite clean. When he learns of the threat to his life, he does not have Hugo killed; he even refuses to have Hugo disarmed, in spite of Jessica's plea. Rather than humiliate Hugo, he chooses to risk his own life. Hoederer says he will lie when necessary (in wartime the soldiers cannot be allowed to know everything that is going on; and even in a proletarian socialist party, leaders have to lie from time to time). But never in the course of the play does Hoederer decide that he has to lie. In contrast to Louis, he is consistently honest and generous.

Pol Gaillard maintains that "this so-called Communist leader most resembles, in fact, Creon in Anouilh's *Antigone*." [28] The similarities, so frequently mentioned in critical commentary on the play, are both obvious and misleading. Hoederer and Creon are political leaders, men who have taken on the responsibilities and the compromises involved in political action. They have accepted life, while Hugo and Antigone have rejected it, preferring to die rather than corrupt their ideal of purity. Creon says to Antigone: "To say yes, you have to sweat and roll up your sleeves and plunge both hands into life up to the elbows. It is easy to say no, even if saying no means death." But the content of Creon's affirmation is entirely different from that of Hoederer. Creon's act, the edict forbidding that Polynice be buried, is committed solely in the name of order—that favorite word of all dictators. Nor does Creon's concept of order represent a means of achieving a more human life for his people; it is itself the supreme value, justifying both his edict and Antigone's death. Creon can refer to his people as "the brutes I govern." His thinking has nothing in common with Hoederer's humanism: "I love men for what they are. With all their filth and all their vices. I love their voices and their warm grasping hands, and their skin, the nudest skin of all, and their uneasy glances and the desperate struggle each has to pursue against anguish and against death" (Act V).

Part of the blame for the widespread misunderstanding of *Dirty Hands* lies with the many critics who have distorted Sartre's attitude toward his two main characters, Hugo and Hoederer. Sartre has said:

First of all, I wanted a certain number of young people of bourgeois background who have been my students or my friends and who are now twenty-five years old to recognize something of themselves in the hesitations of Hugo. Hugo has never been for me a likable character. . . . Only Hoederer's attitude seems to me healthy.[29]

There is nothing in the play that contradicts these words. Sartre clearly understands Hugo; it is Hoederer he respects.

This statement does not, however, solve the problems posed by the conflict of ideas central to the play's theme. To compare *Dirty Hands* with Sartre's scenario *In the Mesh* is to see how strikingly inappropriate Hugo and Hoederer are for the positions they are supposed to represent. In his scenario, Sartre weighs about equally the arguments of Jean Aguerra, the revolutionary tyrant, and those of his friend and opponent, Lucien Drelitsch. Both are men of dedication, fully committed to the socialist cause. Aguerra, on trial as a dictator who has betrayed his people, slowly emerges through flashbacks as a tortured man, forced into a politics of violence as the only means of saving the revolution. The journalist Lucien, on the other hand, condemns Aguerra's oppression and violence, believing that no end can justify such means, that he must keep "clean hands."

Lucien's hands, unlike Hugo's, are genuinely clean; he acts with courage for his ideas and finally dies for them. Simone de Beauvoir remarks that *Dirty Hands* dramatizes "the confrontation of morality and praxis." [30] But this is not borne out by the play. Hugo, the character speaking for morality, is an adolescent with personal problems; Hoederer, the character who represents praxis, never has to make any drastic or questionable compromise.

Sartre has objected vehemently to the characterization of *Dirty Hands* as an anti-communist play, pointing out that Hoederer, after all, is a Communist. However, political power is finally held not by Hoederer but by Louis, a far less attractive character. Toward Hugo, Louis's attitude is dishonest and contemptuous; the image he has given Hugo of the Party has little in common with its reality. Louis's haste in wanting to get rid of his young disciple at the very beginning of the play, before Olga has even heard his story, cannot be called solely political in motivation. As Olga says, Louis has always been "prejudiced against [Hugo]." At no point does Louis try to find out if Hugo is "salvageable"; he prefers to solve the problem by shooting it out of existence. Hoederer tells Hugo that Louis and his group "belong to my tribe," but the play's plot does not bear this out, except on the simplest level—that of Hoederer and Louis's realism against Hugo's so-called idealism. It is significant that we never see Hoederer and Louis in actual confrontation. Louis does not present any concrete alternative to Hoederer's policy. It is almost the end of the war; the Allies are clearly winning. Meanwhile, is it better to make a pact with the enemies (who are no longer in a position to exert harm), or to sacrifice 100,000 lives? The question seems rhetorical, especially since we are not told what Louis feels could be the deleterious consequences of Hoederer's decision. Louis's only criterion appears to be that of strict adherence to the U.S.S.R. Party line—which he does not know at the time of his decision to have Hoederer assassinated.

Does the end justify the means? Hoederer's means consist of a seeming compromise which in fact compromises nothing. When the problem of means and ends is applied in a practical situation, the means will be justified or condemned according to the kind of end they serve. Hoederer's end is to save 100,000 lives; Louis's end, beyond that of maintaining his own personal power by bending to what he thinks will be Party policy, is not made clear. As a result, his decision to have Hoederer assassinated becomes entirely unjustifiable. Hoederer's statement to Hugo, "In principle, I have no objection to political assassination" (Act IV), implies that political assassination may be a regrettable but necessary means for achieving the revolutionary aim. In order to create sympathy for the Party, Sartre would have had to convince us that the elimination of Hoederer was such a necessity. He does not do this. Whatever Louis's intention may have been, the events prove him absolutely wrong. His decision was worse than a crime: it was a mistake.

Sartre writes in *The Ghost of Stalin:* "It does not matter what a government believes it is doing; what does matter is what it is in fact doing." [31] No matter what Louis thinks he is doing, what he does in fact—through Hugo—is kill the man who has been revealed to us as both generous and supremely able to lead. Francis Jeanson writes that "the main point of the drama lies in the gap between the conflict which opposes Hoederer to his adversaries of proletarian origin and that which opposes him to Hugo." Significantly, however, M. Jeanson does not examine closely the conflict that opposes Hoederer to Louis, although he discusses the conflict between Hoederer and Hugo at great length. He comments only that ". . . Hugo, thinking he is in accord with those who send him to kill Hoederer, finds himself in reality all alone, facing adversaries who continue to

agree on the essential and separate only on a point of tactics." 32 In an ideological essay, it could perhaps suffice to call
the differences between Hoederer and Louis "a point of tactics";
in a play like *Dirty Hands* which depends for its effect on close-
ups, on a sense of the personal reality of its characters, their
differences become not just tactical but essential. Sartre may
consider it his political duty to minimize his profound distrust
of men like Louis, but he is not able to make that duty a
dramatic truth in his play.

In its political theme, *Dirty Hands* is not ambiguous; it is
confused. Hoederer's hands are not dirty and Hugo's hands are
not clean. Nor are Louis and Hoederer "of the same tribe," in
spite of what Sartre would have us believe. Any fair interpretation of the play must confirm as dramatic fact Sartre's intention
(as stated by Simone de Beauvoir and Francis Jeanson) that
Hugo, even in his apparently noble suicide, fails radically to
redeem himself. But the political tragedy—and condemnation
—implicit in *Dirty Hands* lies not in the death and failure of
Hugo, but in the murder of Hoederer.

THE REAL interest of *Dirty Hands* lies in the delineation
of its three main characters: Hugo, Jessica, and Hoederer. None
of them is reducible to an idea; in spite of the social issues
involved, they communicate an immediacy and concreteness
which makes us experience them also as private persons, a rare
phenomenon in Sartre's plays. Sartre's portrait of Hugo, especially, involves an intimacy of understanding which Sartre does
not usually give to his dramatic creations. He reveals Hugo from
within, Hugo as he is for himself, with all the hesitations and
blurs that such a portrait involves. As with Lucien in "Childhood of a Leader," Hugo's childhood is always part of his
present; his actions, unlike those of Orestes and Goetz, convey a

density of experience in time. Hugo's wife Jessica, usually ignored or dismissed by critics, shows the kind of believable unpredictability of intelligence and emotion that makes Ivich a fascinating character in *The Roads to Freedom*. Hoederer, although an entirely admirable character, is neither stiff nor unconvincing. It is the three-way relationship between Hugo, Hoederer, and Jessica which finally makes the play interesting.

Many critics have felt that Sartre identifies with the bourgeois intellectual Hugo, that Hugo expresses Sartre's own hesitations and conflicts in regard to political action. Like Sartre, Hugo finds himself caught between two worlds, unable to belong to either one; he has rejected the bourgeois values of his origin, but his intellectual choice does not make him a member of the proletariat. Although Hugo wants to think of his struggle as a class struggle, his new brothers will not accept him as one of them. Slick and George, Hoederer's guards, instinctively distrust their new "comrade"; his convictions are only in his head and not in his stomach—he has never known what it means to be hungry. Hugo is intensely vulnerable to their dislike and confirms their observations:

For once you're right, my friend. I don't know what appetite is. If you could have seen the tonics they gave me as a kid; I always left half—what a waste! Then they opened my mouth and told me: "One spoonful for Papa, one spoonful for Mamma, one spoonful for Aunt Anna." . . . I have never been hungry. Never! Never! Never! Now perhaps you can tell me what I can do to make you stop throwing it up to me.[33]   (Act III)

In *The Words* Sartre evokes a similar childhood experience of his own with an irony that does not belie Hugo's despair:

Meals, sleep, and precautions against bad weather are the high points and chief obligations of a completely ceremonious life. I eat in public, like a king: if I eat *well*, I am congratulated; my grandmother herself cries out: "What a good boy to be hungry!"[34]

Sartre clearly sees in Hugo something of himself. Hugo's intense shame at his privileged condition in the midst of poverty and oppression goes far in explaining Sartre's own political radicalism. Sartre, too, spoiled and fussed over as a child, grew to hate the solemn rituals of which he was the center.

But these similarities can be misleading, especially when they are used by critics—as has often been the case—to convince us that Hugo represents for Sartre an exemplary hero. Sartre writes in *Saint Genet:* "What is important is not what people make of us but what we ourselves make of what they have made of us." 35 Coming from a bourgeois childhood, Sartre chooses to write committed literature; Hugo chooses "red gloves." Lucien Fleurier, the little fascist-to-be of "The Childhood of a Leader" represents another possible result of the same background.36

In Hugo, Sartre explores many of the themes he deals with less successfully in Orestes and Goetz; Hugo stands as Sartre's modern, humanized version of his two mythical heroes. Like them Hugo finds himself isolated, belonging to no collectivity he can experience as "we" instead of "they" and, as a result, suffers from a constant feeling of unreality. Orestes, although born in Argos, walks "on air," a stranger to his own city; Goetz, half-noble and half-peasant, must turn to God for a confirmation of his identity; Hugo, made up of two selves that do not fit together, frantically seeks in the Communist Party a certainty that will tell him who he is. In common with his larger, more heroic counterparts, Hugo is primarily concerned not with practical consequences, but with a justification for his existence: the salvation of his soul. All three characters need to be seen in order to be sure they exist: Orestes by the people of Argos, Hugo by his comrades in the Party, Goetz by God. They act not for ends, but for spectators. For this reason, the most extreme and irrevocable form of action—murder—becomes their chosen means of acceding to reality, of forcing "them," Sartre's *Autrui*, to take their presence into account. Francis Jeanson writes on this subject: "What Orestes and Hugo aim for, like what Mathieu aims for from the top of his church steeple, is not a particular concrete result in the world but a consecration of his own being in a baptism of blood." 37

A childhood fantasy Sartre recounts in *The Words* gives a perfect image of the central problem of his protagonists, especially Hugo:

> I had sneaked on to the train and had fallen asleep, and when the ticket-collector shook me and asked for my ticket, I had to admit that I had none. Nor did I have the money with which to pay my fare on the spot. I began by pleading guilty. . . . Far from challenging the authority of the ticket-collector, I loudly proclaimed my respect for his functions and complied in advance with his decision. At that extreme degree of humility, the only way I could save myself was by reversing the situation: I therefore revealed that I had to be in Dijon for important and secret reasons, reasons that concerned France and perhaps all mankind. If things were viewed in this new light, it would be apparent that no one in the entire train had as much right as I to occupy a seat. . . . I never knew whether I won my case. The ticket-collector remained silent. I repeated my arguments. So long as I spoke, I was sure he wouldn't make me get off. We remained face to face, one mute and the other inexhaustible, in the train that was taking us to Dijon.[38]

Finding himself without a ticket, Hugo turns to make-believe, playing a heroic role he hopes will eventually replace his own insignificance and give him a place in the train. He takes on the pseudonym Raskolnikov, in order to give himself and his fantasies a dimension of mythical truth. Orestes and Goetz, through their conversion and the "baptism of blood" that accompanies it, finally win their case with the ticket collectors. Hugo never does, even after his assassination of Hoederer; the ticket collectors remain always with him, always asking their question.

Dirty Hands is so constructed that Hugo is revealed to us through the eyes of each of the other characters in turn. Hugo's obsession with his image makes this technique particularly effective. He is constantly looking for himself in the eyes of others, listening to the sound of his words when he speaks. With each relationship, Sartre studies not only a different character but also a specific aspect of Hugo as it reveals itself in his confrontations with that character. It is his adored mentor, Louis, who judges Hugo most harshly: "Salvageable? He is an undisciplined anarchist, an intellectual who thought only of striking an attractive pose, a bourgeois . . ." (Act I). Louis is incapable of thinking in other than categorical terms; nor does he have any sense of what it might be like for someone living those categories. When Hugo hesitates too long in carrying out his assignment to kill, Louis immediately brands him a traitor, as he has already branded Hoederer. Yet Hugo originally takes on his "confidential mission" to gain the confidence of Louis in particular, as if Louis somehow incarnated that great body of mankind from which Hugo seeks recognition. He says to Louis: "Olga and you taught me all I know. I owe everything to you. To me, you are the Party" (Act II).

Olga, although a Communist militant who thinks in much the same way as Louis, sees Hugo differently because of her "weakness" for him, the only personal sentiment she does not completely succeed in repressing. Olga is quite aware that in Party terms, Louis's summary of Hugo is accurate; subjectively, however, she cares about Hugo and wants to believe in him. But she remains first of all a militant. When she throws the grenade into Hoederer's office, she does not know that Hugo is there—but she does know he might be there. When Hugo was in prison and the Party sent him a package of poisoned chocolate, she did nothing to stop them. Hugo admires in Olga's discipline a perfect oneness with what he thinks is Party principle: "I do like you, Olga. You are just as you always were. So pure, so clear. It was you who taught me purity" (Act VII). Hugo is not wrong about Olga's purity, although he mistakes its meaning. It is the purity of *l'esprit de sérieux*, that quality which separates both Louis and Olga from Hoederer.39

Hugo's wife Jessica is a striking contrast to Olga, the *femme de tête*. This does not mean that Jessica is stupid, although she is usually dismissed as exactly that. Raymond Dellevaux's description of Jessica is typical in this regard: "a sparrow-brained hussy who understands nothing of the complexities of her husband." 40 But it is this little sparrow-brain who comes through in moments of crisis when her intellectual husband has lost control. At numerous points throughout the play she succeeds in covering Hugo's blunders without losing her head. When Slick and George's irritation with Hugo's refusal to let them search his room threatens to get out of hand, Jessica quietly solves the problem by suggesting that they call Hoederer. The room is searched, but nothing is found—because Jessica has had enough presence of mind to hide the revolver in her dress. After Olga's grenade explodes, and Hugo, drunk with liquor and humiliation, starts telling all to Slick and George, Jessica calmly announces that Hugo is going to be a father and is trying to adjust to that fact. Nor is it true, as M. Dellevaux maintains, that Jessica does not understand her husband's "complexities." The problem is that she shares them.

When Hugo and Jessica are alone together, *Dirty Hands* changes from the serious drama of Hugo's confrontations with Olga and Louis to comedy. The word "playing" occurs over twenty times. "Are we playing or not?" Hugo asks Jessica, and Jessica asks Hugo. Since they cannot love each other as man and woman, they regress to children acting out exciting adventures, escaping their sexual and emotional inadequacies through fantasy. They live in complete familiarity, but without mutual respect. To Hoederer Jessica says of Hugo: "He's my little brother (Act IV). She knows Hugo because she knows herself. They are orphans, too needful and too much alike to have anything to give to each other. Jessica resembles a petulant child, constantly bored and looking for some distraction that will amuse her. Her *bovarysme* is comic. When Hugo tells her that he, too, will be assassinated, like all political men, she proclaims that if that happened, "I would track down your assassins one by one, then I would make them burn with love for me, and when they began to think that they could console my haughty, despairing grief, I would stick a knife in their hearts."

Hugo reverts to the same kind of comic melodrama. He cannot convince his wife of the reality of his project because he himself is not convinced. This becomes clear after Jessica has discovered the revolver and Hugo has told her he is going to kill Hoederer: "Am I playing? Or am I being serious? There's a mystery for you. . . . Jessica, you are going to be the wife of an assassin!" (Act III). Playing assassin for his child-wife, Hugo is reminiscent of Sartre's shoemaker-prince in *The Words*: "At Saint Anne's Psychiatric Clinic, a patient cried out in bed: 'I'm a prince! Arrest the Grand Duke!' Someone went up to him and whispered in his ear: 'Blow your nose!' and he blew his nose. He was asked: 'What's your occupation?' He answered quietly: 'Shoemaker,' and started shouting again." [41] Jessica is Hugo's feminine counterpart; she lives in a fantasy-world of seductive heroines as he does in a world of heroic assassins. Jessica chooses the role of exotic *femme fatale* because she is unable to respond sexually; Hugo dreams of "red gloves" because he is unable to act. Their attempts to live the pictures painted by their imagination finally succeed—in a distinctly nonheroic way.

After the grenade explosion and Olga's visit to Hugo, a change begins to take place in Jessica. She finally stops seeing Hugo's revolver as a toy; she becomes aware of what is going on around her. When Hugo, warned by Olga that he must act immediately, turns to Jessica for advice, she tells him: "I would go to Hoederer and say to him: 'It's like this. I was sent here to kill you but I've changed my mind and I want to work with you'" (Act V). She does not want to see Hoederer killed; the solution she offers is simple and undramatic. Like her husband, Jessica responds to Hoederer's strength, to the vitality of his presence. But her words come from a personal rather than a political world. Hugo's situation is such that whatever he does, he must be a traitor. He belongs to the Communist Party; he belongs, in a very different sense, to Hoederer. If he does not kill Hoederer, he betrays Louis and the mission the Party has entrusted to him. If he kills Hoederer, he betrays the friendship and confidence that Hoederer alone has offered him. Needing to be at one with himself, willing to do anything to accomplish that end, Hugo finds himself trapped in a position where self-acceptance becomes an impossibility. In this respect, he closely resembles Heinrich in *The Devil and the Good Lord*, caught between contradictory loyalties to the Church and to the poor.

Hugo and Jessica are attracted to Hoederer for much the same reasons. Only Hoederer's confidence can make a man of Hugo; only Hoederer's sexuality can make of Jessica a woman. Both feel in Hoederer a solidity, a reality, that they fail to find in themselves; Hoederer seems at home in his body. From the stage-set in which they live, Hugo and Jessica watch enviously as the world of real objects and real people comes into existence around Hoederer's presence. Just as between themselves the word "playing" occurs over and over again, in relation to Hoederer they use constantly the word "real." Hovering around Hoederer's coffee pot, Hugo suggests Roquentin in *Nausea:* "It seems real when he touches it. [*He picks it up.*] Everything he touches seems real. He pours the coffee in the cups. I drink. I watch him drinking and I feel that the taste of the coffee in his mouth is real" (Act IV). Hugo's general incompetence reduces things to props or toys. Hoederer knows what he is doing and why; for him things are not arbitrary material appearances but signs indicating a specific use.[42] Jessica, less philosophically, also responds to Hoederer's physical reality: "You are real. A real man of flesh and bone. I am actually afraid of you and I think I really love you" (Act VI).

Hoederer sees clearly that he must choose between them; he chooses Hugo. He understands Hugo and wants to help him, to give him the confidence Hugo has sought in vain from his comrades in the Party and from his wife. Hoederer's "I trust you" and Hugo's subsequent admission that he wouldn't be able to shoot Hoederer because of his liking for him marks a moment of fundamental importance in the play. As Jeanson has pointed out, "One perceives in this scene, for the first time in Sartre's plays, the outline of an authentic relationship between two consciousnesses—between which the distance has appeared to us the greatest." [43]

Sartre has depicted elsewhere the intellectual's fascination with the man of action. Canoris as seen by Henri, Brunet as seen by Mathieu, have the same kind of solidity Hugo admires in Hoederer. In *The Age of Reason* Mathieu admits: " 'You know, Brunet, I've finally lost all sense of reality: nothing now seems to be altogether true.' . . . 'Now *you* are very real,' said Mathieu. 'Everything you touch looks real. Since you have been in my room it seems to me an actual room, and it revolts me.' He added abruptly: 'You are a man.' "[44] But what makes the relationship between Hugo and Hoederer unusual in Sartre's work is the reciprocity it involves. Hoederer's interest in Hugo goes deeper than just a desire to convert him to his own ideas, to save his political soul. He has decided that Hugo could become "a fair enough man" and is willing to help him, in spite of the risks involved. Knowing that Hugo has a gun and intends to use it, Hoederer chooses to convince him, thus putting his own life in danger, rather than humiliate Hugo by having him disarmed.

In his prefatory essay to *Dirty Hands*, Oreste Pucciani

states: "The man of good faith is the free man par excellence. . . . He possesses authentic values and his life has meaning. It is significant that Sartre never writes of such a man." 45 Yet surely, Hoederer lives as a free man. Like Brunet or Canoris, he belongs to the Communist Party, but he lacks their *esprit de sérieux* that accepts Party policy as religious truth. Hoederer's mind is open; he knows that every decision involves risk, that judgments can never be more than probable. His disbelief in infallibility, his own or that of his Party, chastens his every act. Hoederer does possess "authentic values," certainly from Sartre's point of view. Committed to what Sartre calls *praxis*—that is, "action in history and on history" 46—Hoederer dedicates himself to the revolutionary cause, not out of a desire for personal salvation, but as a means of creating a more human society. He has transcended gestures—caricatures of the act, the act to be seen rather than to be done—or perhaps he has never had to confront the problem.

Hoederer is the one authentic hero of Sartre's plays, the one fully admirable character. His behavior has nothing in common with the flamboyant heroism of Orestes and Goetz, slaying their respective gods; his concerns are practical objectives in a world of men. Orestes and Goetz must go through the "baptism of blood" before they can feel themselves free. Their ends, we are told, are noble; but we see only the means. Hoederer is more modest. Orestes and Goetz fight dragons; Hoederer simply gets work done. He represents Sartre's more sober ideal of political action, as spelled out in the following passage from *Saint Genet*:

I hate the pretense that trammels people's minds and sells us cheap nobility. To refuse is not to say no, but to modify by work. It is a mistake to think that the revolutionary refuses capitalist society outright. How could he, since he is inside it? On the contrary, he accepts it as a fact which justifies his revolutionary action. "Change the world," says Marx. "Change life," says Rimbaud. Well and good: change them if you can. That means you will accept many things in order to modify a few. Refusal assumes its true nature within action: it is the abstract moment of negativity.[47]

Although Hoederer's life is dedicated to a social cause, he also exists as a private man. In *The Victors* Canoris remarks to Henri, who is obsessed with finding a meaning for the death that confronts him, "I never could interest myself in personal problems. Not other people's nor even my own" (Act I). Canoris's single-minded passion for the cause is useful; he embodies this passion and nothing more. There is a good deal more to Hoederer. Sartre gives us only fragments of facts about his life: we learn that he has had an unsuccessful marriage to a woman not in the Party, we see that he is sometimes tempted by a more private way of life and that he has experienced solitude. When Hugo comments enviously, "You must feel right inside," Hoederer answers, "You think so? Some day I'll tell you about me" (Act VI). The meaning of such remarks is never developed. Although Sartre reveals Hugo from several points of view, giving the spectator the impression of complete familiarity, Hoederer remains elusive, constantly suggesting a complexity which never shows itself fully. It is significant that Hoederer is able to see Hugo, to understand what is going on inside Hugo's head, but for Hugo Hoederer always remains opaque, impenetrable. Discovering Hoederer embracing Jessica, Hugo cries out triumphantly: "I said to myself: he can't be so mad or so generous." Nevertheless, such generosity does exist in Hoederer; his only madness is an adventurer's love of risk.

It is Jessica who finally acts as catalyst of what we have known will be Hoederer's inevitable fate. Hugo kills Hoederer after Hoederer's one moment of weakness, the brief lapse in his will to stay away from Jessica and to ignore her insistent offer of herself. Hoederer's words to Slick and George after Hugo has shot him are characteristic: "Don't hurt him. He was jealous.

. . . I've been sleeping with his wife" (Act VI). Hoederer's final act of generosity is a lie.

Why does Hugo kill Hoederer? Hugo is his act; all that he has been, all his failures are synthesized in that one explosion. Whatever Hugo initially thought his intentions were, his real intentions are revealed by the fact of the murder itself. In *Being and Nothingness* Sartre makes a distinction between the *motif* and the *mobile* of an action. He defines *motif* as the objective grasp of a situation, the understanding of how it can serve as a means for attaining a particular end. *Mobile*, on the other hand, refers to the psychological factors that motivate an act.

Hugo's initial *motif* was to assassinate Hoederer in order to eliminate a political enemy. This long-deliberated *motif*, however, has nothing to do with the crime as it actually happens. Hugo does not kill for political reasons or because his Party has ordered him to kill. In killing Hoederer, it is himself as a failure Hugo wants to kill. He hopes by a single act, a pistol shot, to inaugurate a future that signifies the destruction of his past. In fact he does just the opposite. Had he taken Hoederer's advice and accepted his help, Hugo's past would have become just a painful adolescent stage, the prelude to his manhood; with the act of murder, that past becomes a radical truth of his present and future. Each shot is the despairing confession of his complete alienation, his inability to escape from the prison of his childhood, his solitude, and his weakness. It is an admission that he cannot in any other way win the confidence of his comrades or respect from his wife. Only a dead body can make him feel that he has marked the world.

Analyzing the real-life figure of Heimburger, who was involved in France's famous trial of Henri Martin during the French war in Viet Nam, Sartre describes Heimburger this way: "Seized by the throat, he envisions a lightning act. A second

must suffice for it: a second is time enough to kill, to kill yourself . . . the crime has become a symbol: it is an *ersatz*, trans-
lating a dream of destruction." 48 This is an accurate description of Hugo as well. Rather than confront the slow, painful,
undramatic task Hoederer's offer of friendship would involve,
Hugo prefers to take the easy way out: to "save the tragedy."

When Hugo leaps to the desk to get the revolver and aims
it at Hoederer, he experiences his first moment of liberation.
For the first time he is in a position of strength; he has the pleasure of seeing Hoederer disconcerted. His sense of betrayal has
put him into a state of anger in which he is finally able to take
action. This jealous anger is comparable in its exaltation to
Orestes' joy after his decision to kill Aegistheus. Both are what
Sartre calls *émotions*, the passage from a difficult world that
presents all kinds of obstacles to a world of magic. In *The Emotions, Outline of a Theory* Sartre writes: "Anger is certainly neither an instinct nor a habit nor a reasoned calculation. It is an
abrupt solution of a conflict, a way of cutting the Gordian
Knot." 49 The three shots Hugo fires into Hoederer are like
Hugo's repeated swearing ("the bastards") after Olga throws
the bomb into Hoederer's study. What hits Hugo hardest both
times is that he has been betrayed. It becomes clear after the
bombing incident that he is not greatly concerned with the
murder of Hoederer in itself; what counts is that he, Hugo,
must commit the act. When he finds Hoederer with Jessica, his
mind stops and physiology takes over. Making no attempt to
understand the situation, he falls back on the script that he has
written in his mind.

Finally, after all the meanings of Hugo's crime have been
explained into absurdity, all that remains is the act itself and its
result—the dead body of Hoederer. Notwithstanding Hugo's
long-planned intention, the crime as it takes place is unpremed-
itated. Hugo kills for no real reason; what happens is almost an

accident, like Meursault's killing of the Arab because the sun was in his eyes. Two years after his crime Hugo wonders whether he had anything to do with it, or whether the bullet had not somehow acted independently. He experiences what he has done as an act without an agent; for himself he is still only Hugo the actor, who happened to have real bullets in his play gun. With Olga's admission that the Party line has changed, Hugo's last justification for his crime is taken away. As *his* act, it has been meaningless all along; now he learns that for the Party it was simply an unfortunate mistake that must be covered up.

Most critics of Sartre have interpreted Hugo's suicide at the end of *Dirty Hands* as a last heroic act. Harold Hobson, for instance, asserts: "M. Sartre undoubtedly intended *Dirty Hands* to end with a flourish, and on a note of triumph. . . . It cannot be questioned that Sartre considers that Hugo won a spiritual victory." [50] It can be questioned. Hugo's exaltation as he decides to kill himself is like that of the murder scene. Freed from indecision and self-doubt, he glories in this final liberation, which will give him the purity he desires: that of nonbeing, of death. Hugo wants to believe that by suicide he can save his crime, so that Hoederer will have died not by chance but for his ideas. He sees in suicide a means of giving his act—and himself—a reality which he has not been able to attain otherwise. "The man who commits suicide," Perken says to Claude in *The Royal Way*, "is running after an image of himself: you never kill yourself except in order to *exist*." [51] But Hugo will not have even that. Suicide will not make him exist in Malraux's sense; he will be after his death what he was in life: nobody.

Hugo's suicide changes nothing. What he has done remains irrevocable; Hoederer is dead, and the Party will continue to use its own version of his murder. If Hugo wins our sympathy in the last moments of the play, it is not because he triumphs gloriously, but because he has no better choice; suicide is

all that is left to him. His only alternative would be moral suicide: to forget what has happened by shutting off his mind. In
choosing to open the door to his assassins, Hugo can at least die
at one with himself. Whatever he does at this point must be a
form of failure. For Hugo is "unsalvageable": not for the
Party's reasons, but because he has killed the one man who
could have made him "salvageable."

Dirty Hands, like The Victors, is in a particular realistic
tradition; it deals in a serious, nonmythical way with a contemporary crisis. Both plays involve Resistance movements of
World War II—one in France, the other in a country of East-
ern Europe. But Dirty Hands avoids both the cerebralism and
the sheer physical horror that weaken The Victors. Its intimate
realism is entirely suited to the action of the play. Hugo's initial
mission of assassinating an ideological adversary becomes the
very different task of killing Hoederer; what begins for Hugo as
an abstraction—the problem of "red gloves"—changes into the
terrible demand that he kill the one man who is willing to have
confidence in him, who can help him, and whom he has grown
to love in spite of himself. The relationship between Hugo and
Hoederer foreshadows the "drôle d'amitié" of Schneider and
Brunet in the novel fragment of that name which, like the play,
is set in a context of fierce political disillusionment. Philip
Thody calls Dirty Hands "in many ways [Sartre's] best literary
work so far." 52 This does not seem to me quite true; Dirty
Hands is less original than No Exit before it, less powerful than
The Condemned of Altona after it. But it is the first play we
have considered that escapes Sartre's great fault of sterilizing his
drama with rhetoric; it inhabits a world to which we can give
imaginative assent.

The Respectful Prostitute

> "When I use a word," Humpty Dumpty said, in rather a scornful tone, "it means just what I choose it to mean—neither more nor less."
>
> "The question is," said Alice, "whether you *can* make words mean so many different things."
>
> "The question is," said Humpty Dumpty, "which is to be master—that's all."
>
> LEWIS CARROLL, *Alice in Wonderland*

The *Respectful Prostitute* is taken from the famous Alabama "Scottsboro Case" of 1931, involving two white prostitutes and a group of black men. In his book *Les Etats-Désunis*, Vladimir Pozner gives the account of one of the prostitutes involved:

"The judge and the sheriff came to question us. They just asked us if we had been at the fight and we answered: yes. Then, one of the sheriff's men said to us, to Victoria Price and me, that if we agreed to accuse the Negroes of raping us, that would get us out of going to prison. I refused because it wasn't true. But Victoria Price had more experience than me and right away she accepted. . . . They threatened us so much that finally I couldn't see a way out any more, except to repeat what they told me to say. . . . We stayed in prison for sixteen days, including the trial, and during all that time a mob of people kept on gathering around our windows. They yelled and threatened and I was even more scared of that than of being arrested. I didn't know what they wanted, I didn't understand that they wanted to lynch the niggers. . . . When everything was over and the boys were condemned to the electric chair, they let us go." [1]

Sartre has changed the original story considerably. In his play, the accusation of rape involves one black man and one white prostitute. Sartre introduces the characters of Fred and his father the Senator, who try to convince Lizzie McKay to change her testimony. She finally succumbs not to threats, but to the Senator's patriotic evocations of virtue, motherhood, and the American Way of Life.

The central theme of *The Respectful Prostitute* concerns what Sartre calls *les salauds*—those bourgeois who, because they have property and material success, believe that they represent man, and exist by divine right. They use that sacred privilege to exploit their chosen scapegoats, those who in their eyes do not represent man: Jews, blacks, the poor. Fred exists to be *un chef* like his father, to command other men and to be obeyed by them. Like Lucien in "The Childhood of a Leader," he has been engendered for a specific purpose: to follow in his father's footsteps. Describing Lucien Fleurier's thoughts when he discovers the final solution to his problems, Sartre writes:

He had believed that he existed by chance for a long time, but it was due to a lack of sufficient thought. His place in the sun was marked in Férolles long before his birth. They were *waiting* for him long before his father's marriage: if he had come into the world it was to occupy that place: "I exist," he thought, "because I have the right to exist." [2]

Fred's conception of his right to exist is born of the same logic. He says, "My father is a Senator. I shall be senator after him. I am the last one to carry the family name. We have made this country and its history is ours." For Lizzie to shoot him, Fred informs her, would be to "shoot all of America" (Scene ii).

Fred succeeds in mystifying Lizzie as his father has done before him. Their relationship to each other and to Lizzie expresses satirically Sartre's hatred for the Father-figure, which is apparent in "The Childhood of a Leader," in the characterization of Jupiter in *The Flies*, in Hugo's hatred for his father in *Dirty Hands*, and most profoundly in the relationship between Franz and his father in *The Condemned of Altona*. Born into the dominant class, Fred is merely a continuation of his father, with the same future awaiting him. His social status gives him metaphysical status. Fred and his family are innocent by essence. Speaking of his cousin Thomas, he explains to Lizzie: "He put his hand under your skirt, he shot down a dirty nigger; so what? You do things like that without thinking; they don't count. Thomas is a leading citizen, that's what counts" (Scene i). Since *un chef*, unlike those he governs, has been born for a reason, good is automatically on his side and evil must be attributed elsewhere.

Fred has decided that his position in society is proof of his moral virtue; conversely, the inferior status of Lizzie and the Negro becomes a proof of their immorality and, at the same time, an irrefutable justification of the *status quo*. Fred says to Lizzie: "You are the Devil. The nigger is the Devil too" (Scene i). In *Anti-Semite and Jew* Sartre writes: "The anti-Semite is afraid of discovering that the world is badly made. . . . Thus he localizes all the evil of the universe in the Jew." 3 Projecting onto scapegoats his own evil impulses, Fred's manicheism does not exclude a fascinated attraction to the victim he has named evil. It is after he has joined the crowd to lynch another Negro that Fred comes back to Lizzie to claim her as his property.

Like the Negro, who is simply the victim, the Senator is designated in the cast of characters of *The Respectful Prostitute* not as an individual but as a role, the title of his position in society. His portrait and life history would find their ideal place in an American Bouville Museum. In *Nausea* Roquentin, looking at the portraits of dignitaries assembled around him, feels each one looking at him, seeing him for what he is:

His judgment went through me like a sword and questioned my very right to exist. And it was true, I had always realized it; I hadn't the right to exist. . . .
But for this handsome, faultless man, now dead, for Jean Pacôme, son of the Pacôme of the Défense Nationale, it had been an entirely different matter: the beating of his heart and the mute

rumblings of his organs, in his case, assumed the form of rights to be instantly obeyed. For sixty years, without a halt, he had used his right to live. The slightest doubt had never crossed those magnificent grey eyes. Pacôme had never made a mistake. He had always done his duty, all his duty, his duty as son, husband, father, leader. He had never weakened in his demands for his due: as a child, the right to be well brought up, in a united family, the right to inherit a spotless name, a prosperous business; as a husband, the right to be cared for, surrounded with tender affection; as a father, the right to be venerated; as a leader, the right to be obeyed without a murmur.[4]

When the Senator, *chef* as his son is *chef* after him, seeks to persuade Lizzie to sign the false testimony, he does so not in his own name but in that of the American nation. His "I see you clearly, my child"* (Act I) echoes Electra's relieved submission to Jupiter's truth in *The Flies:* "Yes, yes! I see myself clearly now"* (Act III). In both plays the figure of authority hypnotizes his victim with a barrage of rhetorical eloquence until reality gives way to the power of words. Although Lizzie's acquiescence to the Senator and Fred is less willing than that of Electra to Jupiter, the image of Lizzie's defeat is unmitigated since there is no Orestes to counter its effect. The "respectful" of Sartre's title refers to the prostitute's respect for established order and for the myths that sustain it, even though she is outside that order and gains no rights from it.

Like *The Victors*, with which it appeared as a double bill, *The Respectful Prostitute* created a small furor when it was first produced in Paris. The city councillor objected to the police commissioner; he wanted to know why there should be permitted on a Parisian stage a play "which constitutes a cruel slander of the great American democracy. . . ."[5] In his *Masters of the Drama*, John Gassner describes *The Respectful Prostitute* as "a flagrantly distorted picture of American manners."[6] Curiously, these condemnations, in France and in America,[7] imply that *The Respectful Prostitute* is a bad play because it gives a false image of America; conditions are not, they say, as bad as all that. But we can no longer pretend ignorance.

Henri Peyre, discussing the frequent misinterpretations of Sartre's intentions, comments:

Americans . . . have insisted in seeing [in *La Putain respectueuse*] a crude treatment of the Negro problem. Sartre intended nothing of the kind. The prostitute, Lizzie, and the innocent Negro are, in the eyes of the author, the true villains of the play. They bow to prejudices through sentimentality, inadequate intellectual force, and the same fear of freedom that crushed Electra's early passionate revolt in *Les Mouches*.[8]

In correcting one misconception M. Peyre appears to introduce a new one. Since for Sartre all men are free and responsible by definition, it is true that Lizzie and the Negro could revolt against their situation. But Sartre has explicitly recognized in many of his works that while man is free and not determined, if a man's only choice is between submission and death, or how he will die, to talk of his freedom becomes no more than a lofty abstraction. In *The Flies* and in *The Devil and the Good Lord* Sartre celebrates man's power to rebel against an oppressive system; in *The Respectful Prostitute*, as in *The Victors*, he shows how man can be crushed by that system. This view of man as entirely a creator of his environment on the one hand, and entirely a victim of it on the other, is comparable to the physicists' treatment of energy sometimes as a wave, sometimes as a particle—although each truth seems to exclude the other. In *The Respectful Prostitute* Lizzie and the Negro are not "villains" but victims of a system that has imprisoned them. As Sartre writes in *Anti-Semite and Jew*:

The fact remains, you may answer, that the Jew is free: he can choose to be authentic. That is true, but we must understand first of all that *that does not concern us*. The prisoner is always free to try to run away, if it is clearly understood that he risks death in crawling under the barbed wire. Is his jailer any less guilty on that account? [9]

Sartre does not even give his Negro a name. He is simply "The Negro"—nothing more than a victim. Less lucid than Lizzie, all he can do is plead with her for help and run from his attackers when they come to get him. Even his mind has been violated. He has become the "nigger" his oppressors have made of him to justify their oppression. Sartre writes in *Saint Genet*: "The Indian untouchable thinks that he *is actually* untouchable. He internalizes the prohibition of which he is the object, and makes of it an inner principle which justifies and explains the conduct of the other Hindus toward him." [10] In accepting himself as inferior, the Negro endows whites with the magical superiority with which they have already endowed themselves; thus, he becomes an accomplice to their propaganda. Although he is to be sacrificed for a guilty white man, the old Negro of *The Respectful Prostitute* does not even think of rebelling. When Lizzie gives him a revolver to defend himself against the men who are coming to lynch him, he does not accept it: "I can't shoot white folks. . . . They're white folks, ma'am" (Scene ii). Lizzie's own sympathy for the Negro is tainted with the racism she has adopted from the society that includes her in its contempt. In reply to Fred's suspicion that she had made love with the Negro she says: "I have nothing against them, but I don't like them to touch me" (Scene i).

Lizzie is defeated twice in the play, first by the Senator and then by his son. As Sartre sees it: "When the play ends, she is like those bulls in Spanish bullfights who have been provoked over and over by passes and who stand stupid in the middle of the arena, while the matador turns his back and walks away, with little calm steps." [11] By the end of the action Lizzie no longer believes that Fred and his father, incorporated, are America, but she still cannot shoot Fred; she cannot even resist him. Her second defeat lies in a resignation to things as they are that makes her newly acquired lucidity useless. In agreeing to become Fred's exclusive property, she becomes again the respectful prostitute she was at the beginning of the play.

The similar status of Lizzie and the Negro as outcasts brings them together momentarily in an unstable sense of solidarity.[12] But, ultimately, they respect themselves too little to be able to respect each other.

Sartre intended *The Respectful Prostitute* to be comic. He sees it, in his words, as "a *comédie-bouffe* on an unpleasant subject." [13] The defect of the play is that it vacillates uncertainly between realism and caricature. *The Respectful Prostitute* is meant to be an aggressive work, using ridicule as denunciation. Sartre, however, is unsure of his weapons; as a result, Fred and the Senator are left standing in their inflated state. We cannot recognize the characters as credible persons; nor is their distortion such that we can assent to it as functional caricature. Sartre's unsteady grasp of his characters is particularly evident in the scene in which the Senator dazzles Lizzie into accepting his racism as a form of superior wisdom. The scene is neither convincing farce nor convincing realism; it is not plausible that a prostitute would swallow the Senator's hymn to American motherhood and lily-white virtues. Sartre's problem is not in either of the characters but in their interaction. In order to believe in the Senator we would have to think of Lizzie as a character like Sibilot, the comically gullible "honnête homme" of *Nekrassov*. But given Lizzie's position—and survival—outside respectable society, her stated gullibility becomes simply untrue. Not surprisingly, critics have been left with the erroneous impression that this scene is supposed to be taken as serious drama: Eric Bentley comments that "the characters and situations are simplified to the point where we begin to laugh contrary to the author's intention." [14]

In Paris and in Peter Brook's London production, the *mise*

en scène of *The Respectful Prostitute* emphasized its carica-tural aspects. But everywhere else, Sartre has complained, "They made a drama out of it and this comic play became a ridiculous melodrama." [15] The fault does not lie only with the director. Sartre has said that while the Senator and Fred should be "as crude as marionettes," Lizzie and the Negro are "more realistic than the others." "As with Brecht," he has explained, "the characters have different levels of reality." [16] Neither the Negro nor the prostitute, however, is entirely believable. The naïveté of the poor little girl who says to the Senator, "As things stand, it's too bad the nigger didn't really rape me" (Scene i), is difficult to reconcile with the highly sophisticated shrewdness Lizzie shows when the men come to get the Negro —even if one takes into account all that has happened in the meantime.

FIRST MAN: Don't you want to see him lynched?
LIZZIE: Come for me when you get him.   (Scene ii)

Lizzie's remark implies not only a full awareness of what is going on, but also the toughness needed to contend with it.

In addition, Sartre has written lines a character might think, but which are not plausible when spoken. In the first scene of the play the Negro pleads with Lizzie for help: "When white folk who have never met before start to talk to each other, friendly like, it means some nigger's goin' to die" (Scene i). One could believe such a remark in a book like Rich-ard Wright's autobiography *Black Boy*; growing up black in Mississippi, he might say that to another black or directly to the reader. But given the situation of *The Respectful Prostitute*, it rings oddly to hear these words from a black man terrified for his life, who is speaking to a white woman he does not know and has no reason to trust.

The Respectful Prostitute lacks the authority that makes Sartre's short story "The Childhood of a Leader," dealing with the same themes in a very different context, one of his best works. As Lucien grows up, he becomes more and more sinister; our intimate familiarity with him makes of this *salaud* someone both comic and terrifying. In contrast, Fred and the Senator emerge as no more than parodies of the terrifying. For an American, however sympathetic to Sartre's point of view, *The Respectful Prostitute* inevitably seems second hand: the play of an intelligent Frenchman who was a friend of Richard Wright.

Nekrassov

> L'art du poète comique est de nous faire si bien connaître ce vice, de nous introduire, nous spectateurs, à tel point dans son intimité, que nous finissons par obtenir de lui quelques fils de la marionnette dont il joue; nous en jouons alors à notre tour; une partie de notre plaisir vient de là.
>
> BERGSON, *Le Rire*

THE PLOT of Sartre's "satiric farce" 17 *Nekrassov* is in one of the oldest traditions of French comedy, going back to the medieval *Farce de Pathelin*. It tells the familiar comic tale of the *dupeur dupé*, the clever scoundrel who thinks he is pulling all the strings when, in fact, he is the one who is being manipulated. As in *Pathelin*, the conflict of the play is a struggle between lies; the plot turns on the question of which lie will eventually triumph. Georges de Valéra's adversary, however, is not an individual or a few individuals but a contemporary institution: the anti-communist press. Before the play opened, in June 1955, Sartre declared:

My play is openly a satire on the procedures of anti-communist propaganda. Today when there is a prospect for international entente, systematic anti-communism is, in effect, one of the brakes which attempts to slow down this movement, by means of proce-

dures which are most often fallacious or arbitrary. It is these procedures, this propaganda, this hysteria that I wanted to mock in
Nekrassov.[18]

In *La Putain respectueuse*, Sartre's subject was racism in the
American South; in *Nekrassov* he makes fun of a particular
form of mystification in contemporary French society.

Not surprisingly, the targets of Sartre's satire were less than
pleased. *Nekrassov* was generally condemned by French critics,
with the exception of a few left-wing newspapers and magazines. The wholesale fury of its detractors sometimes got the
better of them; they sputtered invective: "It's a farce which ad-
vances like an elephant, with retorts as heavy as menhirs and
the finesse of a rhinoceros." [19] One of the play's few staunch
defenders in France was Jean Cocteau, who wrote in a letter to
Libération:

I protest against this strange law which seems bound to doom
any new attitude to a kind of failure. . . . One could not imagine
more grace, more ease, more mischievousness without the slightest
malice, than in this opera-bouffe, this fin de siècle revue. I suppose
that the *Marriage of Figaro* must have been an adventure of the
same kind.[20]

The comparison with *Figaro* is appropriate. Beaumarchais,
too, satirizes contemporary institutions rather than eternal
caractères. Irreverent of the powers-that-be, Figaro and Valéra
have managed to get along depending only on their own re-
sourcefulness. "Intrigue and money," Suzanne says to Figaro,
"now you're in your element" (I, i). Like *The Marriage of
Figaro*, *Nekrassov* exists on two levels of comedy. The heroes of
both plays are witty rather than comic; even on the losing end
they are too intelligent and inventive to be made ridiculous. On
the other hand, the journalists of *Soir à Paris*, like Brid'oison in
Figaro, are broad caricatures—believable types distorted into
funny mechanical men with a few immediately recognizable
gestures and attitudes.

It is difficult to see how Cocteau gets the impression of "mischievousness without the slightest malice" in *Nekrassov;* Sartre clearly did not intend his play to be harmless. His targets are specific products of contemporary capitalist society. Naming Aristophanes as a precedent, Sartre takes special delight in mocking individual persons: the editor of *France-Soir,* the editor of the *Figaro,* and Thierry-Maulnier, who was in the audience on opening night to review the play.

Sartre took the idea of writing *Nekrassov* from the Kravtchenko affair that had taken place some years earlier.[21] *Les Lettres Françaises* claimed that Kravtchenko's book *J'ai choisi la liberté* was a fraud; Kravtchenko sued for libel. Nekrassov, too, is a Russian official who supposedly "chose freedom"; Valéra's story is played up by the anti-communist press and later denounced as a fake by a left-wing newspaper. *Nekrassov* is clearly influenced also by America's McCarthy hysteria.

Sartre has since regretted that he centered the plot of his play on the swindler Valéra rather than on the newspaper and that he did not show Valéra "caught in the machinery of the newspaper."[22] In any case, Valéra must be a major character of the play. The inventiveness of his mind acts as a foil to the other characters, making of them so many parts of a huge system that we watch as it reacts to the phenomenon of an individual. Valéra's attempt to take on the system creates livelier action than that contained in the system itself. His existence serves to give a fresh point of view on the workings of *Soir à Paris;* through him the daily routine of the newspaper is magnified into the rise and fall of a myth—how it is created and how it is debunked.

Valéra is the only character in the play who is given a certain complexity and unpredictability. In *Le Figaro littéraire* Jacques Lemarchand wrote: "He should have been the arch *inengagé,* the absolute and ridiculous *salaud* in whose flesh the

Sartrean arrows would have vibrated indefinitely. But no . . ." [23] Valéra, however, has nothing in common with the Sartrean *salaud*, who is always a pillar of society. As an outsider, Valéra cannot enjoy the metaphysical confidence of Lucien Fleurier, or the dignitaries of the Bouville Museum, or the Senator and Fred. Nor has he any pretense to their moral righteousness. He is perfectly lucid about his amorality; as he says to Sibilot: "I am much too cynical, and therefore it is absolutely necessary that I fool myself first" (Scene v). Valéra's "probabilist" anti-Semitism recalls in parody Sartre's Genet, as does Valéra's declaration of a community of interest with Sibilot—since both "l'honnête homme" and the criminal, each in his own way, respect private property.[24] Although he is a professional swindler, Valéra is presented from the outset as a likable character. When he is obliged by his own loquaciousness to name names to Palotin, his immediate instinct is not that the seven "Communists" be fired but that their salaries be raised.

Like so many of Sartre's heroes, Valéra is a "monster of pride." He recoils in comic terror at the thought of owing gratitude to anyone, whether it is the *clochards* who save him from drowning or Veronique who saves him from the police; even when the facts prove otherwise he continues to insist he is a "self-made man." Unlike the typical Sartrean hero, however, the feeling of being only an image, of having no real identity, delights him. Success in his chosen profession depends on his ability to please and convince: "I work with my tongue," he says to Veronique. Since his *métier* is based on make-believe, he enjoys what he considers his freedom from all responsibility, accepting with ease the adoration and hatred his personage inspires.

The turning point of the action occurs with Valéra's discovery that Mme. de Castagnié and the other "Communists" have been fired, against his orders. Until then, Valéra has been the joyous manipulator, intoxicated with his own power and genius. "Little transparent men," he exults, "I see into your hearts, but you can't see into mine" (Scene v). But the myth has slipped out of hand; it is no longer his. The phenomenon Nekrassov has assumed a reality quite separate from Valéra's invention. Impelled by Valéra's lie, the puppets of the press take over; Valéra becomes an unimportant accessory to his own myth. As an unintentional result of Valéra's hoax, people are losing jobs; two journalists of *Libérateur* are to be tried for treason.

At this point, when Valéra's games start having consequences, Sartre begins to lose control of his comic intention. The play changes radically in tone; the playwright becomes an earnest moralizer. This change is exemplified in the redundant and entirely superfluous scene (Scene v) in which Veronique points out to Valéra how he has gone astray. With some justice, newspaper critics pounced on the character of Veronique for their harshest attacks on the play: "This proud leftist appears from time to time in the play to spout what is True, what is Good, what is Righteous, and she says it with the gentle authority and the mechanical assurance possessed by vendors of Salvation Army Bibles." [25] In earlier scenes, Veronique's lapses into the language of the true believer are at least infrequent; when Valéra first breaks into Veronique's apartment to escape the police, she perversely refuses to react to him as he expects a woman to react to an intruder. The situation allows for some good Shavian dialogue between them. The scene between Veronique and her father is in the same tradition. At about the middle of the action, however, Sartre chooses to make of Veronique an explicit political spokesman, with the result that she—and the play—start falling apart. Veronique's moralistic speeches in favor of the communist cause succeed only in making suspect a point of view that Sartre has hitherto made convincing by the deflation and ridicule of its opposition.

The problem is not that, in the words of Le Parisien, "Sartre does not reach eternal truth, in which stupidity and crime belong to no one party." [26] Such an appeal to eternal truth does away in one platitude with satire. To accomplish its purpose, satire makes of its targets objects to be laughed at from a position of superiority. It is hardly relevant, then, to accuse Sartre of being partisan; satire is necessarily partisan. As Kenneth Tynan writes in his review of Nekrassov: "The logical end of that dispute [about partisan plays] is to exact from every playwright a guarantee that he holds no convictions strongly enough to let them influence his writing. And that is like demanding a certificate of intellectual impotence." [27]

Sartre was accused of having written Nekrassov in order to please the French Communist Party, as a kind of penitence that would redeem the suspected anti-communism of Dirty Hands. This theory may be true; as has been indicated earlier, Sartre was distressed with the generally accepted anti-communist interpretation of that play. Certainly Nekrassov has none of the political ambivalence which characterizes Dirty Hands. Its pro-communist bias is clear and open. Sartre has never been a member of the Party; he has judged it personally impossible to accept the rigid discipline that membership would impose upon him.[28] Since his name became famous, he has engaged in frequent and often violent polemics with Party regulars. But his own abortive attempt to create a new left-wing party (the Rassemblement Démocratique Révolutionnaire, in 1948) and his close adherence, since about 1953, to Marxist doctrine have intensified his conviction that the French left, whatever its dislike of certain Party methods, must form a united front with the Communists or be reduced to ineffectiveness.

It is plausible, then, that Sartre wrote Nekrassov for purely political reasons; if so, that fact did not necessarily have to lessen the play's dramatic viability. In the essay quoted earlier Kenneth Tynan writes: "The finest and rarest sort of theatrical teacher is that defined in a dictum of Howard Lindsay's: 'If you are going to write a propaganda play, you had better not let any of your characters know what the propaganda is.' " 29 This is precisely where *Nekrassov* is flawed: Veronique knows exactly what Sartre's propaganda is. She even succeeds in persuading Valéra that the propaganda is true.

The transformation of *Nekrassov* from a satire to a vehicle for edification raises the question of Sartre's trust in comedy as an effective means of attack. Midway through the action, Sartre starts probing into Valéra, studying the meaning of his dilemma, and thus comes close to making of Valéra a traditional dramatic hero. In *The Respectful Prostitute* Sartre was unable to bring off the comic effect because he so often identified the Senator and Fred not with their comic manner but with the horror of what they actually do. Sartre sees the two plays as closely related; he has called *Nekrassov* "*The Respectful Prostitute* on the level of politics." 30 In *Nekrassov*, he is dealing with a less violent subject; but here also, although not as pervasively, he loses the distance necessary to maintain a comic vision intact.

Both Sartre's satires, *The Respectful Prostitute* and *Nekrassov*, are weakened by the scene in which the play's action takes its crucial turn. In all Sartre's dramatic work the turning point occurs as a climactic confrontation between protagonist and antagonist. Only in *Kean*, whose plot Sartre has taken from Dumas père, is there no such scene. Sartre's serious plays are constructed in such a way that this scene is a life-and-death contest between opposing wills: Orestes and Jupiter in *The Flies*, Goetz and Heinrich in *The Devil and the Good Lord*, the resistants and their torturers in *The Victors,* Hugo and Hoederer in *Dirty Hands,* the three *damnés* of *No Exit,* Franz and his father in *The Condemned.* In his two satires, Sartre keeps the climactic confrontation scene but, in both cases, uses it for edification rather than for comic effect. In *The Respectful Prostitute,* the awkward semirealism of Lizzie's contest with the Senator makes of her abdication a sentimental melodrama. In *Nekrassov,* too, Sartre cannot find the right tone for his scene of confrontation, primarily because he has used an irrelevant character to bring the turning point about; the contest to which *Nekrassov's* structure has been leading us finally takes place not between Valéra and Palotin, but between Valéra and Veronique.

Simone de Beauvoir has indicated that Sartre had difficulty ending the play "because he didn't want to make his hero into an out-and-out bastard, but he also didn't want to make him into a convert." 31 Sartre does not actually have Valéra convert, but he cannot resist giving him at least a change of heart. Valéra's pride is a sufficient and believable explanation of his refusal to testify against the two journalists as Soviet agents and of his decision to tell his real story to Veronique after having told the false one to her father. He has been utterly humiliated by the discovery that he has been "manipulated, just like a child! And by everybody." The newspapers have been using him for their own purposes; the government has known his real identity for a long time. Sartre suggests that Valéra's sudden moral behavior is due at least in part to a change of principle. Far more appropriate to *Nekrassov* is Sartre's means of getting rid of his hero so as to end the play with a final tableau of the newspaper: Valéra-Nekrassov, found by all his pursuers at once, lets them fight it out among themselves while he and Veronique disappear in the confusion, out the window and out of the play.

When Sartre stays with his original intention of writing a satiric farce, he creates scenes of frequently brilliant comic technique. The characterizations of Palotin, Sibilot, and Goblet are consistently successful. Sartre does not want us puzzled by his comic types; he wants us to recognize them immediately so we can focus our interest on what happens to them. Except for Valéra and Veronique, who exist on a different level of reality, the characters in *Nekrassov* are deliberately simplified, *du mécanique plaqué sur du vivant*. Palotin, for instance, the powerful editor of *Soir à Paris*, is merely a funny little man. In his infinite vanity he gives himself the role of savior knight and assumes that he should be adored accordingly: "And me, my boy," he says to Sibilot, "do you love me?" (Scene ii). Far from being a hypocrite, this "Napoleon of objective news" is passionately devoted to his calling. Since his newspaper is "an act of love" the headlines must dance out their love for man with rhythmic hatred of the enemy.

Like all comic characters, Palotin, Sibilot, and Goblet are laughable to the extent that they are unaware. Goblet's repetition of "Naturally, Sir, you haven't seen a man five feet ten in height . . ." when, in each case, Valéra is hidden—or not even hidden—right there, is a device which embodies in a comic situation Goblet's doleful conviction that he is destined never to find his man. It is this quality of being possessed by ideas without knowing it that attracts Valéra to Sibilot as a useful ally:

I have ideas. I produce dozens every minute. Unfortunately, they convince no one. I don't pursue them enough. You, you have none, but ideas hold you in their grip, they furrow your brow, and you are blinded by them, and that is just why they convince others. They are dreams of stone; they fascinate all who have a nostalgia for petrification.   (Scene iii)

The ideas of both Sibilot and Goblet are not formed by themselves, from their needs and situation, but from the mystifications of those in power. When Sibilot, in spite of himself, goes along with the Nekrassov scheme, his horror is not of lying, but of lying all by himself. Before, "I lied, but I had the approval of my superiors. I manufactured lies that were controlled, that bore the official stamp, big news lies, lies in the public interest" (Scene v).

The farcical simplification of characters in *Nekrassov* does away with the question of *vraisemblance* that constantly arises in relation to *The Respectful Prostitute*. Sartre convinces us immediately that Palotin believes Valéra's preposterous story that he is Nekrassov. Borrowing from catechism, Valéra reasons for Palotin that Nekrassov exists because Palotin needs his existence. Since Valéra must be Nekrassov in order for Palotin to remain Palotin, "Napoleon of the objective press," it is obvious that Valéra is indeed Nekrassov. Unlike Jules Romains's Knock, the farcically diabolical doctor, Palotin brings to his work no special genius for fraud. He is an exaggeration of the typical rather than of the exceptional. Palotin's vices are part of his job; they are inseparable from his function in society.

Nekrassov's best scenes are in the first part of the play. Scene ii in Palotin's office—especially Valéra's story of radioactive valises and the "Delighted"-"Executed" scene in which Valéra announces to *Soir à Paris* its "Future Victims of the Firing Squad" (a title which immediately becomes a kind of status symbol)—explodes the conspiratorial theory of history. In the scene in which Goblet joyfully recognizes Sibilot as one of his own kind, a fellow "médiocre," Sartre seems on one level to be mocking himself; the scene plays as a parody of Goetz's recognition of Heinrich, in *The Devil and the Good Lord*, as a fellow traitor and "little brother in bastardy."

Roland Barthes, in his spirited defense of *Nekrassov* and denunciation of the hypocrisy of its critics, rightly emphasizes the political significance of Goblet's recognition of Sibilot:

Yet Sartre has presented in *Nekrassov* a scene which is the perfect example of a psychological complexity born entirely of a "simple" political postulate: it is the scene in which Sibilot, the paid professional of anti-communism, and the Inspector *recognize* the identity of their social status. Our good critics have saved this scene . . . but with the wrong meaning: they wanted to see in it—and it was in their interest to do so—only a variation of the idea of "mediocrity" (the moral vice of which Montherlant has made himself the specialist). They have taken away from that vice all the social conditioning which it involves, refusing to understand that with this scene, Sartre was bringing to the theatre a typical case of alienation. Sartre and the Inspector are not "mediocre," they are men alienated by their 78,000 francs a month, united in the same condition of servitude with regard to that Order which compromises them as it employs them.[32]

M. Barthes's point is reinforced by the scene at Mme. Bounoumi's party, when Goblet rejects Sibilot—now the comparatively rich and important transcriber of Nekrassov's memoirs—as a different "tête" from the one he had embraced earlier.

The satiric thrust of the entire play is political rather than moral; that is, Sartre treats his characters not as moral agents but as products of their society. Barthes concludes his "*Nekrassov* juge de sa critique" as follows:

I console myself with the thought that *Nekrassov* will liberate each evening, for as long as possible, Frenchmen like me who are suffocating under the bourgeois sickness. "J'ai mal à la France," Michelet used to say. That's why *Nekrassov* did me good.[33]

The real target in *Nekrassov* is not an individual or a number of individuals but the system that created them. In this respect the play's purpose is entirely different from that of a play like Marcel Aymé's *La Tête des autres*, with which *Nekrassov* has been compared. As Sartre put it, alluding to Aymé's play, "If we find better judges, justice will be better. The situation is reversed in *Nekrassov*." [34]

As the Nekrassov myth takes its course, the identities of all the characters begin to vacillate. When Sibilot continues to doubt what he knows is false, Valéra uses logic to persuade him it is true. Two million people believe Valéra is Nekrassov; only a thousand believe Sibilot is Sibilot; therefore Sibilot is much less Sibilot than Valéra is Nekrassov. Seven random journalists at *Soir à Paris* are suddenly discovered to be Communists. Mouton, at first the formidable publisher of *Soir à Paris*, finds himself suspiciously absent from Nekrassov's list of Future Firing Squad Victims; he learns from Demidoff, to his horror, that he is an "*objective* Communist." "Feodor Petrovitch," he pleads, "decommunize me" (Scene vi). Even Valéra's lie is not so simple as it originally appears. His own Nekrassov is distorted and magnified by the imperious needs of the anti-communist cause. Caught in the machine he has set in motion but cannot stop, Valéra is no longer the independent swindler or the self-created Nekrassov; he is just a cog like everyone else. The Nekrassov myth runs its inevitable course without him, becoming more and more monstrous until it finally explodes altogether. As the machine does its work, persons turn out to be interchangeable and the impossible ending of the play becomes believable. Borrowing the gestures and words of Palotin, Sibilot, the new editor of *Soir à Paris*, becomes at the same time the new Palotin: "Well, boys, do you love me?" (Scene viii).

Kean

Méfiez-vous du théâtre dans la vie.
JEAN COCTEAU, *Les Monstres sacrés*

K*ean*, adapted from the play by Alexandre Dumas, was written at the request of Pierre Brasseur who had played Goetz in *The Devil and the Good Lord* and had become a friend of Sartre. "The interest of Dumas' play," Sartre has remarked, "is that it was commanded by that madman Lemaître, who wanted to bring together in himself both characters." 35 *Kean* is a play written about the actor Kean, for the actor Frédérick Lemaître, which the actor Pierre Brasseur asked Sartre to rewrite for him. In the *Kean* of Dumas the play within a play is *Romeo and Juliet;* Brasseur asked Sartre to change it for him to *Othello,* which he had played earlier in the film *Children of Paradise* in the role of Frédérick Lemaître playing Othello. All three actors —Kean, Lemaître, and Brasseur—are in the tradition of the actor as *monstre sacré.*

Through a mirrored labyrinth *Kean* explores the actor's question: What is my mask, what is my face? Lee Strasberg has written of the actor: "He is the only artist whose basic raw material is himself; he uses his own muscles, brain, emotions, voice, speech, and gesture to identify with and create another human being." 36 This *dédoublement* is such that the actor is both participant and spectator, experiencing his character and, at the same time, observing each word and gesture he performs.

The nature of theatre underlines, then, the ambiguity between man as agent and actor. The performance of Kean as Othello—and of Brasseur as Kean playing Othello—takes place in both a real and an illusionary world. Dramatic vocabulary expresses the pervasive duality of the theatre: "the actor" can refer to an agent or a performer, or both. Part of Sartre's fascination with plays comes precisely from this ambiguity of the idea of acting, an ambiguity which he sees inherent in life and magnified by the theatre.

Dumas's *Kean, ou Désordre et Génie* is a study of the actor as romantic hero, the glorious victim of a society that uses him as its buffoon, unable to understand the true meaning of his "fatal career." Retaining the plot and the characters of Dumas's melodrama, Sartre transforms it into a virtuoso comedy. But, Sartre has emphasized, his intention was not to parody the earlier play: "I adapted *Kean* because I heard people laugh at *Hernani*. I like *Hernani* and the romantic theatre. I didn't want to ridicule Dumas but rather to give to his work the little fillip that it needs in 1953." 37

Kean, like Hugo's Hernani, is a rebel. To vindicate his rights against the injustices of society, Hernani becomes an outlaw; Kean, an actor. Sartre's affection for the Romantics is evident to any reader of *The Words*. As a child, he lived in playacting the romantic myth. For the pleasure of the grown-ups fluttering around him Sartre was a model child, taking his cue from what was expected of him. Like Kean, his identity had fallen into the hands of others. The child Sartre found an escape from that public role by creating the more spectacular private role of make-believe heroism:

But every evening I looked forward impatiently to the end of the daily clowning. I would hurry to bed, reel off my prayers, and slip between the sheets. I was eager to get back to my mad recklessness. I grew older in the darkness, I became a lonely adult, without father and mother, without home or hearth, almost without a name. I would walk on a flaming roof, carrying in my arms an unconscious woman. The crowd was screaming below me. It was obvious to all that the building was going to collapse.[38]

But, Sartre concludes:

However deep my dream might have been, I was never in danger of getting lost in it. Yet I was in a bad way: my truth threatened to remain, to the very end, the alternation of my lies.[39]

Kean, the *monstre sacré*, lives a double imposture as the truth of his adult life; his public and private lies, however, have become indistinguishable. For the pleasure of his audience Kean has transformed himself into an actor instead of a man, losing his real self to the pretended selves of his on-stage and off-stage roles. The child Sartre and the actor Kean are both condemned to the impotence of gestures, imitations of acts. Sartre writes in *Saint Genet*: "The gesture is *sacred*: it is the gesture of an emperor or of a hero; I borrow it from those terrifying beings; it settles on me, tightens my consciousness, which is always a bit slack, imposes an unaccustomed rhythm upon it: it is a sacrament." 40 But it is Kean's vocation to perform gestures; it is his job to imitate an imaginary hero—Hamlet, Romeo, Othello—so as to become that hero for the audience that pays to watch him. His problem is inseparable from his *métier*.41

Sartre leaves intact the social theme of Dumas's play: the actor adored by his audience as a player and despised by them as a man. Outside the theatre, Kean is reduced to the illegitimacy of his birth; he has no rights in the high society that comes to applaud him on the stage. Sartre clearly delights in the revolutionary gusto of certain lines in Dumas's play; he reproduces them almost exactly in his own version: "There is friendship only between equals, prince, and there is as much vanity in your having me ride in your carriage as there is foolishness in my accepting to do so" (IV; IV, xi). In his relations with the Prince of Wales, Kean is forced into the role of Falstaff to Prince Hal: a lusty companion or the Prince's subject, whichever His Highness sees fit to have at a particular time. In his relations with women, Kean plays the grand seducer; only in the beds of the nobility's wives can he successfully assert himself as a man. His notorious exploits are thus a form of revenge as well as pleasure. By conquering the Countess Elena, he hopes both to humiliate the Count and to triumph over the nobility that has excluded him from its ranks.

Sartre does away, however, with the sentimentality that

makes a modern audience smile at Dumas. The *pathétique* of
Kean's situation as victim of society is of less interest to Sartre
than the analysis of that situation. Kean, like Nekrassov, is a
mystifier of society. Both protagonists, the actor and the adventurer, make their livelihood by pretending that they are
what they are not. Each discovers that it is he who has been
mystified, forced by society into a role which does not permit
him to exist as a man. Kean has been created out of society's
need for illusion; his function, simply, is to please. In carrying
out that function, Kean has become an appearance of a reality.
For himself he is only make-believe. Since the subjective sense
of his reality eludes him, he must depend on the image he finds
in the eyes of others. Both for himself and for others, he
emerges as a reflection. Sartre describes Kean in the same terms
as he earlier described Genet: "It was you who took an infant
and turned him into a monster" (Act IV).42 Francis Jeanson
compares Genet and Kean as "monsters," both created by society for its own purposes:

Genet the Thief had been changed into a monster for purposes of
edification, Kean the Actor for purposes of entertainment—in
both cases, for reasons of social usefulness. One is transformed into
a scapegoat; at his expense serious people are reassured: they are
Good, since he is Evil. The other is transformed into an appearance; at his expense serious people divert themselves: through him,
they accede magically to heroism and grandeur, or sometimes they
caress Evil as one dreams of suicide, in all unreality, in all inno-
cence.43

For Dumas, Kean is an actor who can reproduce great passions on the stage because he has experienced them all in his
own life. Sartre's conception of the actor is less exalted. Kean
cannot know great passions precisely because his vocation is to
play them; the constant awareness of his stage roles transforms
his most private responses into *scenes à faire*. As a result, his life
becomes just another role, a theatrical drama for which he is his
own audience when there is no other.44 The constant confu-

sion between stage and life serves only to emphasize the unreality of both.

In Sartre's version, Kean is not the play's only actor. The others, too—with the exception of Anna—are all playing parts, imitating the feelings that belong to their role, dancing their little steps in the social ballet. Elena is in love not with the man Kean but with the legendary *monstre sacré*. The thought of ruining her reputation for the love of Kean excites her imagination; she encourages him just enough to keep that fantasy alive without, in fact, compromising herself. Elena wants Kean in the same way he wants her: as a trophy. When, after the fiasco of his Othello scene, Kean urges her to run away with him, she demands first to be seduced by his words. Her imagination is ready with the appropriately romantic script—that is, the script of Dumas's play. As Kean suddenly refuses to take his cue, she prompts him, inviting him to make a reality of her theatrical lie. At exactly that point, with Kean's sudden awareness that she is following a script, his love for her is dead. Rewriting his part, Kean takes up her vow to follow him to the scaffold, demanding that she follow him to Amsterdam instead. Thus exposed, Elena's passion collapses in turn and the romantic drama turns into comedy. Each has been in love with a *personnage*; Kean with a royal Highness, Elena with a fabulous genius *à la* Dumas. The Prince of Wales completes the play of reflections. He has been courting Elena only because he thinks Kean is in love with her. Without Kean as his rival, Elena is nothing to him. As he says to Kean, "But if you don't love her, what am I to do with her?" (Act V). Suspecting his own unreality, the Prince tries to negate it by playing Kean—imitating his clothes, copying his style, seducing his women. "Three reflections," Kean observes, "each of the three believing in the existence of the other two, that was the comedy" (Act V).

Anna Damby, originally the most conventional of all the

characters, is transformed in Sartre's play into the only one who
is not, ultimately, an actor. The melancholy, tubercular heroine
of Dumas's play, overwhelmed with awe in the presence of the
great Kean, becomes in Sartre's version sure of what she wants
and confident that "I always get what I want." She has decided
that she loves Kean and refuses to be intimidated by him. Although Anna's scenes with Kean retain much of the language of
Dumas's version, Sartre has completely changed the meaning of
the words. In Dumas's play, when Anna is about to confront
Kean, she exclaims: "Here I am in his very room . . . Should I
have the courage to tell him what has brought me here? . . .
Ah, dear God—give me strength, for I feel my courage failing"
(Dumas, II, vii; Sartre, II). Dumas, as usual in his treatment of
Anna, is in deadly earnest. When Sartre gives Anna the same
lines, she is mockingly acting out, on Kean's mocking command, her proper role: the humbly adoring young girl facing
the great actor Kean. At other points, Sartre creates a new effect
by keeping the gist of Kean's questions and entirely changing
Anna's responses. Compare Dumas:

KEAN: Are you prepared to sell your love in order to adorn your
    person?
ANNA: Oh! sir . . .

and Sartre:

KEAN [*in a changed voice*]: Are you prepared to sell yourself?
ANNA [*as herself*]: Is it absolutely necessary?

Anna will cheerfully lie to Kean when it suits her purposes;
there is never any ambiguity, however, in what she does. Her
ambition to be an actress is for the stage only. She alone in the
play is fully a self, outside the maze of reflections where the
others try in vain to find their real image.

In discussing Kean, Sartre has said: "The *acteur* is the opposite of the *comédien*. When he has finished working, the

comédien becomes a man like anyone else; the *acteur* plays himself every second." 45 By this definition Kean is, of course, an *acteur*. Constantly aware of his roles, he makes of their unreality the central truth of his private existence. He plays his own life to the point where it becomes just another part. Too lucid to submerge himself happily, as Dumas's Kean does, in identification with his characters, Sartre's Kean is obsessed with his imprisonment in a world of gestures.

In Kean's Othello scene, this theme reaches its climax. Robert Nelson says of the play within a play as theatrical device: "The relationship of the inner play to the outer play prefigures the relationship between the outer play and the reality within which it occurs: life. The play within a play is the theater reflecting on itself, on its own paradoxical seemings." 46 It is within the context of the play within a play that Sartre has Kean reflect on his own paradoxical seemings as man and actor. As Kean discovers when he falls out of his role as Othello, what the audience comes to applaud and love is not Kean or Othello, but Kean pretending to be Othello. Sartre's use of *Othello* as a play within a play is a good deal more complex than Dumas's use of *Romeo and Juliet*. When Dumas's Kean sees the Prince of Wales in Elena's loge, he announces, outraged, that he is no longer Romeo but Falstaff. His genuine emotion can express itself only in the substitution of one theatrical image of himself for another. Dumas's interpretation of the play within the play depends upon the romantic belief that while the world is a lie, the theatre is truth. To perform well the actor must identify with the role he plays to the point of becoming his role, living within himself the thoughts and passions of his character. Conversely, if he no longer feels the emotions of his character (in Kean's instance, Romeo) he ceases to be able to act the part— for it is no longer himself. Developing this idea quite literally,

Dumas has Kean reject Romeo to take on the role he happens to be feeling at the moment: that of Falstaff, the Prince's buffoon.

For Sartre's Kean, exactly the reverse is true. Sartre, like Diderot in *The Paradox of Acting*, sees the actor as disassociated from the passions of his role; the actor does not feel with his character but, rather, lucidly calculates his every word and movement. In his famous essay Diderot writes:

At the very moment when he touches your heart he is listening to his own voice; his talent depends not, as you think, upon feeling, but upon rendering so exactly the outward signs of feeling, that you fall into the trap. He has rehearsed to himself every note of his passion. He has learnt before a mirror every particle of his despair. He knows exactly when he must produce his handkerchief and shed tears; and you will see him weep at the word, at the syllable, he has chosen, not a second sooner or later. The broken voice, the half-uttered words, the stifled or prolonged notes of agony, the trembling limbs, the faintings, the bursts of fury—all this is pure mimicry, lessons carefully learned, the grimacing of sorrow, the magnificent aping which the actor remembers long after his first study of it, of which he was perfectly conscious when he first put it before the public, and which leaves him, luckily for the poet, the spectator, and himself, a full freedom of mind.[47]

To demonstrate his main point in the *Paradox*, Diderot uses the passion of jealousy as an example: "An actor has a passion for an actress; they come together by chance in a stage scene of jealousy. If the actor is poor the scene will be improved; if he is a real player it will lose: in such a case the fine actor becomes himself, and is no longer the grand and ideal type of a jealous man that he has striven for." [48] This is precisely what happens to Kean: he stops being Othello and "becomes himself." Elena is a spectator rather than the actress playing opposite Kean; her effect on him, however, is the same as that of the actress in Diderot's example. Kean the actor has been able to play superbly the jealousy of Othello. When Kean the man is himself overwhelmed with jealousy, the role becomes impossible for him. Nelson observes, contrasting Sartre's Kean with Dumas's: ". . . the outraged and jealous Othello appears to be the perfect role for the outraged and jealous Kean to play. But it is the very outrage he is feeling which threatens to *prevent* this Kean from playing Othello." 49 Kean's rage cannot be expressed in the language of Shakespeare. When his real passion takes over, Kean is unable to find refuge in a role, however related it might seem to his own emotions.

Sartre, like Diderot, assumes that life and the theatre are quite separate, that what we call true in the theatre must be something quite different from what is true in life. Diderot's theory of what constitutes theatrical truth is entirely applicable to Kean:

Reflect a little as to what, in the language of the theatre, is *being true*. Is it showing things as they are in nature? Certainly not. Were it so the true would be the commonplace. What, then, is truth for stage purposes? It is the conforming of action, diction, face, voice, movement, and gesture, to an ideal type invented by the poet, and frequently enhanced by the player.[50]

Kean, on the same subject, remarks in Sartre's play: "I have always said that Nature was a very inferior copy of Art" (Act II). "Sometimes I wonder if real emotions are not merely false emotions badly acted" (Act I). That is to say, "being true" in life is something less than what would be dramatically true on the stage.

Kean, the drama of the actor, is a comic encapsulation of a theme present throughout Sartre's plays: the difference between gesture and act. Orestes, Goetz, Hugo, and Valéra, like Kean, all act for an audience, performing the role of an imaginary character. Their first concern is not to do, but to be seen, and they use a real or imagined audience as a means of acceding to the identity of hero. After the Othello scene, Kean asks Solomon: "Was it a gesture or an act?" In stepping out of his role as Othello, Kean risks the ruin of his theatrical career. What he does is an act, since it has consequences: Kean is exiled from England. But when Kean reflects on why he committed this act, it is reduced to just another performance of a tragic script: "It was a gesture, d'you hear? The last. I took myself for Othello, and that woman, laughing in her box—I took her for Desdemona" (Act V). Similarly, in *Dirty Hands*, Hugo thinks of his murder of Hoederer in theatrical terms: "It was to save the tragedy that I fired" (Act VII). Hugo, however, in spite of his desperate efforts, never becomes the heroic character of his imaginings. Goetz, in *The Devil and the Good Lord*, plays an heroic role throughout, although its content changes. "Come along, fine actor," Heinrich taunts him, "perform for me. Do you know your part well?" (I, ii). It is entirely fitting that in the Paris productions, the *monstre sacré* Pierre Brasseur played both Goetz and Kean, characters who themselves play imagined roles with all the heroic gestures required.

In *The Devil and the Good Lord*, the grandiloquence of Sartre's lines for Goetz sometimes seems unintentional, especially in the last part of the play. In *Kean* there is no such problem. Sartre joyfully takes his cue from his romantic predecessor, rewriting the play with the same panache as the original. Even in the Othello scene, Kean's confusion does not last long; after the initial surprise, he quickly recovers his eloquence as he addresses the audience, becoming once again—an actor. Sartre prepares the comic effect of this scene by having Anna forget her lines. Spurned by Kean, unable to play her part, Anna has no other theatrical eloquence to fall back on; instead, giving vent to her emotions, she answers Kean's lines with frantic repetitions of "I love you" until he orders her off the stage.

In *Kean*, there are no pauses for earnest moralizing that dissipate the energy and pace of *The Respectful Prostitute* and

Nekrassov. An exchange between Kean and Elena toward the end of the play gives us a clue as to why Sartre does not fall into his usual traps:

ELENA: Tell me—why are we condemned to play drawing-room comedy?
KEAN [*shrugging his shoulders*]: Today love is comical.
ELENA: So there's no more tragedy?
KEAN: Yes: in politics. But that's not our line. (Act V) [51]

Sartre allows himself the luxury of being comic in *Kean* because the play is not intended to be *engagé* in the same sense that *The Respectful Prostitute* and *Nekrassov* clearly are. In his two "serious" comedies Sartre is ultimately less concerned about comic coherence than about the clarity of his social message. But the world of the actor Kean—so like that of the actor-child of *The Words*—is one where politics "is not our line."

No Exit

> The Greeks painted the eyes of marble statues and made out of enamel or glass or precious stones those of their bronze statues, but the Roman was the first to drill a round hole to represent the pupil, and because, as I think, of a preoccupation with the glance characteristic of a civilization in its final phase.
>
> W. B. YEATS, A *Vision*

> MÉPHISTOPHÉLÈS: Après tout . . . Il se peut que je ne serve à rien. Je repose, peut-être, sur une idée fausse . . .
> FAUST: Laquelle?
> MÉPHISTOPHÉLÈS: Que les gens ne sont pas assez . . . malins pour se perdre tout seuls, par leurs propres moyens.
>
> PAUL VALÉRY, *"Mon Faust"*

IN HER *Connaissance de Sartre*, Colette Audry lists what she calls the three essential experiences in Sartre's work:

> First discovery: I exist in the world.
> Second discovery: There are also others in the world.
> Third discovery: I must die; what does that mean? [1]

The most common accusation leveled against Sartre's novels and plays has been that they are too "philosophical," more concerned with ideas than with individuals. In this light, it is perhaps paradoxical that those two literary works generally considered Sartre's masterpieces happen also to be those that proceed most directly from one of his major philosophical works, *Being and Nothingness*. Using Mlle. Audry's list as guide, we can say that Sartre's first discovery is the subject of *Nausea*; the second and third make up the subject of *No Exit*. Sartre devotes large segments of *Being and Nothingness* to a close analysis of what is revealed dramatically in *No Exit*. The section "Concrete Relations With Others" and, even more centrally, the chapter "The Look" serve as an ontological explanation of the play.

Yet *No Exit* is not a thesis play in the conventional sense, any more than *Nausea* is a conventional thesis novel. What makes *No Exit* a masterpiece is that Sartre is able to translate philosophy into dramatic form. *No Exit*—in contrast to Sartre's other plays—does not contain a lot of ideas; it is, in itself, a powerful literary idea. Francis Jeanson describes *No Exit* as "a kind of ontological tragedy in which one of the essential components of our condition has been isolated from context and carried mythically to its limit." [2] Garcin, Estelle, and Inez are not independently interesting characters endowed, as the expression goes, with "a life of their own." What gives them interest is that they are incarcerated together. And it is their existence together, for eternity, that creates Sartre's idea and maintains it in dramatic action.

The three characters are configured according to a certain vision of life that is realized with both intensity and formal completeness. Examining the nature of Sartre's power in his best literary creations, Gaëtan Picon writes in his essay on Sartre's novels:

Sartre's greatness is that he has a universe to reveal to us. Not the universe but his universe: a universe which he translates, as others do, through fiction with the help of a certain number of unforgettable obsessions. There is a world of Sartre as there is a world of Kafka, a world of Faulkner, and it is this world which holds us in its power. [3]

Nausea is an individual confrontation with the world lived to such intensity as to be an obsession. Sartre's other fundamental obsession—his other philosophical myth—is expressed in its purest form in *No Exit*: the self petrified into an object by the Medusa-like look of other people.

For Sartre, "My original fall is the existence of the Other." 4 The existence of the other is directly revealed to me by his look. The look that sees me endows me with an identity, a nature. To make his point, Sartre goes back to Scripture:

> It is before the Other that I am *guilty*. I am guilty first when beneath the Other's look I experience my alienation and my nakedness as a fall from grace which I must assume. This is the meaning of the famous line from Scripture: "They knew that they were naked." 5

Sartre connects the fall, then, not with any particular sin but with my discovery in shame of a symbolic state of nakedness, of my defenseless state as an object in the eyes of the other.6 I experience his gaze as a form of possession and even of theft; he has me as I can never have myself. This fundamental alienation explains the lure of the mirror, which gives me the illusion of seeing myself as the other sees me, of becoming the other looking at me while still remaining myself. But in spite of my efforts, "The Other holds a secret—the secret of what I am." 7 The self that I am for the other is in no way commensurate with my own experience of myself. My behavior has a particular meaning for me; seen by another it is defined, captured as by a photograph, given another meaning over which I have no control.8

The look makes itself felt in Sartre's first story, "The Wall," when the Belgian doctor who is there in the cold cell to examine Pablo and the other prisoners before they are to be killed "never took his hard eyes off me. Suddenly I understood and my hands went to my face: I was drenched in sweat. . . . [He had] thought: this is the manifestation of an almost pathological state of terror; and he had felt normal and proud because he was cold." 9 Scrutinized by the doctor, Pablo's suffering is reduced to a medical category. In "The Room" Eve watches in humiliation as her father looks at Pierre: "I hate him when he looks at him, when I think that he *sees* him." [10] Alone with Pierre, she can almost believe in a special complicity between them, from the sheer effort of trying to enter into Pierre's madness, of being with him as he is with himself. Her father's presence destroys that fragile complicity. She is forced to see Pierre from without, as her father does. Pierre becomes simply a poor thing, one of the mentally ill.

To become an object through the look of the other can be desired as well as feared. In *The Words* the child Jean-Paul depends upon the eyes of the grown-ups around him for a reassuring identity: "I would run and jump across that gaze, which preserved my nature as a model grandson, which continued to give me my toys and the universe." [11] For many of Sartre's dramatic heroes, the look serves as an escape from the painful elusiveness of self-examination. Orestes poses as a savior, Hugo as a heroic revolutionary, Goetz as devil and then as saint. Daniel in *The Reprieve*, like Goetz, longs to be petrified as anything—as long as it is something. Through his religious conversion he finds the absolute spectator he has been seeking:

Last night, as he lay sweating in his bed, he had been conscious of God's presence, and had felt like Cain: Here am I, as thou hast made me, cowardly, futile, and a pederast. And then? The look was there, and everywhere, dumb, transparent, and mysterious. . . . The butcher passed, a large and florid man who wore spectacles of a Sunday to dignify the occasion; a missal in his hairy hand; he will be seen, the look will reach him through the stained-glass windows; they will all be seen; half of humanity lives beneath a look. . . . He turns the thumbed pages of his missal, and says with a groan: "Lord, lord I *am* a miser." Medusa's petrifying gaze will fall upon him from above. Stone virtues, stone vices—how restful! [12]

The look becomes Hell when the other refuses the image of myself I want him to see. In *No Exit* this happens to each character in turn as he finds himself the one who looks and the one who is looked at, the torturer and the victim. As the play

circles downward and inward to its conclusion, the three realize
in horror their complete interdependence. "I don't suppose if
God had given us the clear knowledge of how closely we are
bound to one another," Bernanos writes in *The Diary of a
Country Priest*, "that we could go on living." As the layers of
lies are torn away, the three "others" of *No Exit* are given a
clear knowledge of this unlivable solidarity. Each is at the mercy
of another who will not give him what he wants and can get
only from that one person.(5) Inez wants Estelle who wants Garcin who wants the reassurance of Inez. Every move of one of
the three, in word or gesture, sets the cycle of punishment re-
peating its inevitable round. Inez and Estelle will eternally desire and be frustrated; Garcin will eternally seek his impossible
salvation.(6)

When the play opens, Garcin seems to be Everyman. For
the first several minutes, he and the spectator have no idea what
is to take place in the strange Second Empire room to which
Garcin has been led. At first it seems to be a hotel, or perhaps a
prison, or perhaps a mental institution. Gradually, in this ugly,
windowless room Hell takes form. Objects have lost their com-
forting aspect of things to be used; they serve no function.
There is a paper knife, but no book to be cut. The bell to call
for the bellboy sometimes works but just as often does not. Beyond the room, Garcin learns, there are only hallways and more
rooms. Nor will he be able to find escape from himself. There is
no sleep in Hell. Garcin begins to see how this room is in itself a
punishment: "Why, now, should it be disagreeable? . . . Ah, I
see; it's life without a break." The electric lights are on per-
manently.13 Nowhere is there relief; eyes are always open and
there is no darkness. The only ornament in the room is a
Barbedienne bronze statue, ugly to look at and too heavy to
throw at the electric light.

Damned in Hell, Garcin is still desperately seeking salvation. For him most of all, the action of the play is a movement toward increasingly painful self-knowledge. Like Everyman in the medieval morality play he learns; unlike Everyman, his final lucidity comes too late to help him. Of the three of them in Hell, Garcin's truth takes the longest to come out. He has lived his life with the image of himself as a tough; that ideal alone has been important. First, he presents himself as a courageous pacifist, shot and killed because at the crucial moment he chose to stand up for his principles. His initial admission of guilt involves his wife. Bored with her adoration, he continually made her suffer because "it was so easy." Garcin tells the others how he brought a mulatto woman into the house to live with him and made his wife serve them breakfast in bed. As we understand more clearly later, the story costs him nothing to tell. Since his wife in no way contradicts the image he holds of himself, his treatment of her becomes in his mind merely an aspect of his virility. Although Garcin is aggressively heterosexual, he is not really concerned with women. Their admiration has always been easy for him to win; it was in the world of men that he wanted to make his mark. It is entirely fitting, then, that Hell should put Garcin for eternity with two women. Estelle couldn't care less about what he is "provided he kisses well"; Inez wishes him only the worst.

The truth that Garcin has been trying to hide finally comes out: Garcin the tough, at the moment of danger, took the train to Mexico and was shot as a deserter. If either Estelle or Inez will believe that he could not possibly have fled, that he is not a coward, he is convinced that he will be saved. Estelle is more than willing to tell Garcin what he wants to hear. But the accusing presence of Inez makes any complicity with Estelle impossible. As Garcin soon realizes, it is Inez whom he must convince: Inez knows him because she knows what cowardice and self-hatred are all about. And in the eyes of Inez, he is a coward as surely as he has his own nose and eyes and mouth and body, as surely as he is Garcin.14

When the door of Hell suddenly opens to Garcin's frantic pounding, he decides to stay where he is. To leave that room would be to leave forever the image of Garcin the coward in Inez's eyes. By staying, Garcin hopes to convince Inez to change her mind. Yet his staying rests on a hope which is one more self-deception and which results in an added torture. Garcin has something which Inez wants: Estelle. Inez must continue to call Garcin coward for her own protection; only that epithet can guarantee her power to prevent Garcin and Estelle from becoming a couple. The unexpected opening of the door gives all three of them a kind of reprieve, a possible second chance. In rejecting it, they all show themselves to be cowards, imprisoned by themselves before they were imprisoned by a higher Judgment. Their Hell becomes a chosen one. From that moment when they are free to leave, they all truly create their own Hell.

As has often been remarked, Inez is the most lucid of the trio. She is the first to realize that nothing has happened by chance; they have been put together in order to do each other the most harm possible. Inez can afford to laugh contemptuously at the noble masks behind which the other two try to hide. She does not need to lie. Long before her death Inez had thought of herself as *une femme damnée*; now, in this Second Empire room with Estelle and Garcin, she waits to repeat what she has already lived many times. In life, her vampire lust lived on and in her victims, draining their vitality. She succeeded in making Florence, her last victim, see her husband with the eyes of Inez and hate him with Inez's hatred; he was finally driven to his death. Florence became Inez's creature, totally possessed by her, until the day Florence turned on the gas and killed them both.

Inez's sadism is a way to burn an ineffaceable image of herself into another. The diabolical nature of the image does not matter, since she has the pleasure of knowing that she is responsible for it. Inez is aware of herself only through what she does to her victims, the pain that she causes them and the fascination that she exerts upon them.

For Inez, then, damnation is nothing new; she had already made it her destiny in life. She is, as Genet described one of his characters, "a joyous moral suicide." 15 When Garcin advises her to keep quiet and try to put her life in order she answers him: "My life's in perfect order. It tidied itself up nicely of its own accord. So I needn't bother about it now." Inez does not learn about herself in the course of the play; from the outset— and as far back as we know—everything has been clear. Her self-chosen epithet of *femme damnée* is entirely appropriate. As Delphine gazes at Hippolyte in Baudelaire's poem "Femmes damnées," Inez gazes at Estelle:

> Delphine la couvait avec des yeux ardents
> Comme un animal fort qui surveille une proie.

Even before being finally damned in Hell, Inez has seen herself as a fixed, eternal essence of evil. What Sartre would call her *mauvaise foi* resembles that of Baudelaire who, as Sartre sees him, refused all his life the freedom to change. While he continually complained of the cruelties of his fate, he savored the horror of his self-chosen role: an elect of the damned. Sartre writes:

He chose to consider his life from the point of view of death as though it had been suddenly frozen by a premature end. He pretended to have killed himself; and, if he often laughed at the idea of suicide, it was also because it allowed him at any moment to imagine that he had just put a stop to his life. At every moment, though still alive, he was already on the other side of the grave. He had performed the operation of which Malraux speaks; his "irremediable existence" was there under his eyes like a destiny.16

In Hell, Inez waits to re-enact her destiny, to repeat with Estelle her possession of Florence. Working to fascinate Estelle with her look, Inez offers her eyes as a mirror, there to create Estelle as hers. But Inez has lost her power to seduce; Estelle is not Florence. The efforts of Inez to make Estelle see Garcin through her own lesbian contempt only serve to kindle Estelle's desire for him. In her unaware frivolity, Estelle is to be Inez's torturer, inflicting upon her the one suffering that Inez cannot bear: to be nothing. When Inez tells her that she has not put her lipstick on very well, Estelle answers: "I thought as much. Luckily [*she throws a quick glance at Garcin*] no one's seen me." Later, after Estelle has confessed that she murdered her child, Inez tries again to lure Estelle, promising her whatever image she desires. Estelle's rejection is definitive: "Oh, leave me in peace. You haven't any eyes." Damned in life because she made others her possessions, Inez is now in turn possessed, "Beauté forte à genoux devant la beauté frêle." Inez's power over others existed to the extent that her victims recognized that power. Thus, as with Sade himself, she was far from self-sufficient; her power *depended* upon others—upon their acceptance of the role of victim. When Estelle by her contemptuous indifference refuses that role, it is Inez who becomes the victim. Tortured by jealousy and frustrated desire, she is condemned to be forever at Estelle's mercy.

Inez used her mind as an instrument of fascination; Estelle, more simply, dominated others through her physical beauty. In life and after life she exists only through her body. It is Estelle who is most upset by the absence of mirrors in Hell: "When I can't see myself I begin to wonder if I really and truly exist. I pat myself just to make sure, but it doesn't help much. . . . When I talked to people I always made sure there was [a mirror] near by in which I could see myself. I watched myself talking. And somehow it kept me alert, seeing myself as the others saw me." She has lived as an appearance, completely mindless, with no sense of herself from within. Now, in Hell, she must depend on the look of Inez who, as another woman, hasn't any eyes and the look of Garcin who, until prodded by Inez, is too preoccupied with what has become his eternal soul to pay any attention to her.

Estelle chose to count as real only the pretty thing that she was for others. Her essence as she would like to see it resembles a delicate *objet d'art*, radiating aristocratic elegance and refinement. She moved in a *décor* of which she was the most beautiful part. To save her cherished appearance, Estelle asks the others to speak of themselves as "absent" rather than dead; she even invites them to believe with her that surely they must have been sent to Hell by mistake. Estelle's punishment will be the impossibility of continuing to seem. When her story finally comes out, Estelle the crystal object is shattered by the reality of her acts. Married to an old man for his money, she became pregnant by a lover and drowned their baby in a lake. Estelle's effortless *mauvaise foi* creates much of the black humor that is part of the play's atmosphere. After telling the others that her lover had seen everything, then shot himself, she remarks: "It was absurd of him, really, my husband never suspected anything." That one sentence, worthy of Voltaire or Swift, exposes with savage clarity the morality of "what people think." All three characters of *No Exit* are trapped, in different ways, by the opinion of others. The character of Estelle expresses in terms of middle-class banality what the play is all about. She embodies the theme of the play, robbed of its complexity and made into a joke.

Robert Campbell states: "It was necessary to put together a man, a woman, and a homosexual in order to permit successively all the possible combinations of jealousies and intimacies. But as for the conditions of deserter, murderess, and infanti-

cide, they are perfectly unnecessary." 17 His criticism implies
that each of Sartre's characters in *No Exit* is somehow com-
posed of two categories, a sexual category and a criminal category, arbitrarily connected to one person. He ignores the intimate relationship that Sartre establishes between each character's sexual behavior and his other actions. Estelle is an obvious
example, although an analogous case can be made for Inez or
Garcin. Estelle thought of herself as a beautiful object; for that
identity she depended upon the admiration of a number of
lovers. At the same time, she lived in a world of high society in
which the appearance of respectability had to be maintained.
From both points of view, she could not accept the situation in
which she found herself, that of mother of an illegitimate child.
Killing the baby was the most direct way out. Iris Murdoch re-
minds us that "Sartre, like Freud, finds in the abnormal the
exaggerated forms of normality." 18 Sartre's characters in *No
Exit* express attitudes that are common enough in their basic
form; Sartre takes those attitudes to their extreme possible consequences.

We begin to see why Garcin, Inez, and Estelle have been
damned in Hell. Even before their deaths, they were never
completely alive. All three treated others as their possessions,
objects to be used. Their punishment is appropriate to their sin.
They existed through domination and sadism, taking pleasure
in the suffering of their victims. Each one finds now that he
himself is a victim, tortured unmercifully by his dependence on
the others. When Inez talks about Florence's husband as
"rather pathetic really. Vulnerable," Garcin smiles, "Because I,
anyhow, am not vulnerable." Inez answers prophetically: "That
remains to be seen." By mocking Garcin's heroic self-image,
Inez has complete power over him. But she is equally vulnerable to Garcin; the enslavement works both ways. He can have
at any time what she wants and will never have. Each of the
three in turn is congealed by the look of the other into what he

cannot bear to recognize as himself: Garcin is fixed as a coward in the eyes of Inez, Estelle as an infanticide in the eyes of Garcin, Inez as nothing in the eyes of Estelle.

Without the presence of Inez, Garcin and Estelle could establish a love relationship based on their mutual lies. Garcin is able not to see Estelle the infanticide as long as she will reassure him that he could not be a coward; Estelle is willing to tell him what he wants to hear if it means that he will finally make love to her. For each other and thus for themselves Garcin could be a hero and Estelle a saint. Inez destroys this complicity based on self-deception. She forces Garcin to see that Estelle merely wants Garcin as an available man's body and that she neither knows nor cares what Garcin is.

In a last effort to find a way out of their unbearable situation, Estelle takes the paper knife and stabs Inez several times. "Each consciousness seeks the death of the other," Hegel writes in his famous analysis of the Master-Slave relationship. This statement serves as an epigraph for Simone de Beauvoir's novel *She Came to Stay*; it is an idea which informs most of Sartre's plays. For him, as for Hegel, the fundamental relationship is conflict rather than *Mitsein*. Both Orestes and Goetz, Sartre's two heroic heroes, have recourse to murder as a means of annihilating another consciousness with whom they cannot coexist. But in *No Exit*, the antagonists are already dead: Estelle's attempt ends in ludicrous failure.

It is because they are dead that Inez's retort to Garcin's last attempt to defend himself is a statement of horror: "You are— your life, and nothing else." For someone on the threshold of life, those same words could be exhilarating. For Garcin, Estelle, and Inez, they are a final damnation. As Jacques Guicharnaud explains: "The traditional idea that man commits such or such act because he is thus and so, is replaced with its opposite: by committing such or such act, man makes himself thus and so. Nothingness to start with, man spends his life giv-

ing himself an essence made up of all his acts." [19] The three
characters of No Exit have botched their lives and their lives are
now finished. If existence precedes essence, they have become
their essence. They are what they have been, irrevocably. For all
three of them, that essence is a form of failure. Since they are
dead, they can no longer change; there is precisely nothing that
they can do. In life, our actions in the future can always modify
the meaning of our pasts. But for them it is too late. They are
left with no future except an endless repetition of the present,
which itself is merely an image of the past for which they were
condemned. With the possibility of action unavailable to them,
they are truly in a world à _huis-clos,_ forced to endure without
respite the condemning gaze of the others.

On one level, No Exit can be seen as a dramatic image of
Sartre's sense of death. He writes in a crucial passage of Being
and Nothingness:

The very existence of _death_ alienates us wholly in our own life,
to the advantage of the Other. To be dead is to be a prey for the
living. . . . So long as I live I can escape what I _am_ for the Other
by revealing to myself by my freely posited ends that I _am_ nothing
and that I make myself be what I am; so long as I live, I can give
the lie to what others discover in me, by projecting myself already
toward other ends and in every instance by revealing that my dimension of being-for-myself is incommensurable with my dimension
of being-for-others. Thus ceaselessly I escape my outside and ceaselessly I am reapprehended by the Other; and in this "dubious
battle" the definitive victory belongs to neither the one nor the
other of these modes of being. But the _fact of death_, without
being precisely allied to either of the adversaries in this same
combat, gives the final victory to the point of view of the Other
by transferring the combat and the prize to another level—that is,
by suddenly suppressing one of the combatants.[20]

In No Exit this analysis is given form and intensity. Before Hell
has completely closed in on the three _damnés_, they are able to
see what is becoming of them on earth. Garcin sees Gomez at
the newspaper office telling the others about Garcin who ran
away, Garcin the coward. His wife who admired him too much

has died of grief. Those who are left to think of him at all have fixed him in their minds as a coward. "I've become public property,"* he laughs. Estelle, looking back, sees her lover (he had called her his "crystal") dancing with her best friend (she had not wept at the funeral, fearing her mascara might run). As Estelle watches them with helpless dismay, she hears her best friend tell him Estelle's whole story. The image she has acted all her life to appear is definitively broken. Inez is forced to see the room in which she lived with Florence rented to strangers, a man and a woman. They talk quietly on her bed and turn off the lights, oblivious to her presence. Those whose life Inez had invaded, Florence and her husband, are dead. She has become on earth what she is now in Hell for Estelle, nothing.

Sartre has quoted a few times Malraux's statement in *Man's Hope*: "The tragic thing about death is that it transforms life into a destiny." 21 The characters of *No Exit* are identified by a past over which they have no control; it has become their destiny. Garcin, for example, cannot prove his courage by acting courageously, since he is no longer able to act. He has already been labeled by Gomez and his co-workers at the newspaper. The only way out for him now would be to convince Inez that he is what he wants to think he is; but that, too, is impossible. What was a relative fact has become an absolute.

Death in *No Exit* thus becomes analogous to the Christian idea of the Last Judgment. Sartre remarks in *Being and Nothingness*: "The Reverend Father Boisselot in a private conversation with me gave me to understand that the 'Last Judgment' was precisely this closing of the account which renders one unable any longer to recover his stroke and which makes one finally *be* what one *has been*—irremediably." 22 The dramatic idea of *No Exit* depends upon the existence of some Supreme Power that has seen what Inez, Garcin, and Estelle *are* and has condemned them to eternity in Hell. Throughout the play Sartre uses Christianity as the cultural myth that gives force to his own secularized version of what the Last Judgment means.[23] His characters' fate is decided, finally, not by God but by those left on earth—the living—and by the three of them for each other.

Echoing Sartre's formula, "To be dead is to be a prey for the living," is a statement in the same passage: "The unique characteristic of a dead life is that it is a life of which the Other makes himself the guardian."[24] In this sense, Inez, Garcin, and Estelle were already dead in life, for even then the Other was the guardian of what they were. Each of them had chosen to live as an appearance—Garcin as the tough, Inez as Evil, Estelle as the lady of exquisite refinement and sensitivity. Their existence in Hell is a kind of photographic negative of their life on earth.

It is with this added dimension of death—death after life and death in life—that Garcin's final discovery reaches its full significance. "Hell is—other people" is the central truth of *No Exit*. Within the play, it serves as a summing up of what has been dramatically revealed to us by the interaction of its three characters. It is important to remember, however, that within Sartre's philosophy that formula has a limited and specific meaning. Sartre has emphasized this point: "The only valid relationship is with other people. That can go even to hell. In order for it not to be hell, *praxis* must exist. The characters of *No Exit* are in a passive, changeless situation in which each of them is inevitably fixed in his essence by the others."[25] Hell, then, is other people when they brand us with an image we cannot bear to accept as our own, and when we have no possibility to act so as to change that image.

Eric Bentley has commented: "Intending no slur, I would call *No Exit* philosophic melodrama."[26] In an important sense, this description applies to all Sartre's plays; they make use of sensational effects to create serious drama. Sartre himself has spoken of his plays as "false melodrama." As he explains in more specific terms: "The theatre is fascination, magic. It must be used to contest all magic." 27 *No Exit* is uniquely successful in realizing this intention. Theatrical fascination serves not only as a means of conveying an idea, but also as an integral part of the idea, embodied in dramatic form.

In his "Forgers of Myth" speech, given in the United States in 1946, Sartre described as follows the new French plays born during the Occupation:

Our plays are violent and brief, centered around one single event; there are few players and the story is compressed within a short space of time, sometimes only a few hours. As a result they obey a kind of "rule of the three unities," which has been only a little rejuvenated and modified. A single set, a few entrances, a few exits, intense arguments among the characters who defend their individual rights with passion.[28]

No Exit entirely fits that characterization; it is the only one of Sartre's plays to do so.[29] It is also the only Sartrean play to contend successfully with the problem of dramatic language, which Sartre has recognized as the fundamental problem of theatre. Questioned on this subject in an interview with *Théâtre Populaire*, Sartre replied: "It's a question of finding a structure of word and act in which the word does not seem superfluous, in which it keeps a power beyond all eloquence. That is in fact the first condition of a truly effective theatre." [30] In *No Exit* Sartre creates a language bare of extraneous rhetoric: the words act. Language can even be considered one of the themes of *No Exit*. In an essay on Brice Parain's studies of language, Sartre shows his preoccupation with the relationship between language and the existence of the other:

If, when I speak, I have the agonizing certainty that words escape me and that they will take on elsewhere, outside me, unexpected aspects and unforeseen meanings, does not this mean that it is inherent in the very structure of language to be understood by a free individual other than myself? In short, is it not the Other who makes language, is it not the Other who comes first? . . . Language is being-for-another. What need have we for God? The

Other is sufficient, any other. He enters, and I cease to belong to myself. It is he who interpolates himself between me and myself, not in the silent privacy of the *cogito,* but between myself and all that I am on earth.[31]

Garcin, Estelle, and Inez speak in order to convince. Neither silence nor solitude will help them, for alone they can do nothing. Whatever their hatred of the other, the three of them are bound in complete interdependence. Their passion is to talk. Only by talk can they hope to change their lot, to escape from the cycle of torture. As Sartre has said, "Passion is a way of sensing that one is right, of relating oneself to a social world of exigencies and values. To justify wanting to keep something, to take, destroy, construct something, passionate men do nothing but reason." [32]

In *The Devil and the Good Lord* Goetz says to Hilda: "We shall be alone together" (Act III). His words herald his new awareness of the solidarity that binds each man in his solitude to others. Garcin, Inez, and Estelle are also "alone together." The discovery of that solidarity as a fact underlies Goetz's conversion to action—which is, as we have seen, his salvation. The same discovery by the characters of *No Exit* reveals to them their damnation. Living their death in Hell, action is definitively cut off; the three are condemned forever to be themselves and forever to be together.

Every detail of *No Exit* is configured to inhabit a physical as well as a cerebral world. The debilitating power of the look makes itself felt in brutally direct images, as when Estelle stares into the pupil of Inez's eye, looking for her image. Just as objects have lost their function, bodies are out of control. The bellboy's eyes cannot blink. Garcin's mouth twitches obsessively; his face shows the fear he tries in vain to hide. A kind of nausea pervades *No Exit* as it does Sartre's story of Roquentin. Gaëtan Picon writes of Sartre's world:

Cut off from the external universe, it spreads out in its narrow human frontiers; it is always a room closed to the outside where no breath penetrates and where the suspicious fragrances of the human body, the smoke and the artificial lighting soon compose a suffocating density. It is Pierre's room with the shutters always closed, the lamps always lit; it is Marcelle's room which resembles the inside of a shell; it is the room where Inès, Estelle and Garcin are face to face for eternity. The scene is always a closed place where the air does not renew itself.[33]

There is constantly in *No Exit* a sense of things closing in, of the room becoming ever smaller. At first the three can look outside the room to what is happening to them in the world. These glimpses soon fade into darkness, leaving only the relentless light of the room. For a while they can hide in lies, but that recourse too is taken away as gradually each exposes the others until they all find themselves "naked right through." Finally there is only the glaring room and the three of them together, each with his truth and with his two fellow torturer-victims. The end of the play comes as an awareness, in grotesque laughter, that they will forever be saying the same words and using the same gestures, like a religious ritual. "Let's get on with it" is the last line before the curtain falls.

> If all time is eternally present
> All time is unredeemable.[34]

Time coagulates in *No Exit* as surfaces do in *Nausea*. When the action reaches its conclusion, past and present and future have become undifferentiated in the eternity of Hell. *(21)*

The Condemned of Altona

> . . . this madhouse, this prison, this charnelhouse, this earth.
>
> AUGUST STRINDBERG, *Ghost Sonata*

FIFTEEN YEARS after *No Exit*, Sartre takes us once again into the closed world of characters imprisoned in what they have done, condemned to play out, until their final awareness of failure, the acts of an irrevocable past. In *The Condemned of Altona,* as in both *No Exit* and *Dirty Hands,* Sartre uses the stage as a tribunal. Final judgment is passed on acts that have been committed before the beginning of the play; the characters must, in the course of the action, suffer their punishment for these acts. For Franz, Leni, and their father, as for the three *damnés* of *No Exit,* the chips are down. Their past completely defines their present and they have no future.

No Exit portrays the interaction of three characters in one room. In *The Condemned* there are five characters and two rooms: Franz upstairs with his visions, the rest of the von Gerlach family downstairs—two levels of reality whose relationship forms the structure of the play. The triangle of relationships in *No Exit* is set in a circle, with Inez needing Estelle who needs Garcin who needs Inez. In *The Condemned* the five characters exist primarily in relation to Franz, whose sequestration has sequestered them as well. Old von Gerlach lives for the manipulations that will ultimately enable him to see Franz one last time. Leni is bound to Franz in incestuous love. And Werner, Franz's younger brother, has obeyed the demand that he sacrifice himself and his wife Johanna to stay in the Altona mansion for the rest of Franz's life.

In the plot of *The Condemned,* it is the father who controls events, playing Johanna against Leni and then Leni against Johanna until he achieves what he wants. Old von Gerlach is Sartre's most complex embodiment of the *chef,* portrayed satirically in the Bouville Museum portraits of *Nausea,* Lucien's father in "The Childhood of a Leader," and Fred's father the Senator in *The Respectful Prostitute.* As Sartre describes him, "Franz's father is in the image of those German industrialists whom the journals and magazines now baptize 'giants who have reconstructed Germany' while in fact they helped Hitler try to destroy it. They are the same people." 35 Von Gerlach was not a Nazi; he despised them as "the plebeians on the throne." Yet he was willing to put his power at the service of the Nazis, supplying them with ships for their navy and with land for a concentration camp, on the theory that his industrial empire would remain long after Hitler's empire had ceased to exist. Von Gerlach's collusion with the Nazis was based on the reality of Nazi power: to remain a *chef* was primary and to remain a *chef* during the war meant to collaborate with Hitler.

When the play opens, old von Gerlach is dying of cancer. He has decided to commit suicide, deciding also that his beloved Franz must die with him. Franz had been formed for absolute power over his father's great industrial empire—his future was to be his father's past. But the increasing prosperity of von Gerlach's naval firm since the end of the war has been accompanied by a severe decline in his personal power; he is now only a figurehead. Madeleine Fields sees the firm as "an enormous opaque presence, alienated from man, which after the death of the Father will continue by itself without him, like a monstrous child." 36 Von Gerlach still owns the firm but no longer commands it: the monarch has been destroyed by the kingdom that he himself created.

Like so many of Sartre's *chefs*, von Gerlach's public role is duplicated in private life by his position as a father. In contrast to the other main characters of *The Condemned*, von Gerlach is designated in the cast listing not by his name but by his central function: he is "The Father." A characteristically Sartrean father, von Gerlach has created his son in his own image. "Nine months before my birth," Franz says to Johanna, "they had chosen my name, my career, my character and my fate" (Act II). Franz was conceived and raised to be just like his father, a *chef*, with his father's pride and his father's passions.

Like Hugo in *Dirty Hands*, Franz is defined in relation to

his childhood. Hugo joins the Communist Party as a rebellion against the role that his family life, and particularly his father, have created for him. Although there are no flashbacks to Hugo's life at home and his father never appears in the action, Sartre makes us aware of the influence of Hugo's childhood in his every gesture. In an attack against contemporary Marxist writing, Sartre has protested:

> Today's Marxists are concerned only with adults; reading them, one would believe that we are born at the age when we earn our first wages. They have forgotten their own childhoods. As we read them, everything seems to happen as if men experienced their alienation and their reification *first in their own work*, whereas in actuality each one lives it *first*, as a child, *in his parents' work*.[37]

While Hugo seeks his identity by revolting against his father the *chef*, Franz, in fighting Hitler's war, becomes completely assimilated to his designated role, with all its consequences. Both, in very different ways, are what their fathers have made of them.

Sartre seems to have formed his conception of the von Gerlach family from his studies of Flaubert. In the *Search for a Method* Sartre alludes to Flaubert's father who "terrorized everyone with his own worth and ability, his Voltairian irony, his terrible angers and his fits of melancholy." The family "was a little behind the industrial families which the father Flaubert cared for or visited"; [38] von Gerlach, also behind his times, is described by Leni and Franz as "old Hindenburg." Flaubert's mother had little influence on the family; in *The Condemned* the mother is dead. Werner's relationship to Franz and to his father clearly duplicates, however feebly, Gustave's relationship to Achille and to his father: hatred and jealousy of the older brother; unrequited love for the father who gives all his affection to his first born, molded in his own image. In a fragment entitled "Père et Fils," part of his work on Flaubert, Sartre describes father, son, and their house:

The child doubly possesses *the House*. He possesses it first of all because the Owner has devoured it, digested it, assimilated it to his own substance, but also because the House contains him and encloses him. In this sense, it becomes the fixed image of the Father. Everywhere in the House, the paternal power makes itself seen; from top to bottom nothing is there that he did not want or allow. Within its walls space is furrowed by the paths which he marked out. Gustave walks within an omnipresent, materialized will. It is that will which he loves in these rooms, that will which hides from him their sinister ugliness.[39]

Sartre uses Flaubert's family to illustrate his idea of the family as one "mediation" between the life of a particular individual and the social and economic forces of history. In *The Condemned* it seems evident that Sartre is attempting to dramatize this approach. The von Gerlach family, exemplifying a certain segment of the German bourgeoisie, contains inherently both Franz the individual case and Hitler's Germany with its systematic atrocities. In a speech at the Sorbonne in 1960, Sartre noted that bourgeois drama means "you always have the right to speak ill of the bourgeois as a man, but not as a bourgeois." [40] *The Condemned* is, among other things, an indictment of the bourgeoisie as a particular Weltanschauung that makes the von Gerlachs, both father and Franz, possible. The nature of Franz's obsession with "grandeur"—power for its own sake, at any price—implies Hitler's power. What made Hitler successful was not the minority of dedicated Nazis, but the much larger number of Germans who, to protect their own power, were willing to collaborate with Hitler. In Sartre's words, "They think against him and they act for him." [41]

Although Franz and his father do not confront each other until Act V (except in flashbacks), the force of their relationship is constantly felt. Raised with his father's ardent love of power, Franz once was compelled to learn what it is to be powerless. Von Gerlach had agreed to sell some of his land to Himmler, to be used as the site for a concentration camp.

Franz, then in his early twenties, saw the prisoners behind the barbed wire and was horrified by his father's act. When a Polish rabbi managed to escape, Franz hid him in his room. To protect his son, the father called Goebbels. Shortly thereafter, S.S. men arrived and massacred the rabbi; Franz watched, helpless to intervene. Owing to the power of his father, Franz is left unpunished for what he has done. The dangerous risk he thought he was taking existed in fact only for the rabbi. Franz sees then that he is not responsible for his acts because, as his father's son, he himself counts as nothing.

Franz has learned that to rebel against Nazi brutality means to suffer impotence. The Biblical principles von Gerlach had instilled in his family have proved themselves expendable, to be honored only when they do not interfere with expediency. Unlike his father, Franz takes very seriously the Protestant ethic whose tenets have been part of the family ritual. Yet Sartre emphasizes that even Franz's act of protecting the rabbi is not particularly admirable in its motivation. When Franz sees the prisoners in the concentration camp, huddled in terror, his first reaction is not compassion but disgust. He does not feel with them as a man witnessing the suffering of other men; what shocks him is "their squalor, their vermin, their sores." They have been transformed in his eyes from fellow human beings into repulsive objects that he cannot help despising, although his Protestant conscience tells him such emotions are wrong. A pride in principle, rather than imaginative sympathy, makes him rebel against the concentration camp that his father's pride in power made possible. By hiding the rabbi he hopes to redeem both his father and himself, since they are one: "It is for us. You and I are one" (Act I).

When, after this incident, Franz must enlist, he seeks to flee from his shame. He wins numerous decorations for military valor—for his failure to escape into death. Power, he later tells his father, became his vocation. Only by serving Hitler could he be a *chef*, could he assume the power for which he was born. Absolute powerlessness, it has been said, corrupts absolutely; rather than be powerless against evil, Franz makes evil his own. Franz follows his obsession to its limit of damnation. On the Russian front he tortures two partisans. After that initiation, he goes on to become the butcher of Smolensk.

Sartre sees in the von Gerlach family a mediation between Franz and the history of which he had been a part. To connect the members of the family Sartre depends on a conventional plot, which does not adequately translate the meaning of that mediation. In *No Exit*, Sartre transforms the conventional triangle situation into a powerful image of Hell. But the romantic triangles of *The Condemned* (Werner-Johanna-Franz, Leni-Franz-Johanna) are not integrated into the play's theme. They are just one part of the melodrama that centers on the father's maneuverings of the two women and Werner. All Sartre's dramatic work depends upon melodramatic devices; where they are successful, these devices are part of the play's meaning. *The Condemned of Altona* gives, rather, the impression of two quite separate plays.

The von Gerlachs are interesting to the extent that they figure directly as part of Franz's madness. Johanna downstairs, whose marriage with Werner is threatened by the father's intrigues, does not hold us. It is only upstairs, in her confrontations with Franz, that Johanna takes on dramatic force. Dressed sumptuously, she appears to Franz as an image of death; her extraordinary beauty tempts him out of his solitude, threatening to destroy his madness and with it, his only reason for living.

Unlike Leni, Johanna exists for Franz with frightening

reality as a separate person; her very presence challenges the reality of his imaginary world. Leni, because of her identity with Franz, poses no such threat. As Oreste Pucciani has pointed out, in Leni "the implicit incest of the von Gerlach family becomes explicit." [42] With the exception of Werner, the von Gerlachs are as one being, Franz in his father, Leni in Franz. Leni's incestuous love for Franz is her pride as a von Gerlach and her only identity. To keep Franz, she reads him made-up newspaper stories, tells him what he wants to hear about Germany, talks to his crabs. In return for protecting his madness, he allows her to take care of him and occasionally makes love to her.

With Johanna's intrusion into the room, however, Franz must fight for his madness. Since he cannot dismiss her, his madness will survive only if he can persuade her to submit to it. Fascinated by her beauty, as his father had guessed he would be, Franz tries to fascinate Johanna in turn. His recognition of Johanna as a prisoner like himself, obsessed with an impossible beauty as he was with an impossible grandeur, draws her into his madness. He tempts her to live upstairs, outside time in eternity, where each can be his desire in the other's eyes. Having come to Franz determined to tell him the truth, Johanna finds herself instead almost believing his lies, almost ready to join with him to protect his madness in a "double delirium." But their mutual ruse cannot succeed. While Johanna is drawn into Franz's madness, Franz is pulled away from it by her presence. When Johanna brings a watch into the room, Franz uses it to count impatiently the minutes she is late. The crabs begin to fade out; Franz turns to Johanna to pass judgment on him.

Franz asks Johanna to judge him only when he is convinced that she may pronounce the favorable verdict he has been trying for years to elicit from his crabs. He knows that

Johanna loves him; unlike the three who judge each other in
No Exit, she wants to acquit him. Except for the single fact
that Franz cannot bear to divulge, Johanna understands his
madness. Although an outsider, she feels his suffering with him.
Since she is separate from him, as Leni is not, she can judge
him; at the same time, he knows that Johanna's love will assure
a more favorable judgment from her than from any other
human being.

Still, he cannot bring himself to tell Johanna the whole
truth. His admissions are merely further evasions. In the two
flashbacks that he lives before Johanna, Franz accuses himself
of a false guilt, knowing in advance that she will acquit him. In
the first flashback of confession, Franz sees an old woman lying
on the ground; her legs have been blown off. She blames him
and all those like him who did not go far enough into the hell
of war, who kept their principles at the cost of Germany's defeat. The memory of that woman—perhaps a fantasy—has been
reassuring to Franz in spite of its hideousness. It is the only
alibi he has to vindicate his crimes. He at least has gone all the
way, "to hell and beyond." With Johanna, Franz uses that story
for the opposite purpose of making himself appear guilty of the
old woman's accusation.

The second flashback was clearly a real event. In Smolensk,
cut off by the partisans and with hardly any rations left, Franz's
men find two Russian peasants. Franz almost tells Johanna
what actually happened and then pulls back, sensing her reaction. His guilt, he says, lies in his innocence: he did not torture.

The arrival of Leni breaks down Franz's lies and his madness as well. Her intention remains what it has always been, to
possess Franz completely and exclusively. As she says to him
proudly: "Dead or alive, it's right that you should belong to me,

for I'm the only one who loves you as you are" (Act IV). Her
obsession with Franz precludes any concern for what he is, as
long as he is hers. To keep him now, she tells Johanna the end
of his story about the two partisans. The audience learns, with
Johanna, what it has suspected for some time. Franz, witness of
man before history, is a torturer.

Earlier, when Franz first chooses Johanna to be his judge,
Johanna wants to refuse that role:

JOHANNA: I'm not your judge. One doesn't judge those whom one
loves.
FRANZ: And suppose you stop loving me? Won't that be a judgment? The last judgment? * [*Pause. He looks quite mad.*] A day
will come, just like any other day. I shall talk about myself, and
you will listen. Then, suddenly, love will be shattered. You will
look at me with horror, and I shall again become [*going down
on his hands and knees and walking sideways*] . . . a crab.
JOHANNA: [*looking at him with horror*]: Stop!
FRANZ [*on his hands and knees*]: You will look at me with those
eyes, exactly like that.   (Act IV)

What Franz foresees with panic is precisely what happens.
When Leni tells everything, Johanna's horror, even stronger
than her love for Franz, is the "last judgment"; it is as definitive
as Inez's judgment, in hatred, of Garcin. If the woman who
loves him cannot accept him, an impartial judge could only find
him guilty. To escape from Johanna's judgment, Franz makes a
last effort to hide in his madness. But it is too late; he can no
longer believe the lies he had been telling himself. Leni has
brought with her a newspaper which she forces him to read. His
father, he learns, is one of the "Giants Who Have Rebuilt Germany." With the clear realization that his martyred Germany is
actually a rich and powerful nation, Franz's madness falls in
ruin. His only alibi has proved false. He has staked everything
on an acquittal from his chosen judge and he has lost.

The intense attraction that Johanna initially feels for Franz affects our own response to him. It is essential to Sartre's intention that we see Franz, in spite of his madness, in spite of the Nazi who still inhabits him, as a man who can be loved. Johanna's love, unlike that of Leni and the Father, who are bound to him as one being, does not preclude the possibility of judgment. At the same time, the recognition between Franz and Johanna allows her to enter into Franz's madness. With each meeting, she becomes increasingly involved in his visions and gradually comes to see herself in Franz. It is this understanding of Franz that gives her final rejection its full meaning. Her love cannot survive the horror; she—and the audience—must judge Franz, in the words of *Dirty Hands*, "unsalvageable."

In Acts I and III, Sartre gives us a realistic portrait of von Gerlach as family tyrant. But that portrait in its carefully situated detail seems less real than von Gerlach as he exists for Franz in his semimadness: the Father who created him in his own image, the Father his "old Führer," the Father who has been "my cause and my fate, right to the end" (Act V). Sartre has said: "The whole play centers on the problem of filial and paternal love." 43 Franz is the only human being his father has ever loved; it is a love that hardly differs from self-love. The hatred Franz now feels in return, inseparable from the passion he turns against himself, is merely another form of that same love. As he tells Johanna, he loves his father "As much as I do myself and less than cholera." Franz has been so enveloped in his father that his own identity seems to him nothing more than an image existing only in old von Gerlach's mind. The relationship between them parallels Sartre's description of what God as creator—if there were a God—would be in relation to his creature:

The tragedy of the absolute Creator, if he existed, would be the impossibility of getting out of himself, for whatever he created could only be himself. Where could my creation derive any objectivity and independence, since its form and its matter are *from me?* [44]

Franz's meeting with his father corresponds to the final confrontation, characteristic of all Sartre's plays, in which one antagonist attempts to assert his power over the other by some irrevocable act. In many of the plays that act is murder. In Sartre's first play, Orestes symbolically kills the Father Jupiter by triumphantly rejecting the god's power. Franz, unable to free himself from the power of his father, must finally die with him.

Alone in his room and mad with pride, Franz assumed full responsibility for himself, his country, and his century. In *Saint Genet,* Sartre defines pride as "the reaction of a mind which has been beleaguered by others and which transforms its absolute dependency into absolute self-sufficiency." [45] But face to face with his father, Franz accepts that absolute dependence. One lie has given way to another: upstairs, Franz refused to recognize his act; downstairs, he denies the self that committed the act. He accuses the father of being responsible for the crimes of his son: "It's because you're an informer that I'm a torturer."

His fear of being judged by his father soon changes into a desperate need for that judgment. Only to his father can he confess everything. Both father and son are criminals; yet, without God to believe in, the son looks to his father as his "natural judge." His father becomes for him what he always has been, the one who knows him completely because he has made him. The lies Franz told himself in his room turn out to have been in vain; for three years his father has known that he was "the butcher of Smolensk." Nevertheless, von Gerlach neither can nor wants to judge his son. Bound to Franz in whatever he is, von Gerlach rejects Franz's acts but continues to love him totally. His paternal love, born of identity, makes judgment impossible.

The identity of son in father is brought to its resolution when von Gerlach takes on Franz's responsibility for his crimes as butcher of Smolensk. Left with nothing, Franz allows his father to sanctify that nothingness. In a momentary illusion that he, Franz, has never really existed, that his father was all, his hatred vanishes and he can accept the paternal gift of grace: "I made you. I will unmake you. My death will envelop yours, and in the end I shall be the only one to die" (Act V). As Madeleine Fields has pointed out, Franz dies without a trace:

> In Argentina, no tomb carries his name, since he is not dead. In Germany, his death will be "enveloped" in that of his father. Franz will drown with him in the Elbe where their bodies will not be found. The newspapers will mention only the death of the father since, officially, Franz died in South America.[46]

The von Gerlach power—the father who gave Hitler ships and the son who gave him corpses—ends inevitably with a *Götterdämmerung* that extends symbolically beyond father and son to the decadent civilization they represent. Imprisoned in a past that has left them without a future, they have no way out except in death.

S ARTRE's great achievement in *The Condemned of Altona* is his dramatization of Franz. In Brecht's play *A Man's a Man,* a mild little Irish dockworker living in a fantastical setting of colonial India undergoes complete transformation to become another man—the ferocious soldier Jeriah Jip. At first, we begin to identify with the likable Gayley Gay; then, as he is changed before our eyes into something horrible, we recoil, watching from comic distance the performance of this person-thing. But the profound originality and excitement of *The Condemned* lies in a direction opposed to Brecht's alienation effect. Sartre

presents his Nazi lieutenant in such a way that we not only con-
demn him, we also identify with him. In a discussion of his
technique Sartre has explained:

Distancing should not destroy the *Einfühlung* dear to the ex-
pressionists. The two should go together. How does one make
the public understand what it is to come back from a war and
to remember that one was a torturer? The public must be able to
identify with the protagonist. It must be able to *hate itself in
him*.[47]

For thirteen years, Franz tried to escape the memory of his
war crimes. In keeping with the von Gerlach tradition, Franz
was raised on the Bible; its principles had instilled in him a
strict sense of right and wrong. Unable to stand the contradiction between his acts and his conscience, he sought to find a
resolution in madness. There is nothing of the clinical, detached observer in Sartre's creation of Franz. He presents
Franz's delirium as a subjective experience, making us understand it from within. We see Franz's madness and the particular form it takes as a solution he has invented, the only way he
can live an unlivable situation.

Yet Franz's madness, for all the self-deception it involves,
ultimately does not save him from understanding. His ravings
depend upon an intuition of truths that those who are "normal" manage not to see. The very effort to exorcize his past
makes that past intensely present. In his self-created prison
Franz has installed a permanent tribunal. He is cut in two, one
half a traitor to the other. While he has a need to be judged, he
needs also to be acquitted. His long speeches to the tribunal of
crabs are the elaboration of a grandiose lie. He must escape
from the act he has committed; to accomplish that end, he assumes the voice of the German nation, which he determinedly
believes is being systematically destroyed by the war's victors.
Only in the apocalyptic vision of a martyred Germany, the beginning of humanity's extinction, can he find absolution for his

own crimes. Franz's suffering is the result of his remaining lucidity: he is not mad enough to believe his lies totally. Man's witness, loudly proclaiming that his century is not guilty, constantly becomes the accused, defending himself from an invisible accuser whom he serves as opponent and accomplice.

For thirteen years, Franz lives imprisoned in his upstairs room, defending himself and his century before his thirtieth-century judges. His presence in that room controls the destiny of all the von Gerlachs; all find themselves sequestered, dependent on Franz. While they look upstairs to him, constantly aware of the bolted door above them, Franz thinks only of the crustaceans who in turn are above him, "Masked inhabitants of the ceilings," looking at him with the eyes of history.

As we have seen in *No Exit*, the petrifying look of the other is one of Sartre's fundamental images; it pervades both his literature and his philosophy. The characters of *No Exit* exist in a timeless reality in which each is eternally condemned to suffer being looked at by the other two. The look becomes a Last Judgment or, in other terms, an ontological reality. Even in Sartre's early work the look often takes on a social and historical dimension; he uses it as an expression of class struggle in a particular situation. We have seen in *Dirty Hands* the effect on Hugo of Slick and George looking at him, reducing him to the bourgeois identity he has joined the Party to escape. Beyond even the class struggle, the eyes of the crowd watching France's defeated soldiers in a famous passage of *Troubled Sleep* become transformed into the look of history:

"We're being looked at." A crowd growing more and more dense was watching them swallow this bitter pill of history. The crowd grew older and backed away from them, muttering: "There stand the vanquished of 1940, the army of defeat. By their fault, we are in fetters." There they stood, unchanged beneath the changing scrutiny of the crowd, judged, summed up, explained, accused, excused, condemned, imprisoned within this ineffaceable day, buried beneath the drone of insects and the rumble of guns, in

the hot smell of growing things, in the air quivering above beds of carrots; there they stood, guilty forever in the eyes of their sons, of their grandsons, and of their great-grandsons, they, the conquered of 1940 to all eternity. . . . [Mathieu] looked at his comrades, and his mortal eyes met the timeless, petrified eyes of history.[48]

The look of history is even further distanced in *The Condemned* with Sartre's use of the crustaceans. Franz demands of his crabs: "But why have you kept your eyes? That was the ugliest thing about us. Why?" (Act II). But it is for their eyes that he has invented these masked inhabitants of the ceiling. In their imagined look, Franz tries to discover how he might appear to an entirely alien species. He needs the absolute judgment of an inhuman being: since he can no longer believe in God, he turns instead to a subhuman form of life.

The crabs in *The Condemned* supply the play's most powerful metaphor. Crustacean imagery appears frequently in Sartre's work, dating from an experience in 1938 when he took mescaline in order to study on himself its hallucinatory effects. The result was a nightmarish deformation of ordinary objects, described as part of Roquentin's sickness in *Nausea*. One of the visions that most haunted Sartre was a variety of sea creatures: a lobster crawling behind him, an octupus that threatened to overwhelm him.[49] In Franz's room, crustaceans and mollusks, emblems of his madness, are omnipresent. He speaks to the crabs on the ceiling. His preferred food is oysters; he lives surrounded by their discarded shells, which he nervously rubs together or uses to bombard the portrait of Hitler on the wall.

In *Saint Genet* Sartre writes:

We feel that we are being judged by the masked men who will succeed us and whose knowledge of all things will be such that we cannot have the slightest inkling of what it will be; our age will be an object for those future eyes whose gaze haunts us. And a guilty object. They will reveal to us our failure and guilt.[50]

Why do the "masked men who will succeed us" become in *The*

Condemned "masked inhabitants of the ceilings," no longer men but crabs? Franz's obsession with crustaceans points not only to the inhuman beings who look at him; it points also to the inhuman being within himself.

There is a scene in *Nausea* in which Roquentin remembers himself at the age of eight, playing in the Luxembourg gardens. He sees passing "one of these fishy-eyed men with an inward look and with whom no agreement is possible. . . . We felt that he was shaping thoughts of crab or lobster in his head. And that terrified us, the fact that one could conjure thoughts of lobsters on the sentry-box, on our hoops, on the bushes." 51 But Sartre, describing the child Jean-Paul in *The Words*, sees the crustaceans not in another, but as an image of himself: "What flowed from my pen at that point—an octopus with eyes of flame, a twenty-ton crustacean, a giant spider that talked—was I myself, a child monster; it was my boredom with life, my fear of death, my dullness and my perversity." 52

The generalized metaphysical horror that the crustaceans represented for Sartre up to the period of *Nausea* takes on, in *The Condemned*, an historical significance. The terror of metamorphosis—brute physical being triumphing over the human—is still there. But that metamorphosis now takes place as a result of man's acts, the atrocities he has committed in history. In "Paris sous l'Occupation" Sartre describes the enemy as "an octopus: it seized our best men in the dark and made them disappear. It seemed to be all around us, silently swallowing them up." 53 When, under Johanna's influence, Franz's madness begins to disintegrate, we see the real meaning of the crabs. To Johanna's question about the truth he supposedly tells to his crabs, Franz retorts:

What crabs? Are you mad? What crabs? [*Pause. He turns away.*] Ah, yes, yes . . . [*With a sudden thought*] The Crabs are men. [*Pause.*] What? [*He sits down*] Where did I discover that?

[*Pause.*] I knew it . . . once . . . Yes, yes, yes. But I've got so much on my mind. [*Pause. In a decided tone*] Real men, good and handsome, on all the balconies of the centuries. When I was crawling in the yard, I thought I heard them saying: "What's that, brother?" And that . . . was me. [*He stands up, springs to attention, gives a military salute, and speaks in a loud voice.*] I, the Crab.   (Act IV)

In a premonition of what is to follow, Franz crawls on his hands and knees as if he were a crab. Johanna looks at him with horror. When the revelation comes that Franz is a torturer, Johanna looks at him with that same horror, the horror of watching a human being transformed into a beast. Franz who has tortured ceases to be human; he is metamorphosed into an animal—in Sartre's imagery, a crab.

Franz speaks to the crabs in a public voice; what he wants them to understand, however, is intensely private. His defense of man does not concern itself with the facts; he leaves those to the "false witnesses." His task is to communicate another truth: "Centuries, I shall tell you how my century tasted and you will acquit the accused" (Act II). For Franz, the subjective *moi* who has inflicted horror, his acts remain with him like a bad taste; the image recurs frequently in Franz's ravings. "Where does it come from, this rancid, dead taste in my mouth? From man? From the beast? From myself? It is the taste of the century" (Act V).

He registers his defense into a tape recorder. For the benefit of his judges, he gives an eloquent performance, improvising fabulous ruses as he goes along. An able lawyer, he knows that his job is to acquit his client. But when Franz plays back what he has said, the words seem to belong to someone else: "I didn't mean to say that. But who's speaking? Not a word of truth" (Act II). Unable to find the right words, he is condemned to testify interminably. Herbert Blau has alluded to "the affinity between Krapp's tape and Gerlach's. . . . The tape is Krapp's defense against extinction." 54 In Franz, as in Krapp, there is a painful intimacy between the voice listening and the voice speaking, like two persons who need each other but cannot communicate. The Franz who listens to his tapes wants to hear the truth; he knows that the Franz talking into the recorder has been telling lies. Since Franz cannot reject one for the other, the ritual must continue.

By means of the tape recorder, *je* becomes *un autre*. In *Man's Fate* Kyo remembers "that record, *his* voice which he had not recognized a while ago, at Hemmelrich's. He thought of it with the same complex uneasiness that he had felt when as a child, he was shown his tonsils which the surgeon had just removed." 55 Franz's tape recorder involves the same kind of anxiety. His voice has become externalized; it is something over there, like someone else.

Hoping that his truth will somehow become the truth, Franz continues his endless conversation with posterity. When Leni points out that his tapes can be stolen, he invents a new device: "Imagine a black window. Finer than ether. Ultra-sensitive. It records the slightest breath. The *slightest* breath. All history is engraved on it, from the beginning of time to this snap of my fingers" (Act II). Franz's omnipresent window pane, like the tape, replaces an absent God. They are Franz's attempt to guarantee that his life will not end without significance. What he fears most is not death but meaninglessness: somewhere, something must register that he, Franz von Gerlach, has lived and has taken responsibility for his century.

Franz's real wish, as he tells his father, is not to have been born. He continually acts out this desire for nonbeing. In one of the best polemic images of the play, a kind of political sacrilege, Franz eats his medals. They are made of chocolate and we are given the impression that he eats them every day. When Leni brings him a birthday cake with his name written on it in pink sugar, he eats it as his body and drinks champagne as his blood, in a grotesque parody of the Last Supper. At the end of the play, Franz brings these gestures of negation to realization in his death—by drowning—as decided by his father. Religious imagery and allusions occur throughout the play. Both father and son use the Bible as sacred, although they no longer believe in it. In his room, Franz informs the crabs of his new station identification: D.P.C., *De profundis clamavi*.56 The crabs themselves are an inversion of God's tribunal of angels.

In Franz's madness his own existence is indistinguishable from the existence of man. Thus, he transforms his desire for self-negation into a vision of man's extinction. Without a future himself, he has decided that mankind has no future either. The destruction of man by the beast in himself has resulted in a universal apocalypse. He proclaims: "Man is dead and I am his witness" (Act II). Franz lives as if his vision of man's death were an accomplished reality. In the void that he both desires and fears, Franz imagines his tapes long after his death: they testify in defense of man, who has been replaced by the crab as lord of creation.

W HEN *The Condemned* was first presented in Paris in 1959, the critics and the audience understood that Franz was also a symbol: Sartre was talking to them not only about a former S.S. lieutenant but also about French torture in Algeria.57 Had Sartre written the play that he really wanted to write, no theatre in Paris, as he said to Oreste Pucciani in an interview, would have produced it.58 Although Sartre attempts on one level to root the von Gerlachs within a specific family tradition, Franz himself evokes both the French soldier returned from Algeria and the French nation marked by its experience of the Occupation and the Algerian war. "It has been midnight for twenty years this century," Franz tells his crabs. "It's not very easy to keep your eyes open at midnight" (Act II).

Franz becomes a torturer because of an experience of unbearable powerlessness. After the failure of his attempt to resist the Nazis, Franz determines that he will pay any price not to repeat that humiliation. Since power is on the side of the Nazis, he joins with them to make that power his own. Like many French collaborators after the French defeat, he never really believed Nazi doctrines; he did believe that Nazi power would triumph. Franz tells his father: "I was Hitler's wife" (Act V). Sartre has noted in his essay "Qu'est-ce qu'un collaborateur?" that "everywhere in the articles of Chateaubriant, Drieu, Brasillach, you will find curious metaphors which present the relations of France and Germany as a sexual union in which France plays the female role. And most certainly, the feudal *liaison* of the collaborator to his master has a sexual aspect." 59

But those who actively collaborated with the Nazis after France's defeat represented a small minority of the French population. Most of the French suffered the Nazi domination of France as victims; they looked at the German soldiers and their French collaborators as inhuman monsters. With the Algerian war, the nation's horror of torture shifted from "they" to "we." Sartre's point is that the French in 1959 found themselves in the same relation to the Algerians as that of the Germans to the French during World War II. The anger in *The Condemned* reverberates very differently from that in *The Victors*, which takes place at a time when the moral question, at least, was simple: evil clearly stood on the other side. Sartre describes the transformation that he was later to dramatize in Franz:

During the war, when the English radio and the clandestine Press spoke of the massacre of Oradour, we watched the German soldiers walking inoffensively down the street, and we would say to ourselves: "They look like us. How can they act as they do?" And we were proud of ourselves for not understanding.

Today we know there was nothing to understand. The decline has been gradual and imperceptible. But now when we raise our heads and look into the mirror we see an unfamiliar and hideous reflection: ourselves.[60]

What Sartre wants to achieve with his characterization of Franz is recognition as well as condemnation.

The central fact about Franz and *The Condemned of Altona* is torture. What does it mean for a man of both conscience and intelligence to torture and to have to remember that he has tortured? To say that a man is what he does is meaningful only if it includes an awareness of the complexity involved in every act:

The fact is that an act can no more be reduced to what it is than can a man: it transcends itself. Viewed subjectively, it escapes by virtue of its objectivity, and sooner or later its objective significantion returns in the most unexpected way to strike it directly even in its subjective depths: sooner or later, "objective" betrayal becomes subjective and taints our innocence. Viewed objectively, the act escapes by virtue of its subjective reality.[61]

More than any other Sartrean play, *The Condemned* succeeds in dramatizing this unresolvable tension between subject and object. What moves us in Franz is the constant strain he experiences as he lives out the suffering of his century: he exists for us both as the man who has tortured and as the man who is tortured. The executioner is also a victim. All his life he has been possessed: first by his father, then by Hitler, now by his memories. To accept himself is impossible. Unlike Leni, Franz cannot say with conviction "I have done what I wanted, and I want what I have done."

In his essay "A Victory" Sartre celebrates the victory of one man, a Frenchman, over the fellow Frenchmen who tortured him. Amidst all the horror of the Algerian war, Henri Alleg's account becomes a testimony that the human man can triumph. By presenting his torturers as merely other men who should and can be stopped, Alleg wrests us from our fascination with "the abyss of the inhuman." "The inhuman does not exist," Sartre proclaims, "except in nightmares engendered by fear."* 62

In that same year (1958), the other, less confident Sartre, was writing *The Condemned of Altona,* a play that gives life to these nightmares of the inhuman:

One and one make one—there's our mystery. The beast was hiding, and suddenly we surprised his look deep in the eyes of our neighbors. So we struck. Legitimate self defense. I surprised the beast. I struck. A man fell, and in his dying eyes I saw the beast still living—myself.   (Act V)

In the murderer and his victim lives the same beast; murder is suicide with a case of mistaken identity. The murderer tries to kill in the other what he hates and fears in himself. Forced to choose between the terrified and the terrifying, he becomes the latter, if he has the means to do so. Man is eating his fellow man, the crab; nevertheless, "the accused is dying of hunger." His ever more voracious appetite for violence cannot be satisfied, since it is finally the whole human race that he wants to devour. Franz's last tape records his vision of the unlimited capacity for murder that threatens to become humanity's suicide.

The room in *The Condemned* contains a reality radically different from that of the rooms in Sartre's works before 1945. *Nausea,* "The Room," and *No Exit* take place in an essentially ahistorical world. Dominique Fernandez, in a generally negative review of *The Condemned,* contends:

There is an excellent theatrical idea in *The Condemned:* the struggle of this man, both mad and reasonable, against the ghosts of his memory and of his conscience. Sartre at his best can be found there, the pre-war Sartre of *Nausea,* of *No Exit* also, who had chosen to account for the human condition by isolating it within the four walls of a cell. Having reached maturity Sartre, like Goethe with the second *Faust,* wanted to enlarge this cell to the dimensions of history. Result: a bourgeois drama, complete with the pater familias, the unsuccessful son, the incestuous daughter, the adulterous daughter-in-law, and which is not saved by the brilliant extravagances of the prodigal son, mirror and conscience of the world.[63]

Such a judgment misses the point. It is true that *The Condemned* is cluttered by a plot of family intrigues. Inside the "cell," however, Franz's struggle draws its meaning from the history that he has made and that has made him. For Sartre in 1959, to "account for the human condition" inevitably means—as it did for Malraux—the human condition in history. History is not an arbitrary superstructure in *The Condemned*; Franz's room exists in history with the same necessity that the room of *No Exit* exists in Hell. "One and one make one—there's our mystery," Franz tells his tape. In *No Exit* the three *damnés* who prey on each other cannot do without each other. In *Dirty Hands* Hugo's murder of Hoederer leads directly to his own suicide. The terrible interdependence of man and his human prey, fixed by eternity in *No Exit*, dramatized in individual nonmythical terms in *Dirty Hands*, becomes in *The Condemned of Altona* the tragedy of history.

Most of Sartre's plays are concerned with man and history. *The Condemned*, however, is the first play in which man's struggle with history takes place in the claustrophobic world of Sartre's best early works. In Franz's room, enclosed behind the bolted door, history assumes a life and a tragic reality that is singularly absent from the open spaces of *The Flies* and *The Devil and the Good Lord*.

Simone de Beauvoir has written of Sartre and herself:

One of our inconsistencies was our refusal to accept the idea of the subconscious. Yet Gide, the surrealists, and, despite our resistance, Freud himself had all convinced us that in every person there lurks what André Breton called *un infracassable noyau de nuit*, an indestructible kernel of darkness, something that . . . does, now and then, burst out in a peculiarly scandalous fashion.[64]

In contrast to so many of Sartre's heroes who are reduced to schematic formulas, Franz, in the best moments of the play, puts us in touch with that "infracassable noyau de nuit" at the point where our individual and collective history meet.

Conclusion

A driving force in all his writing is his serious desire to change the life of his reader.

IRIS MURDOCH, *Sartre*

THE Sartrean hero, both an agent and an actor, belongs in the theatre. In action, usually violent action, he plays out his desire to achieve an heroic image in the eyes of others. Orestes, Goetz, Hugo, Garcin, Franz—all are obsessed with salvation through heroism, possible and realized for Orestes and Goetz, unrealized for Hugo, impossible for Garcin and Franz.

It is worth noting that the much talked about "existentialist hero," considered a "positive" figure, does not appear at all in Sartre's novels or stories; he appears only in *The Flies* and *The Devil and the Good Lord*. Orestes and Goetz belong to no collectivity. Their past has left them only with a sense of what they are not. *Engagement* expressed in violence thus becomes their means of acceding to reality. In Sartre's heroic mythology, violence for a liberating cause is both a ritual of initiation into the human community and the exact price of his hero's salvation.

Speaking to a critic from *Théâtre Populaire* about his own plays as opposed to those of Brecht, Sartre took this position: "We must make our public—which might not react to a purely critical spectacle—participate in the actual demystification of certain characters." [1] In theory this position is valid. But it is Sartre's *No Exit*, one of the two plays he might call a purely critical spectacle, that is also his most perfect: the only play in which Sartre fully realizes what he sets out to do. Both *The Flies* and *The Devil and the Good Lord* concern "the actual demystification" of the hero, as brought about by a radical conversion. Sartre goes beyond the idea of recognition (*anagnorisis*) in which the hero sees the flaw that has led to his destruction. His two heroes have both the will and the means to act upon their new knowledge. The future is all.

We are not convinced that the future *is* all, perhaps because Sartre himself—in spite of Orestes and Goetz—does not quite believe in the possibility of individual salvation:

The retrospective illusion has been smashed to bits; martyrdom, salvation, and immortality are falling to pieces; the edifice is going to rack and ruin; I collared the Holy Ghost in the cellar and threw him out; atheism is a cruel and long-range affair: I think I've carried it through. I see clearly, I've lost my illusions, I know what my real jobs are, I surely deserve a prize for good citizenship. For the last ten years or so I've been a man who's been waking up, cured of a long, bitter-sweet madness, and who can't get over the fact.[2]

Sartre wrote this passage in 1964; he would date his awakening, then, from 1954. Yet, as early as 1943 Orestes' salvation through the salvation of others seems less a conviction than a cherished fantasy, passionately wished for but never entirely believed.[3] This element of fantasy is even more apparent in *The Devil and the Good Lord*.[4] It is surely not a coincidence that neither of Sartre's heroic plays takes place in modern times. The transposition of *The Flies* into ancient legend was made necessary by the Occupation; one feels in *The Devil and the Good Lord* that Sartre chose an historical spectacle as a necessary means to make the extraordinary feats of his hero more credible.

We have seen in these spectacles that the hero must use violence to achieve his goal of liberation: the conversion that redeems Orestes and Goetz is marked by murder. But whatever their revolutionary ends may be, we are shown in these plays only the violent means. Sartre's remarks about Brecht point up a fundamental difference between the two playwrights in their presentation of heroism:

If only there were a hero: the onlooker, whoever he may be, likes to identify himself with those exalted characters who, for themselves and for everyone, reconcile opposites and make Good overcome Evil. . . . But Brecht puts no heroes on the stage. . . . That is to say that there is no individual salvation, it is the whole of society that must change: and the function of the dramatist remains that "purification" of which Aristotle spoke; he shows us what we are: victims and accomplices at the same time. This is why the plays of Brecht move us.[5]

When Brecht directly advocates revolutionary violence in his plays, his favorite spokesman is the well-intentioned young woman like Joan Dark or the Good Woman of Setzuan. Her ineffectiveness speaks more convincingly in dramatic terms than the total efficacy of Sartre's two heroes.

In *The Condemned*, written during the Algerian war, heroism expressed by violence takes on a very different meaning from that embodied by Orestes and Goetz. "In this play," Sartre has explained, "I tried to demystify military heroism by showing the link which unites it to unrestrained violence." [6] The meaning of Franz's military heroism is made dramatically convincing, as Goetz's liberating heroism never is. Sartre's adaptation in 1965 of Euripides' *The Trojan Women* continues certain preoccupations manifested in *The Condemned of Altona*. The voices of the Trojan women, lamenting and damning their fate, serve as a kind of counterpoint to Franz's protests before the tribunal of crabs. *The Condemned* centers on a father and son who were agents of an oppressive history; in *The Trojan Women*, Sartre focuses on the people at whose expense history has been made. The would-be hero has left the center of the stage; in his place stands what is left of an oppressed people.

In an introduction to the play, Sartre explains how he first became interested in adapting it:

The Trojan Women was produced during the Algerian War, in a very faithful translation by Jacqueline Moatti. I was impressed by the way this version was received by a public favorable to negotiations with the F.L.N.; it was this aspect of the play which first interested me. The play had a precise political significance when it was first produced. It was an explicit condemnation of war in general, and of imperial expeditions in particular.*7

Sartre has tried to make the play more accessible to a modern audience by developing certain legends and omitting others; by "dramatizing" static oppositions of characters; by choosing a poetic language faithful to the language of the original "but which modified [its] tone."*

Euripides' tragedy expressed his opposition to his fellow Greeks; it is a memorial to the victims of their war. Sartre has accentuated and modernized Euripides' condemnation of colonial wars:

> Men of Europe,
> you despise Africa and Asia
> and you call us barbarians, I believe,
> But when vainglory and greed
> throw you on our land,
> you pillage, you torture, you massacre.
> Where are the barbarians, then? 8

The final words of Sartre's adaptation are left to the sea god Poseidon:

> Make war, stupid mortals,
> ravage the fields and the cities,
> violate the temples, the tombs,
> and torture the victims.
> You will die of it.
> All of you.*

SARTRE's myth of salvation takes two forms, distinct but closely related: salvation through the creation of a work of art and salvation through heroic action. He writes in *The Words*:

"I was of the Church. As a militant, I wanted to save myself by works; as a mystic, I attempted to reveal the silence of being by a thwarted rustling of words and, what was most important, I confused things with their names: that amounts to believing." 9 The past tense indicates that this state of believing no longer obtains. The break occurred in the mid-1950s when Sartre, increasingly involved in direct political action, began to question the assumptions about literature that had informed all his earlier work.

Sartre the "mystic" first reveals himself in *Nausea*. At the end of the book, Roquentin goes back for the last time to the Bouville café; he listens to his favorite record, turned on, appropriately, by Madeleine. The song is a popular jazz blues, "Some of These Days." Listening to "this little jeweled pain" Roquentin feels a kind of joy, the possibility of a way out of nausea: "She sings. So two of them are saved: the Jew and the Negress. Saved. . . . They are a little like dead people for me, a little like the heroes of a novel; they have washed themselves of the sin of existing." 10 Only art is not *de trop*; it simply is, beyond existence in a world of essence. Something of the necessity of the work of art passes to its creator.

This almost Proustian belief in salvation through art did not survive intact Sartre's experience of France's defeat and the Occupation. Sartre the "militant" makes his appearance in the theatre, where the myth of salvation takes on a new form: salvation through heroic action. His first idea of *littérature engagée*, born during the war, rests on a faith that stage action can somehow incite the audience to political action. The mediator of this transformation is the dramatic hero. His action in the imaginary world of the stage assumes a magical power to create changes in the real world.

Jeanson has said that Sartre tries in his literary works to reconcile "esthetic demands and a certain idea of effectiveness." 11

Such a distinction implies that a work of literature can be effective beyond its realization as art, that it can be effective as action. In his *What Is Literature?*, written in 1947, Sartre contrasts the prose writer with the poet or painter. He defines prose as essentially utilitarian, using words as signs that point to a particular meaning. The poet, on the other hand, like the artist with his paint, creates an object with words; as such it is opaque and self-contained. The context of Sartre's definitions implies a faith that prose literature can act in the real world.

This utilitarian conception of prose bears directly on Sartre's sense of literature as salvation. The connection lies in his position that "the 'engaged' writer knows that words are action. He knows that to reveal is to change and that one can reveal only by planning to change." 12 In this definition Sartre does not distinguish between action and the image of action, or, as he so frequently puts it, between act and gesture. A magical leap has been made from the word to the world.13

Although *What Is Literature?* contrasts in some detail the language of poetry with the language of prose, Sartre does not concern himself with the language of literature as it differs from prose in general. He rejects unequivocally the idea of revolutionary art as it is expressed by Soviet realism; the two modern writers for whom he has most frequently expressed admiration are Kafka and Faulkner. It is not a question of committed literature as opposed to so-called "pure art" or "art for art's sake." Sartre's great strength lies in his continuing insistence on what Gomez, the painter and Spanish civil war general in *Troubled Sleep*, calls the "embarrassing questions." 14 More than any other contemporary French dramatist, Sartre sees what those questions are. His central problem in the plays is one of language: his demand that words become action conflicts with their power as words.

No Exit is the only Sartrean play that triumphs completely over this problem. Its structure has the kind of mathematical purity that Maurice Blanchot has described as the essence of theatre:

In the theatre, neither ideas nor words count in themselves. What counts is the relationships that they sustain, the transitions that they assume, the general action for which they provide the momentary fulcrums. There is no genre in which language is closer to the terms of mathematical analysis.[15]

The entire action is in the interaction of the three characters as they create their hell. Once the infernal machine is set in motion, it functions with its own automatic necessity. Nothing external intervenes to alter the initial situation; we simply watch the inevitable take place in a single dramatic movement that repeats itself again and again, each time with greater intensity until the final *prise de conscience* which is the play's climax.

The Condemned of Altona does not achieve the integration of form and content that gives *No Exit* its peculiarly classical beauty. The achievement of *The Condemned* is Franz. Earlier, in *Dirty Hands*, Sartre created in Hugo a character perhaps equally complex; as with Franz, we are given an intimate awareness of his public and private truths. Hugo, however, lacks the stature to embody those issues that the play requires him to embody. *Dirty Hands* nevertheless succeeds as effective drama because of the vitality of its central relationships. In *The Condemned*, a more ambitious and original effort than *Dirty Hands*, Sartre creates with Franz a character both fascinating in himself and large enough to support the themes with which the play contends. The scenes of Franz's madness, his attempts to find the words that will proclaim him innocent to the tribunal of crabs, are equal to the best in Sartre's writing.

Like *No Exit* and *The Condemned* Sartre's satiric comedies dramatize a negative image. *The Respectful Prostitute* and *Nekrassov* miss their mark, however, to the extent that Sartre distrusts the critical function of comedy. At crucial moments, he abandons his chosen weapon. For the critics who had forgotten "The Childhood of a Leader," and who considered his comic plays negligible, *The Words* was something of a revelation. In fact, its dominant style of comic irony is not really new in Sartre's work; the difference is that in *The Words* he is able to sustain and control this style. Much of the irony of *The Words* lies in the discrepancy between grandiose heroic postures and the little boy Jean-Paul who assumes those postures. With obvious pleasure, Sartre dismantles the bourgeois image of a happy child. While he feels entirely free to mock the impostures of childhood, he does not allow himself the same freedom when he is dealing with the more directly political subjects of *The Respectful Prostitute* or *Nekrassov*. Rather than allowing his characters to speak as themselves, Sartre the political moralist, fearful of not being clear, periodically intrudes to explain what he really means.

Sartre often speaks of literature as an act of "disclosure," but the majority of his plays reach impatiently for a more concrete kind of action. In so doing, they rarely by indirections find directions out; instead, they rely on straightforward, didactic prose. As Sartre sees clearly in *Saint Genet*, literature can accomplish its ends only by making of language a force persuasive in its own right:

Genet is careful not to propose: he *demands*—therein lies his diabolical cleverness. In order for him to fight against the restive attention of his readers, in order to force them to have thoughts which are distasteful to them, there must be a categorical imperative—constantly lurking behind the words—that requires unconditional adherence. In short, the work must be beautiful.[16]

It is precisely this beauty that Sartre, more puritanical than Genet, rarely allows himself. Sartre has always been fascinated by the absolute of literature and, at the same time, distrustful of its attraction. As a choice of the imaginary over the real, literature becomes suspect, since it is the real world that Sartre wants to change. His plays, like his philosophy, struggle with Marx's famous eleventh thesis on Feuerbach: "The philosophers have only *interpreted* the world, in various ways; the point, however, is to *change* it." From that point of view, beauty becomes something almost contemptible: it cannot do; it can only be.

Many critics have insisted that Sartre does not take his writing for the theatre seriously. Thus, R.-M. Albérès writes: "It is obvious, moreover, that Sartre's dramatic work constitutes for him only a rather secondary illustration of his thought, a recourse to the 'mass-media.' "* 17 This point of view seems mistaken on two counts. First of all, it ignores Sartre's delight in the panache of theatre, dating from his childhood:

But, regardless of author, I adored the works in the Hetzel series, little theatres whose red cover with gold tassels represented the curtain; the gilt edges were the footlights. I owe to those magic boxes—and not to the balanced sentences of Chateaubriand—my first encounters with Beauty.18

Second, far from thinking of theatre as "recourse to the mass media," Sartre sees the impasse of literature in general in its inability, at this point in history, to speak to all.19 His sense that literature must be *concretely* universal is particularly frustrated by the theatre as it exists institutionally. In *The Words*, Sartre expresses his dislike for the bourgeois, hierarchical aspect of theatre, which he opposes to the mingled, popular audience of films. Speaking of "that sense of everyone's direct relationship to everyone else," he recalls his experience as a prisoner in Stalag XII D. 20 Significantly, it was in that situation that he wrote his first play, *Bariona*.

It is true that while Sartre has complained of theatre as a bourgeois institution, his own plays do not attempt to change the old forms. The subject of all Sartrean plays is subversive; their end is to undermine the established system of values. Sartre sees the writer as a mediator who gives society a "bad conscience" by creating an awareness that contests its basic assumptions. But he presents this subversive content within a conventional form. Sartre has expressed great admiration for the dramas of Brecht, Genet, and Beckett; in his own plays, however, he has chosen to use traditional dramatic techniques rather than experiment with new ones. This traditionalism has often proved inadequate to sustain what he wants to say. Robert Brustein, in an article on *The Condemned of Altona*, calls Sartre "The Janus of Modern Dramatists":

His virtues stem from an adventurous mind, his faults from an inability to be equally adventurous in his use of the stage. As a thinker, Sartre has no peers among contemporary playwrights, but he has not yet learned to forge his ideas into powerful myths. He is certainly a dramatist, but one who presently looks backward, even as he is pushing forward intellectually to the limits of human thought.[21]

In *What Is Literature?* Sartre relates committed literature specifically to political action that is directed toward a democratic, socialist society. In the same essay, dropping his distinction between poetry and prose, he expresses as the final end of art: "to recover this world by giving it to be seen as it is, but as if it had its source in human freedom."[22] As in *Nausea*, art again becomes an absolute, separate from any moral imperatives outside it; the artist asserts his power to redeem the world by giving it beauty through the creative act. Questioned in 1960 about the meaning of committed literature, Sartre used Mallarmé's work as an example and explained: "I mention him to show you that pure literature is a dream. . . . If literature is not *everything* then it is not worth an hour of trouble.[23] That is what I mean by 'engagement.' "[24]

For Sartre the idea of literature as an absolute is intimately connected with a faith in salvation. His most recent position, expressed in *The Words*, indicates that his loss of faith in one has meant loss of faith in both:

For a long time, I took my pen for a sword; I now know we're powerless. No matter. I write and will keep writing books; they're needed; all the same, they do serve some purpose. Culture doesn't save anything or anyone, it doesn't justify. But it's a product of man: he projects himself into it, he recognizes himself in it; that critical mirror alone offers him his image.[25]

Sartre, writing about the hero seeking salvation, was himself pursuing salvation through the act of writing. But a play, in his own words, enacts "the image of the act"; [26] writing is "a gesture-creating act." [27] *The Words* involves a rethinking of the relationship of literature and action. It is perhaps not a coincidence that both Sartre's most recent play and his adaptation of Euripides present only a "critical mirror." In *The Condemned of Altona* Franz conveys an image irreducible to the schematic formulas for right action that characterize Orestes and Goetz. *The Trojan Women* has no hero, nor does it offer any answers. Sartre seems to have become more willing to leave to his essays the task of pointing the way to solutions.

Sartre's contradictions as a writer exemplify with particular clarity the crisis in contemporary literature that has occupied such critics as Jean Paulhan, Gaëtan Picon, and Roland Barthes: the writer's distrust of language, his desire to realize a truth beyond the possibilities of literature. In Sartre's plays that truth lies in action. However, as Roland Barthes has said, clearly with Sartre in mind:

The intellectual is still only an incompletely transformed writer, and unless he scuttles himself and becomes forever a militant who no longer writes (some have done so, and are therefore forgotten), he cannot but come back to the fascination of former modes of writing, transmitted through Literature as an instrument intact but obsolete. These intellectual modes of writing are therefore unstable, they remain literary to the extent that they are powerless, and are political only through their obsession with commitment.[28]

From this point of view, even Sartre's failures become enormously interesting insofar as they question literature itself, at the point where the real and the imaginary meet. In *The Words* Sartre expresses his long ambivalent relationship with words, his love and his despair for them. Sartre has constantly vacillated between the conviction that literature is everything and that literature is nothing, between the desire to capture in words a total reality and the frustration that that reality can be captured only in the imaginary. His autobiography relates his present disillusionment with literature; the words embody a power denied by their contents.

Since the mid-1950s, Sartre has been creating fewer plays and giving proportionally more of his time to writing political and philosophical essays. There is no indication, however, that he intends to stop writing for the theatre altogether. As *The Words* confirms: "I wanted to write novels and plays long before I knew what philosophy was. I want to do so still; I have wanted to all my life." 29 Although well into middle age, Sartre has not been tempted by institutionalized honors that would fix his past work into a monument at the expense of the living writer. Much of the excitement in following his work lies precisely in this readiness to question past certainties, to remain faithful to himself by betraying old ideas that he no longer considers valid. He refuses to take refuge in esthetic solutions or in the timeless truths to which everyone can too easily assent, preferring to think of himself as a kind of permanent revolution: "Adolescence, manhood, the year which has just rolled by, these will always be the Old Regime. The New is ushered in this very hour but is never instituted: tomorrow, everything goes by the board." 30

FIRST PERFORMANCES OF THE PLAYS
OF JEAN-PAUL SARTRE

Les Mouches
> April 1943, Théâtre de la Cité-Sarah Bernhardt, directed by Charles Dullin, sets by Adam.

Huis-Clos
> June 1944, Théâtre du Vieux Colombier, directed by Raymond Rouleau.

Morts sans sépulture
> November 8, 1946, Théâtre Antoine.

La Putain respectueuse
> November 8, 1946, Théâtre Antoine.

Les Mains sales
> April 2, 1948, Théâtre Antoine, directed by Pierre Valde, sets by Emile and Jean Bertin.

Le Diable et le bon Dieu
> June 7, 1951, Théâtre Antoine, directed by Louis Jouvet, sets by Felix Labisse.

Kean (adaptation of Dumas père)
> November 17, 1953, Théâtre Sarah Bernhardt, directed by Pierre Brasseur, sets by Alexandre Trauner.

Nekrassov
> June 8, 1955, Théâtre Antoine, directed by Jean Meyer, sets by Jean-Denis Malcles.

Les Séquestrés d'Altona
> September 23, 1959, Théâtre de la Renaissance, directed by François Darbon, sets by Yvon Henri.

Les Troyennes (adaptation of Euripides)
> March 10, 1965, presented by the Théâtre National Populaire at the Théâtre du Palais de Chaillot, directed by Michael Cacoyannis.

Notes

INTRODUCTION

1. "Forgers of Myth: The Young Playwrights of France," *Theatre Arts*, XXX (July 1946), 324–35. This article was originally a speech, given by Sartre during his visit to the United States in 1946.
2. *The Prime of Life*, p. 385. Some brief fragments of *Bariona* have been published in Francis Jeanson's *Sartre* (Collection Les écrivains devant Dieu), pp. 135–37.
3. "Rencontre avec Jean-Paul Sartre," *Nouvelles Littéraires*, February 1, 1951. [CR]
4. Quoted in Jeanson, *Le Problème moral et la Pensée de Sartre*, p. 309.
5. "Modern Theatre," *Evergreen Review*, IV, 11 (January–February 1960), 144.
6. A part of *La Dernière Chance* entitled "Drôle d'amitié" appeared in *Les Temps modernes*, November and December 1949.
7. "Modern Theatre," *Evergreen Review*, IV, 11 (January–February 1960), p. 143.
8. *Stages on Sartre's Way*, p. 64.
9. *Six Plays of Strindberg*, trans. by Elizabeth Sprigge (New York, Doubleday, 1955), p. 64.
10. "Sartre and Camus: A Study in Incarceration," *Yale French Studies*, XXV (1960).
11. *Sartre, Romantic Rationalist*, p. 81.
12. *The Words*, pp. 84–86.
13. "Beyond Bourgeois Theatre," *Tulane Drama Review*, V (March 1961), 4.

1. ACTION AS SALVATION

1. In the English translation of the play, Stuart Gilbert consistently identifies the Greek god by his proper name, Zeus. In the original version, however, Sartre gives the name Jupiter

to both the character and his statue. An exception is the conversion scene: when Orestes beseeches Zeus, Jupiter replies. Jeanson gives this explanation: "Zeus is the symbol of Good, the absolute principle. Jupiter is the patron of every Aegistheus: he is the coercion exercised in the name of Good, the religion of repentance, the temporal Church and its mummeries, the order of Nature as a justification of that 'moral order' invoked by every tyranny." *Sartre par lui-même*, p. 15.

2. *The Reprieve*, p. 363.   3. *Stages on Sartre's Way*, p. 86.

4. *Being and Nothingness*, pp. 475–76.

5. *Ibid.*, p. 412.   6. *Sartre par lui-même*, p. 25.

7. *The Emotions, Outline of a Theory*, p. 69.

8. Compare these words with Mathieu's in *The Reprieve*, p. 362: "I am my own freedom. He had hoped that one day he would be filled with joy, transfixed by a lightning-flash. But there was neither lightning-flash nor joy."

9. "Jean-Paul Sartre nous parle de théâtre," *Théâtre Populaire*, XV (1955).

10. In 1947 Erwin Piscator created an epic-theatre style production of *The Flies* in New York City using a film "tracer" as a prologue to remind his audience that Sartre wrote the play during Hitler's conquest of Europe.

11. *What Is Literature?*, p. 62.

12. *Notes de théâtre, 1940–1950*, p. 123.

13. *The Prime of Life*, p. 386.

14. Slochower, "The Function of Myth in Existentialism," *Yale French Studies*, I, 46.

15. It is astounding that the German censors could have failed to understand the subversive intention of *The Flies*. This obtuseness can be explained to some extent by the fact that Sartre was known at the time primarily as the author of philosophical works that had been greatly influenced by Heidegger and other German thinkers. The Germans showed the same kind of unawareness with other plays produced as dramas of revolt. At the end of 1940, Shaw's *Saint Joan* appeared, followed in July 1941 by Péguy's *Jeanne d'Arc*. The censors took literally those lines portraying Joan as a martyred victim of the English and thus were glad to encourage plays that, they thought, supported their own anti-English propaganda. See Dussane, *Notes de théâtre*, p. 121.

16. *Stages on Sartre's Way*, p. 103.

17. "On Modern Drama and Modern Theatre," in Toby Cole, ed., *Playwrights on Playwriting* (New York, Hill and Wang, 1960), p. 19.

18. In 1951, at the time of a revival of *The Flies*, Sartre made the following statement: "My play *The Flies* is linked for me

to the memory of Charles Dullin. He needed a great deal of courage to agree to stage this play. First of all, I was an unknown author; secondly, *The Flies* had, among other meanings, that of being a 'political play.' It was 1943 and Vichy wanted to drive us into repentance and shame. In writing *The Flies* I tried to contribute as best I could to the extirpation of this sickness of repentance, this abandonment to shame that Vichy was soliciting from us. The collaborators made no mistake about it. Violent press campaigns rapidly forced the Sarah Bernhardt theatre to withdraw the play, and the remarkable work of the man who was our greatest director was not rewarded. But the interest that Charles Dullin had taken in my first play was to be for me a most precious encouragement." "Ce que fut la création des *Mouches*," *La Croix*, January 20, 1951. [CR]

19. *Situations, III*, pp. 43–61.
20. *Jean-Paul Sartre: Philosopher without Faith*, p. 20.
21. Sartre may have gotten the idea of using flies as his structural symbol from this line in Giraudoux's *Electra* (Act I): "GARDENER: Move along, won't you! Get going! Can't you leave us alone? You buzz like flies." The gardener is speaking to the three little girls (the Eumenides or Erinyes) who, in Giraudoux's version, grow bigger and bigger as the play progresses. According to Hazel Barnes, Sartre has given the Erinyes what was probably their original form: "The Erinyes almost certainly developed from the Keres, tiny winged creatures who seem in the beginning to have functioned almost like bacteria, causing putrefaction, disease, etc." *The Literature of Possibility: A Study in Humanistic Existentialism*, p. 390.
22. *Situations, III*, p. 35.   23. *Théâtre & Destin*, p. 179.
24. "Man and His Acts: Jean-Paul Sartre and Albert Camus," in *Modern French Theatre from Giraudoux to Beckett*, p. 137.
25. *Sartre par lui-même*, p. 28.   26. *Saint Genet*, p. 477.
27. *The Reprieve*, p. 406.   28. Quoted in *Saint Genet*, p. 162.
29. Sartre has taken pleasure in pointing out that he borrowed extensively in *The Devil and the Good Lord* from Christian writers: "'The church is a whore,' Nasty says. That's a phrase of Savonarola. 'You are a bastard.'—'Yes,' Goetz answers, 'like Jesus Christ.' I took that from Clement VII. You will see reading the play an unorthodox monologue which was cut on stage: it's from Saint John of the Cross." [Sartre is referring here to Act III, scenes viii and ix: ". . . For Thou art the One who is present in the universal absence, whom we hear when all is silence, whom we see when we can see no more."] "And this outburst of Goetz in front of Hilda: 'Give me the eyes of the Boetian lynx so that my gaze may

penetrate this skin!' " [The passage continues: "Show me what is hidden in your nostrils and inside your ear holes. I who would shudder to touch dung with my finger tips, how can I desire to hold in my arms this bag of excrement?"] "That's a quotation from Odilon of Cluny, a monk of the Clunisian reform." *Le Figaro Littéraire*, June 30, 1951. [CR]

30. *Saint Genet*, p. 174.   31. Quoted in *Saint Genet*, p. 161.

32. *Trends in Twentieth Century Drama*, p. 161.

33. According to Simone de Beauvoir, this scene, taken from Cervantes, was what first gave Sartre the idea of writing *The Devil*: "Barrault had once told Sartre the story of Cervantes' *Il Rufio Dichoso* in which a bandit decides to reform on a throw of the dice. At La Pouèze, Sartre began to write a play inspired by this episode, though not without altering it: in his version the hero cheated in order to lose." *Force of Circumstance*, p. 237.

34. In *The Words*, Sartre writes of himself: ". . . I accepted the loathsome myth of the Saint who saves the populace because, in the last analysis, the populace was myself: I declared myself a licensed redeemer of crowds so as to win my own salvation on the sly and, as the Jesuits say, into the bargain." *The Words*, p. 181.

35. Sartre may have taken the idea for this scene from Kafka's story "The Judgment": "He used to tell us the most incredible stories of the Russian Revolution. For instance, when he was on a business trip to Kiev and ran into a riot, he saw a priest on a balcony who cut a broad cross in blood on the palm of his hand and held the hand up and appealed to the mob." *Selected Short Stories of Franz Kafka*, trans. by Willa and Edwin Muir (New York, Random House, 1952).

36. *Jean-Paul Sartre*, p. 107.   37. *Ibid.*, p. 105.

38. Interview with Sartre, January 7, 1964.

39. *Stages on Sartre's Way*, p. 124.

40. Quoted in *Le Figaro*, June 3, 1951. [CR]

41. *Stages on Sartre's Way*, p. 127.

42. *The Communists and Peace*, *passim*.

43. *Métamorphose de la littérature* (Paris, Editions Alsatia, 1952), p. 236.

44. *Humanisme et Terreur: Essai sur le problème communiste* (Paris, Gallimard, 1947), pp. xxxvi–xxxvii.

45. Preface to Fanon, *The Wretched of the Earth*, p. 21.

46. In an interview in 1964 Sartre stated this decision unequivocally: "From the period when I wrote *Nausea* I wanted to create an ethics. My evolution consists in my no longer dreaming of doing so." *Le Monde*, April 18, 1964.

47. *Saint Genet*, p. 186.   48. *The Words*, p. 114.

49. *Force of Circumstance*, p. 243.
50. *Opéra*, January 3, 1951. [CR]
51. *Saint Genet*, p. 155.   52. *The Words*, p. 237.
53. *Force of Circumstance*, p. 242.   54. *Saint Genet*, p. 584.
55. Quoted in "Portrait de l'aventurier," in *Situations*, VI, p. 18.
56. "L'Autre dans le théâtre de Jean-Paul Sartre," in *Théâtre &
   Destin*, p. 178.
57. Such a comparison is more unjust to Sartre's existentialism
   than to *The Devil and the Good Lord*. Sartre writes in the
   preface to his *Search for a Method*, p. xxxiii: "I do not like
   to talk about existentialism. It is the nature of an intellectual
   quest to be undefined. To name it and to define it is to wrap
   it up and tie the knot. What is left? A finished, already out-
   dated mode of culture, something like a brand of soap—in
   other words, an idea."
58. Interview with Sartre, January 7, 1964.

2. ACTION AND REALISM

1. *What Is Literature?*, p. 211. 2. *Force of Circumstance*, p. 112.
3. "Portrait de l'aventurier," in *Situations*, VI, p. 9.
4. Interview with Christian Grisoli, *Paru*, December 1945, p. 10.
5. Introduction to Alleg, *The Question*, p. 30.
6. "Jean-Paul Sartre: Philosopher as Dramatist," *Tulane Drama
   Review*, V, 3 (March 1961), 46.
7. Interview with Christian Grisoli, *Paru*, December 1945, p. 10.
8. *The Wall*, p. 33.
9. "A Reader's Hesitations," *Yale French Studies*, XXX, 100.
10. *L'Express*, March 3, 1960.
11. "Forgers of Myth: The Young Playwrights of France,"
   Theatre Arts, XXX, 6 (July 1946), 324–335.
12. *Jean-Paul Sartre: A Literary and Political Study*, p. 86.
13. *Franc-Tireur*, November 10, 1946. [CR] Sartre agreed to
   shorten the torture scenes and made a few changes in them.
   He also had an *avertissement* read before the opening of the
   play in which he declared he was not looking for a scandal.
14. *Essays in Aesthetics*, p. 62. 15. *L'Express*, March 3, 1960.
16. Interview with Sartre, January 7, 1964.
17. *Le Figaro*, March 30, 1948. [CR]
18. *L'Ordre*, March 31, 1948. [CR]
19. *Les Lettres Françaises*, April 8, 1948. [CR]
20. *Métamorphose de la littérature*, p. 196.
21. See Philip Thody, *Jean-Paul Sartre: A Literary and Political
   Study*, p. 99.
22. There have been exceptions. Simone de Beauvoir notes that

Sartre—and the Communists—allowed the play to be produced in Yugoslavia. Sartre authorized another production of *Dirty Hands* for the spring of 1964, sponsored by a left-wing group in Turin, Italy. Interview with Sartre, January 7, 1964.

23. *Jean-Paul Sartre: A Literary and Political Study*, p. 100.
24. *Force of Circumstance*, p. 149.
25. *The Mind of an Assassin* (New York, Farrar, Straus, 1959), p. 107.
26. The title of the preface refers to the following: "Some scientists, says a song, performed experiments on rabbits. The objective results of this experiment were established in advance by strict reasoning. The rabbits already knew what they were supposed to verify. It happened that the experiment did not confirm the foreseen results. To explain this absurdity, the scientists concluded that the rabbits were false rabbits. Very good; and we understand that Tito is a false rabbit, Yugoslavia a false Yugoslavia." "Faux Savants ou Faux Lièvres," *Situations*, VI, p. 51.
27. *Ibid.*, p. 43. 28. *Les Lettres Françaises*, April 8, 1948. [CR]
29. Quoted in Jeanson, *Sartre par lui-même*, p. 48.
30. *Force of Circumstance*, p. 150.
31. *The Ghost of Stalin*, p. 158. 32. *Sartre par lui-même*, p. 38.
33. The young bourgeois Philippe in *The Reprieve* makes the same kind of protest: "He saw himself with their eyes, and he couldn't bear it. . . . 'You're such brutes—the whole lot of you. . . . it isn't my fault if I'm rich. It's much easier to be poor.' " *The Reprieve*, p. 191.
34. *The Words*, p. 32. 35. *Saint Genet*, p. 49.
36. The opening scene of "The Childhood of a Leader" comes right out of Sartre's own childhood, and could issue from Hugo's as well: " 'I look adorable in my little angel's costume.' Mme. Portier told mamma: 'Your little boy looks good enough to eat. He's simply adorable in his little angel's costume.' . . . Everybody thought he was so charming with his gauze wings, his long blue robe, small bare arms and blond curls." *The Wall*, p. 157. Compare this incident with the following one from *The Words*: "At the anniversary party to celebrate the founding of the Institute, there are more than a hundred guests; light champagne is served; my mother and Mlle. Moutet play four-handed Bach; in a blue muslin robe, with stars in my hair and wings on my back, I made the rounds offering tangerines in a basket; the guests exclaim: 'He's really an angel!' " *The Words*, p. 39.
37. *Sartre par lui-même*, p. 132. 38. *The Words*, p. 110.
39. Sartre's description of Brunet (as he appears in the first two volumes of *The Roads to Freedom*) would be applicable also

to Olga and Louis: "Brunet incarnates *l'esprit de sérieux* which believes in transcendent values, written in the sky, intelligible, independent of human subjectivity, placed like things. For him, there is an absolute meaning of the world and of history which commands his enterprises. Brunet commits himself because he needs a certainty in order to live." Interview with Christian Grisoli, *Paru*, December 1945.

40. *L'Existentialisme et le Théâtre de Jean-Paul Sartre*, p. 15.
41. *The Words*, p. 208.
42. Francis Jeanson wrote in an article: "If I dared, I would advance this hypothesis: Hoederer is the only positive image that Sartre has ever had of himself." "Le Théâtre de Sartre, ou les Hommes en proie à l'homme," *Livres de France*, XVII, 1 (January 1966).
43. *Sartre par lui-même*, p. 44.   44. *The Age of Reason*, p. 153.
45. *The French Theater since 1930: Six Contemporary Full-length Plays*, p. 318.
46. *What Is Literature?*, p. 233.   47. *Saint Genet*, p. 344.
48. *L'Affaire Henri Martin*, p. 109.
49. *The Emotions, Outline of a Theory*, p. 36.
50. *The French Theatre of Today: An English View*, p. 107.
51. André Malraux, *The Royal Way* (New York, Random House, 1955), p. 12.
52. *Jean-Paul Sartre: A Literary and Political Study*, p. 89.

3. COMIC INTERLUDES

1. "Le Viol," *Les Etats-Désunis* (Paris, Bibliothèque Française, 1948), pp. 104–107. Although Pozner's book was not published until 1948, it is probable that Sartre talked to him about his experiences in the U.S. well before that date.
2. "The Childhood of a Leader," in *The Wall*, p. 268.
3. *Anti-Semite and Jew*, p. 40.   4. *Nausea*, p. 115.
5. Reported in *Le Figaro*, November 21, 1946. [CR]
6. *Masters of the Drama*, p. 718.
7. In France, if not in America, *The Respectful Prostitute* has also been enthusiastically admired. Arthur Adamov, in a speech in New York in 1965, spoke of it as his favorite Sartrean play. And Gide noted in his journal in 1947: "I consider Sartre's *La Putain respectueuse* as a sort of masterpiece. I did not at all like his last two long and boring novels; but *La Putain* . . . Since the excellent stories of *Le Mur* he had written nothing stronger or more perfect." *The Journals of André Gide*, trans. by Justin O'Brien (New York, Knopf, 1951), IV, 274.

8. "Existentialism and French Literature: Jean-Paul Sartre's Novels," in *The Contemporary French Novel*, p. 228.

9. *Anti-Semite and Jew*, p. 136.   10. *Saint Genet*, p. 34.

11. *Libération*, October 30, 1946. [CR]

12. Sartre describes their one brief, physical expression of closeness in a favorite image: "[*Instinctively she steps closer to him. He trembles but puts his arm around her shoulders*. . . .] LIZZIE: Well, look at us, now! Aren't we alone in the world? Like two orphans" (Scene ii). In *The Age of Reason* Sartre writes of Boris and his sister Ivich: "They drew together, feeling like a a pair of orphans" (p. 293). And Electra says to Orestes at the beginning of *The Flies*: "I look at you and I see we're just two orphans" (II,i). See *The Words*, p. 54: "I thought for a long time of writing a story about two lost children who were discreetly incestuous. Traces of this fantasy can be found in my writings. . . . What attracted me about this family bond was not so much the amorous temptation as the taboo against making love."

13. *Le Figaro*, November 1, 1946. [CR]

14. "Sartre's Struggle for Existenz," *Kenyon Review*, X (1948), 329.

15. Interview with Bernard Dort, "*Les Séquestrés d'Altona* nous concernent tous," *Théâtre Populaire*, XXXVI (1959), 5.

16. Interview with Sartre, January 7, 1964.

17. "It should be called a satiric farce, because it is a satire that I wanted to make farcical." *L'Humanité*, June 8, 1955. [CR]

18. *Libération*, June 7, 1955. [CR]   19. *Arts*, June 13, 1955. [CR]

20. *Libération*, June 20, 1955. [CR]

21. The actual Kravtchenko case, of course, led to conclusions about the Soviet Union very different from those we are supposed to draw from the fictional Nekrassov.

22. *L'Express*, March 3, 1960.

23. *Le Figaro littéraire*, June 18, 1955. [CR]

24. Cf. *Saint Genet*, p. 203. "Genet is anti-Semitic. Or rather he plays at being so. . . . Genet is repelled by the Jews because he recognizes that he and they are both in the same situation." Also, p. 579: "How could Genet find the delicious taste of sacrilege in his thefts if he did not, like you, consider property sacred?"

25. Jacques Lemarchand, *Le Figaro littéraire*, June 18, 1955. [CR]

26. *Le Parisien*, June 13, 1955. [CR]

27. "Art for our Sake," in *Curtains*, p. 116.

28. Simone de Beauvoir cites this unpublished note of Sartre: "The contradiction was not one of ideas. It was in my own being. For my liberty implied also the liberty of all men. And all men were not free. I could not submit to the discipline of

solidity with all men without breaking beneath the strain. And I could not be free alone." *Force of Circumstance*, p. 243.

29. *Curtains*, p. 117.
30. *France-Observateur*, June 9, 1955. [CR]
31. *Force of Circumstance*, p. 320.
32. "*Nekrassov juge de sa critique*," *Théâtre Populaire*, XIV (July 1955).
33. *Ibid.*   34. *L'Humanité*, June 19, 1955. [CR]
35. *Lettres Françaises*, November 12, 1953. [CR]
36. Introduction to Denis Diderot, *The Paradox of Acting*, trans. by Walter Herries Pollack, and William Archer, *Masks or Faces?* (2 vols. in one; New York, Hill and Wang, 1957), p. xiii.
37. *Le Figaro*, November 4, 1953. [CR]   38. *The Words*, p. 115.
39. *Ibid.*, p. 134.   40. *Saint Genet*, p. 322.
41. Camus writes: "Always concerned with better representing, [the actor] demonstrates to what a degree appearing creates being. . . . At the end of his effort his vocation becomes clear: to apply himself wholeheartedly to being nothing or to being several." "The Absurd Man," in *The Myth of Sisyphus*, trans. by Justin O'Brien (New York, Knopf, 1961), p. 79. Camus, like Sartre, saw in the actor an exemplary figure. Camus's actor is one of the representative types of the absurd man, affirming and rebelling against his absurdity by an ethics of quantity. Sartre's Kean, a critical conception of the actor, is first of all a man constantly aware of performing for an audience; his actions—in life as well as on the stage—become unreal, nothing but gestures.
42. Cf. *Saint Genet*, p. 23: "They took a child and made a monster out of him for reasons of social utility." Cf. also *The Words*, p. 83: "My truth, my character, and my name were in the hands of adults. I had learned to see myself through their eyes. I was a child, that monster which they fabricated with their regrets."
43. *Sartre par lui-même*, p. 77.
44. Talma wrote in his *Réflexions sur Lekain*: "I hardly dare confess that, in a passage of my life in which I was undergoing a deep distress, my histrionic obsession was so overmastering that, crushed as I was by a genuine enough unhappiness, in the very moment of shedding tears I took involuntarily a quick, fleeting notice of how my voice altered and acquired a kind of spasmodic vibrancy as I wept. And—I set it down not without some shame—I was thinking automatically how I could make use of the fact on occasion; indeed, that experiment on myself has often stood me in good stead." Quoted in Archer, *Masks or Faces?*, p. 146.

45. *Combat*, November 5, 1953. [CR]
46. *Play within a Play: The Dramatist's Conception of his Art*, p. 10.
47. *The Paradox of Acting*, p. 19.   48. *Ibid.*, p. 39.
49. *Play within a Play*, p. 103.   50. *The Paradox of Acting*, p. 23.
51. This passage is omitted from Kitty Black's translation of *Kean*.

4. ACTION AS DAMNATION

1. *Connaissance de Sartre*, Cahiers de la Compagnie Madeleine Renaud–Jean-Louis Barrault, XIII, 22.
2. "Le Théâtre de Sartre, ou les Hommes en proie à l'homme," *Livres de France*, XVII, 1 (January 1966), 9.
3. *Panorama de la nouvelle littérature française*, p. 109.
4. *Being and Nothingness*, p. 263.   5. *Ibid.*, p. 410.
6. God, in this context, is merely "the concept of the Other pushed to the limit." *Ibid.*, p. 266.
7. *Ibid.*, p. 364.
8. Iris Murdoch writes that "The striking symbol of the petrifying Medusa is interpreted by Freud as a castration fear (*Collected Papers*, Vol. V). Sartre of course regards as its basic sense our general fear of being observed (*L'Etre et le Néant*, p. 502). It is interesting to speculate on how one would set about deciding which interpretation was correct." *Sartre, Romantic Rationalist*, p. 90. The two interpretations do not seem mutually exclusive, and in fact, can support each other. In *No Exit* the petrifying Medusa reduces all three characters to different kinds of impotence.
9. "The Wall," in *The Wall*, p. 16.
10. "The Room," in *The Wall*, p. 61.
11. *The Words*, p. 83.   12. *The Reprieve*, p. 197.
13. *No Exit* was first performed during the Occupation. At one point the bellboy says, "We have unlimited electricity." His line, Simone de Beauvoir tells us, "brought the house down— something which Sartre had not anticipated." *The Prime of Life*, p. 461. All the actors in *No Exit* had worked for the Resistance. Gaby Sylvia, who played Estelle, had been transporting arms in a baby carriage. Reported in *Libération*, September 8, 1944. [CR]
14. Within a very different relationship in *The Reprieve*, Pierre finds himself similarly trapped as a coward in the eyes of his mistress Maud and, as a consequence, completely in her power: " 'I'm a coward. . . . Coward. I would never have thought it.' One day had sufficed for him to find out his true character; but for these threats of war he would never have known.

. . . It isn't fair, he thought. . . . She would never have known, she would have continued to look at me with her adoring air, she would have lasted no longer than the rest, I would have got rid of her in three months. But now she knows; she knows. The bitch—she's got me." *The Reprieve*, p. 163.

15. Quoted in Sartre, *Saint Genet*, p. 99.
16. *Baudelaire*, p. 161.
17. *Jean-Paul Sartre, ou Une Littérature philosophique*, p. 137.
18. Sartre, *Romantic Rationalist*, p. 17.
19. *Modern French Theatre*, p. 136.
20. *Being and Nothingness*, p. 543.
21. Quoted in "John Dos Passos and '1919,'" in *Literary and Philosophical Essays*, p. 91.
22. *Being and Nothingness*, p. 538.
23. *No Exit* was given as a college production at Langston University in Oklahoma, formerly Langston Colored Agricultural and Normal University. Like its counterparts, Langston is almost uniformly Christian. For obvious reasons, its students tend to carry to an extreme the middle class's anxiety about image, how they appear to others. The late Professor M. B. Tolson, who directed the production of *No Exit*, was a Marxist Afro-American poet who grew up in a family of preachers. He chose to create a *mise-en-scène* that superimposed on the stage set described by Sartre a Christian inferno, dominated by serpents. According to students and teachers with whom I talked, the production was enormously effective. Although Tolson's interpretation was not quite what Sartre had in mind, it gave his audience a frame of reference familiar enough to make the insights of *No Exit* meaningful.
24. *Being and Nothingness*, p. 541.
25. Interview with Sartre, January 7, 1964.
26. *The Playwright as Thinker*, p. 200.
27. Interview with Sartre, January 7, 1964.
28. "Forgers of Myth: The Young Playwrights of France," *Theatre Arts*, XXX, 6 (July 1946), 324–35.
29. Describing the inspiration of *No Exit*, Simone de Beauvoir notes that "The idea of writing a short play, with a single set and two or three characters only, intrigued Sartre. He at once thought of a situation *in camera*, as it were: a group of people shut up in a cellar during a lengthy bombardment. Then he had the inspired notion of placing his characters in Hell, for all eternity. The actual writing of Huis Clos [*No Exit*] was easy and quick. Originally he entitled it *Les Autres*, and it was thus that it appeared in *L'Arbalète*." *The Prime of Life*, p. 439.

30. "Jean-Paul Sartre nous parle de théâtre," *Théâtre Populaire*, XV (September–October 1955), 3–9.

31. "Departure and Return," in *Literary and Philosophical Essays*, p. 162.

32. "Beyond Bourgeois Theatre," *Tulane Drama Review*, V, 3 (March 1961), 3–11.

33. *Panorama*, p. 110.

34. T. S. Eliot, "Four Quartets," *The Complete Poems and Plays*, 1909–1950 (New York, Harcourt, 1952), p. 117.

35. *Les Lettres Françaises*, September 17, 1959. [CR]

36. "De la *Critique de la raison dialectique* aux *Séquestrés d'Altona*," PMLA, December 1963, p. 625.

37. *Search for a Method*, p. 62.   38. *Ibid.*, p. 62.

39. *Livres de France*, XVII, 1 (January 1966), 19.

40. "Beyond Bourgeois Theatre," *Tulane Drama Review*, V, 3 (March 1961), 6.

41. Interview with Bernard Dort, "*Les Séquestrés d'Altona* nous concernent tous," *Théâtre Populaire*, XXXVI (1959).

42. "*Les Séquestrés d'Altona* of Jean-Paul Sartre," *Tulane Drama Review*, V, 3 (March 1961), 23.

43. *Le Figaro*, September 11, 1959. [CR]

44. *Being and Nothingness*, p. 590.   45. *Saint Genet*, p. 57.

46. "De la *Critique de la raison dialectique* aux *Séquestrés d'Altona*," PMLA, December 1963, p. 626.

47. Interview with Bernard Dort, *Théâtre Populaire*, XXXVI (1959), 6.

48. *Troubled Sleep*, p. 85.

49. See Simone de Beauvoir's account in *The Prime of Life*, pp. 168–70, 219.

50. *Saint Genet*, p. 598.   51. *Nausea*, p. 17.

52. *The Words*, p. 152.   53. *Situations, III*, p. 21.

54. "The Popular, the Absurd, and the *Entente Cordiale*," *Tulane Drama Review*, V, 3 (March 1961), 119–51. Blau notes in the same article that "Beckett, who was about to start rehearsals of *Krapp's Last Tape*, thought Sartre's play too long but admired it." Mr. Blau directed the 1966 New York production of *The Condemned of Altona*.

55. André Malraux, *Man's Fate* (New York, Random House, 1934), p. 32.

56. Justin O'Brien, who translated *The Condemned of Altona* for the London and New York productions, has compared Franz's *De profundis clamavi* with Camus's name for his protagonist in *The Fall*. Franz, like Jean-Baptiste Clamence, is both judge and penitent. See program of New York production at the Vivian Beaumont Theater, Spring 1966.

57. Sartre has insisted on this point. "None of the spectators took

literally the Germany that I presented. No one believed that I really wanted to talk about what happened to a German ex-soldier in 1959. Behind that Germany, they all read Algeria—everyone, even the critics." Interview with Bernard Dort, *Théâtre Populaire*, XXXVI (1959). If we can judge from the Paris newspaper and periodical reviews of *The Condemned of Altona*, Sartre's claim is justified. In 1966, with the New York production of the play, it was equally clear that Herbert Blau had chosen *The Condemned* for what it had to say about America's war in Viet Nam.

58. "An Interview with Jean-Paul Sartre," *Tulane Drama Review*, V, 3 (March 1961), 13.
59. *Situations, III*, p. 58.   60. *Ibid.*, p. 14.
61. *Saint Genet*, p. 432.   62. "A Victory," p. 20.
63. "Les Séquestrés d'Altona," *La Nouvelle Revue Française*, LXXXIII (November 1959), 896.
64. *The Prime of Life*, p. 107.

CONCLUSION

1. "Jean-Paul Sartre nous parle de théâtre," *Théâtre Populaire*, XV (1955).
2. *The Words*, p. 252.
3. In a revealing passage of "Paris sous l'Occupation" Sartre writes: "But the Resistance was only an individual solution and we always knew it: without the Resistance the English would have won the war; with it they would have lost if they were going to lose. In our eyes, the Resistance had primarily a symbolic value. That is why many Resistance fighters were in despair." *Situations, III*, p. 30.
4. Note the numerous mock-heroic passages of *The Words*. (For example, see above, p. 36.)
5. "Brecht as a Classic," *World Theatre*, VII, 1 (1958), 11–19.
6. Interview with Bernard Dort, *Théâtre Populaire*, XXXVI (1959).
7. Euripides, *The Trojan Women*, adapted by Jean-Paul Sartre.
8. These lines do not appear in Ronald Duncan's English version of Sartre's adaptation.
9. *The Words*, p. 251.   10. *Nausea*, p. 236.
11. *Sartre par lui-même*, p. 173.   12. *What Is Literature?*, p. 17.
13. Sartre remarked in an interview: "[The aspiration to write] is rather strange all the same and doesn't happen without a 'crack.' The kid who dreams of being a boxing champion, or an admiral, or an astronaut, chooses the real. If the writer chooses the imaginary, it is because he confuses these two

domains." "Jean-Paul Sartre s'explique sur *les Mots*," *Le Monde*, April 18, 1964.

14. See the scene between Gomez and Ritchie in *Troubled Sleep*, pp. 25–32.
15. *La Part du feu*, p. 273. M. Blanchot's analysis, of course, characterizes a specifically French tradition, more relevant to Racine than to Shakespeare.
16. *Saint Genet*, p. 496.
17. *Jean-Paul Sartre: Philosopher without Faith*, p. 141.
18. *The Words*, p. 73.
19. In his interview with *Le Monde* (1964), Sartre commented: "Like ethics, literature needs to be universal. . . . As long as the writer cannot write for the two billion men who are hungry, he will be oppressed by a feeling of malaise." In the meantime, he adds, the writer can prepare for the time when everyone will read, not by communicating at the lowest level, but by posing problems "in the most radical and intransigent manner."
20. See *The Words*, p. 121.
21. "Sartre: The Janus of Modern Dramatists," *The New Republic*, February 26, 1966.
22. *What Is Literature?*, p. 51.
23. Gomez says in *Troubled Sleep*, p. 31: "If painting is not *everything* then it is merely a bad joke."
24. Quoted in Madeleine Chapsal, "To Show, To Demonstrate," *Yale French Studies*, XXX, 30–44. Excerpt from interview with Sartre in *Les Ecrivains en personne*. It is striking that all Sartre's biographical essays have dealt with writers conspicuously noncommitted in any political sense, writers whose art reflects, as Sartre said of Genet, an "inhumanism." Sartre's *Baudelaire* was published in 1947; his *Saint Genet* appeared in 1952. He is completing at present a long study of Flaubert and is also writing a book on Mallarmé.
25. *The Words*, p. 253.   26. See above, p. 6.
27. *Saint Genet*, p. 421.   28. *Writing Degree Zero*, p. 27.
29. *Les Ecrivains en personne*, p. 209.   30. *The Words*, p. 239.

Selected Bibliography

I. Works by Sartre, including selected interviews and speeches, through June 1968. Arranged by date of French publication. The place of French publication is Paris, unless otherwise indicated.

"La Transcendence de l'ego," *Recherches philosophiques*, VI (1936–37), 85–123. The Transcendence of the Ego. Translated by F. Williams and R. Kirkpatrick. New York, Noonday Press, 1957.

L'Imagination. Felix Alcan, 1936. Imagination. Translated by Forest Williams. Ann Arbor, University of Michigan Press, 1962. London, Cresset, 1962.

La Nausée. Gallimard, 1938. Nausea. Translated by Lloyd Alexander. Norfolk (Conn.), New Directions, 1959. Same translation appears as The Diary of Antoine Roquentin. London, J. Lehmann, 1949.

Le Mur. Gallimard, 1939. The Wall and Other Stories. Translated by Lloyd Alexander. Norfolk (Conn.), New Directions, 1948.

Esquisse d'une théorie des émotions. Hermann, 1939. The Emotions: Outline of a Theory. Translated by Bernard Frechtman. New York, Philosophical Library, 1948.

L'Imaginaire, psychologie phénoménologique de l'imagination. Gallimard, 1940. The Psychology of Imagination. Translated by Bernard Frechtman. London, Rider, 1949.

L'Etre et le Néant, essai d'ontologie phénoménologique. Gallimard, 1943. Being and Nothingness. Translated by Hazel Barnes. New York, Philosophical Library, 1956.

Les Mouches. Gallimard, 1944. The Flies. Translated by Stuart Gilbert. London, H. Hamilton, 1946. New York, Knopf, 1947.

Huis-Clos. Gallimard, 1945. No Exit. Translated by Stuart Gilbert. New York, Knopf, 1947. Same translation appears as In Camera. London, H. Hamilton, 1946.

L'Age de raison (Les Chemins de la liberté, I). Gallimard, 1945. The Age of Reason. Translated by Eric Sutton. New York, Knopf, 1947.

179

Le Sursis (Les Chemins de la liberté, II). Gallimard, 1945. The Reprieve. Translated by Eric Sutton. New York, Knopf, 1947.

"Qu'est-ce que l'existentialisme? Bilan d'une offensive," Les Lettres françaises, LXXXIII (November 24, 1945), LXXXIV (December 1, 1945).

Interview with Christian Grisoli. Paru, December 1945.

L'Existentialisme est un humanisme. Nagel, 1946. Existentialism. Translated by Bernard Frechtman. New York, Philosophical Library, 1947. Existentialism and Humanism. Translated by Philip Mairet. London, Methuen, 1948.

Morts sans sépulture. Lausanne, Marguerat, 1946. "The Victors," in Three Plays. Translated by Lionel Abel. New York, Knopf, 1949. Men without Shadows. Translated by Kitty Black. London, H. Hamilton, 1950.

La Putain respectueuse. Nagel, 1946. "The Respectful Prostitute," in Three Plays. Translated by Lionel Abel. New York, Knopf, 1949. Also translated by Kitty Black. London, H. Hamilton, 1950.

"Forgers of Myth: The Young Playwrights of France," Theatre Arts, XXX, 6 (July 1946), 324–35.

Réflexions sur la question juive. P. Morihien, 1947. Gallimard, 1954. Anti-Semite and Jew. Translated by George J. Becker. New York, Shocken Books, 1948. Portrait of the Anti-Semite. Translated by Eric de Mauny. London, Secker and Warburg, 1948.

Théâtre (Les Mouches, Huis-Clos, La Putain respectueuse). Gallimard, 1947.

Baudelaire. Gallimard, 1947. Translated by Martin Turnell. Norfolk (Conn.), New Directions, 1950.

Les Jeux sont faits. Nagel, 1947. The Chips Are Down. Translated by Louise Varèse. Lear, 1948. London, Rider, 1951.

Situations, I. Gallimard, 1947. Literary and Philosophical Essays. Translated by Annette Michelson. London, Rider, 1955. Includes selected essays from Situations, I on Mauriac, Camus, Giraudoux, Blanchot ("Aminadab or the Fantastic Considered as a Language"), Faulkner, Dos Passos, Parain ("Departure and Return"), and Descartes. Also, from Situations, III: "Individualism and Conformism in the United States," "American Cities," "New York, the Colonial City," "Materialism and Revolution."

L'Engrenage. Nagel, 1948. In the Mesh. Translated by Mervyn Savill. London, Dakers, 1954.

Les Mains sales. Gallimard, 1948. "Dirty Hands," in Three Plays. Translated by Lionel Abel. New York, Knopf, 1949. Crime Passionel. Translated by Kitty Black. London, H. Hamilton, 1950.

Situations, II. Gallimard, 1948. What Is Literature? Translation of "Qu'est-ce que la littérature?" by Bernard Frechtman. New York, Philosophical Library, 1949.

Entretiens sur la politique with David Rousset and Gerard Rosenthal. Gallimard, 1949.

La Mort dans l'âme (Les Chemins de la liberté, III). Gallimard, 1949. Troubled Sleep. Translated by Gerard Hopkins. New York, Knopf, 1951.

"Drôle d'amitié" (excerpts from La Dernière Chance, Les Chemins de la liberté, IV), Les Temps modernes, November and December, 1949.

Situations, III. Gallimard, 1949. Essays in Aesthetics. Translated by Wade Baskin. New York, Philosophical Library, 1963. Includes selected essays from Situations, III: "The Mobiles of Calder," "The Quest for the Absolute." Also, from Situations, IV: "The Venetian Pariah," "The Paintings of Giacometti," "The Unprivileged Painter: Lapoujade."

Le Diable et le bon Dieu. Gallimard, 1951. The Devil and the Good Lord. Translated by Kitty Black. New York, Knopf, 1960. Same translation appears as Lucifer and the Lord. London, H. Hamilton, 1952.

"Rencontre avec Jean-Paul Sartre," Les Nouvelles littéraires, February 1, 1951.

"Ma pièce est avant tout une pièce de foules," Le Monde, May 31, 1951. On The Devil and the Good Lord.

"Jean-Paul Sartre répond à la critique et offre un guide au spectateur pour suivre le Diable et le bon Dieu," Le Figaro littéraire, June 30, 1951.

Saint Genet, comédien et martyr (Oeuvres complètes de Jean Genet, Tome I). Gallimard, 1952. Saint Genet. Translated by Bernard Frechtman. New York, Braziller, 1963.

Preface to Poésies, Stéphane Mallarmé. Gallimard, 1952.

L'Affaire Henri Martin, commentaire de Sartre, textes de Hervé Bazin et al. Gallimard, 1953.

Kean par Alexandre Dumas, Adaptation de Jean-Paul Sartre. Gallimard, 1954 (with Dumas text). Translated by Kitty Black. London, H. Hamilton, 1954. New York, Knopf, 1960.

Nekrassov. Gallimard, 1955. Translated by Sylvia and George Leeson. London, H. Hamilton, 1954. New York, Knopf, 1960.

"Jean-Paul Sartre nous parle de théâtre," Théâtre Populaire, XV (September–October 1955), 3–9.

"Brecht as a Classic" (in French and English), World Theatre, VII, 1 (1958), 11–19.

Interview with Bernard Dort, "Les Séquestrés d'Altona nous concernent tous," Théâtre Populaire, XXXVI (1959), 1–13.

"Deux heures avec Sartre," *L'Express*, September 17, 1959.
"Modern Theatre." Translated by Richard Seaver. *Evergreen Review*, IV, 11 (January–February 1960), 143–52.
Critique de la raison dialectique, précédé de Question de méthode (Tome I, Théorie des ensembles pratiques). Gallimard, 1960. Question de méthode translated as Search for a Method. Translated by Hazel Barnes. New York, Knopf, 1963.
Les Séquestrés d'Altona. Gallimard, 1960. The Condemned of Altona. Translated by Sylvia and George Leeson. New York, Knopf, 1961. Same translation appears as Loser Wins. London, H. Hamilton, 1961.
"Sartre répond aux jeunes," *L'Express*, March 3, 1960.
Interview with Madeleine Chapsal. In Les Ecrivains en personne. Julliard, 1960, pp. 205–233. Excerpts translated as "To Show, To Demonstrate," *Yale French Studies*, XXX.
Sartre on Cuba. Ballantine Books, 1961. A collection of newspaper articles that appeared in the French Press. No equivalent collection printed in French.
"An Interview with Jean-Paul Sartre," *Tulane Drama Review*, V, 3 (March 1961), 12–18.
"Notes sur le théâtre," *Paris-Théâtre*, XIII, 166 (1961), 2–5. "Beyond Bourgeois Theatre." Translated by Rima Drell Reck. *Tulane Drama Review*, V, 3 (March 1961), 4. Parts of a lecture given in the Sorbonne in the spring of 1960.
Controverse sur la dialectique with Roger Garaudy, Jean Hyppolite, Jean Pierre Vigier, J. Orcel. Plon, 1962.
Théâtre (Les Mouches, Huis-Clos, Morts sans sépulture, La Putain respectueuse, Les Mains sales, Le Diable et le bon Dieu, Kean, Nekrassov, Les Séquestrés d'Altona. Avec 32 aquarelles par H. G. Adam, A. Masson, R. Chapelain-Midy, L. Coutaud, F. Labisse). Gallimard, 1962.
Les Mots. Gallimard, 1964. The Words. Translated by Bernard Frechtman. New York, Braziller, 1964. Words. Translated by Irene Clephane. London, H. Hamilton, 1964.
"Jean-Paul Sartre s'explique sur les Mots," *Le Monde*, April 18, 1964.
Situations, IV. Gallimard, 1964. Situations. Translated by Benita Eisler. New York, Braziller, 1965. Includes selected essays from Situations, IV on Tintoretto, Gide, Camus, Paul Nizan, Giacometti, Nathalie Sarraute, Leibowitz ("The Artist and his Conscience"), Merleau-Ponty, and Gorz ("Of Rats and Men").
Situations, V. Gallimard, 1964. Preface to Frantz Fanon, The Wretched of the Earth. Translated by Constance Farrington. Evergreen, 1966. "A Victory," Introduction to Henri Alleg, The Question. New York, Braziller, 1958.

Situations, VI. Gallimard, 1964. The Communists and Peace. Translation of essay "Les communistes et la paix." New York, Braziller, 1968.
Interview with Yves Buin. Clarté, LV (March–April 1964).
"Palmira Togliatti," Les Temps modernes, October 1964.
Situations, VII. Gallimard, 1965. The Ghost of Stalin. Translation of essay "Le fantôme de Staline." New York, Braziller, 1968.
Les Troyennes par Euripide, adaptation de Jean-Paul Sartre. Gallimard, 1965. The Trojan Women. English version by Ronald Duncan. London, H. Hamilton, 1967. New York, Knopf, 1967.
"L'Ecrivain et sa langue," Revue d'Esthétique, IV (1965).
"Les Livres de poche," Les Temps modernes, May 1965.
"Père et Fils" (inédit), Livres de France, XVII, 1 (January 1966).
"Entretien avec Jean-Paul Sartre." Livres de France, XVII, 1 (January 1966), 14–18.
"La Conscience de classe chez Flaubert," Les Temps modernes, May and June 1966.
"Kierkegaard," La Quinzaine littéraire, June 15, 1966.
"Mythe et Réalité du théâtre," Le Point, January 1967, pp. 20–25.
"Le Génocide," Les Temps modernes, December 1967.
"Les Bastilles de Raymond Aron," Le Nouvel Observateur, June 19–25, 1968.
"L'Idée neuve de mai 1968," Le Nouvel Observateur, June 26–July 2, 1968.

II. Selected works wholly or partially about Sartre, arranged alphabetically by author. The place of French publication is Paris unless otherwise indicated.

Albérès, R.-M. Jean-Paul Sartre. Editions Universitaires, 1953. Jean-Paul Sartre: Philosopher without Faith. Translated by Wade Baskin. New York, Philosophical Library, 1961.
Audry, Colette. Connaissance de Sartre. Cahiers de la Compagnie Madeleine Renaud–Jean-Louis Barrault, XIII. Julliard, 1955.
———. Sartre et la Réalité humaine. Seghers, 1966.
Barnes, Hazel. The Literature of Possibility: A Study of Humanistic Existentialism. Lincoln, University of Nebraska Press, 1959.

Barthes, Roland. Le Degré Zéro de l'écriture. Editions du Seuil, 1953. Writing Degree Zero. Translated by Annette Lavers and Colin Smith. New York, Hill and Wang, 1968.

——. "Nekrassov juge de sa critique," Théâtre Populaire, XIV (July 1955).

Beauvoir, Simone de. La Force de l'âge. Gallimard, 1960. The Prime of Life. Translated by Peter Green. Cleveland and New York, World, 1962.

——. La Force des choses. Gallimard, 1963. Force of Circumstance. Translated by Richard Howard. New York, Putnam, 1964.

Bentley, Eric. "Sartre's Struggle for Existenz," Kenyon Review, X (1948).

——. The Playwright as Thinker. Cleveland and New York, World, 1964.

Blanchot, Maurice. La Part du feu. Gallimard, 1959.

Blau, Herbert. "The Popular, the Absurd, and the Entente Cordiale," Tulane Drama Review, V, 3 (March 1961).

Boros, Marie-Denise. "Le Thème de la séquestration dans l'oeuvre littéraire de Jean-Paul Sartre." Unpublished doctoral dissertation, U.C.L.A., 1964.

Brombert, Victor. The Intellectual Hero. Studies in the French Novel, 1880–1955. Philadelphia and New York, Lippincott, 1961.

Brustein, Robert. "Sartre: The Janus of Modern Dramatists," The New Republic, February 26, 1966.

Campbell, Robert. Jean-Paul Sartre, ou Une Littérature philosophique. Editions Pierre Ardent, 1945.

Carat, Jacques. "Sartre, le séquestré," Preuves, CV (November 1959).

Champigny, Robert. "God in Sartrean Light," Yale French Studies, XII (1953).

——. Stages on Sartre's Way. Bloomington, Indiana University Press, 1959.

Cormeau, Nelly. Littérature existentialiste: Le Roman et le Théâtre de Jean-Paul Sartre. Liège, Thône, 1950.

Cranston, Maurice. Jean-Paul Sartre. New York, Grove, 1962.

Dellevaux, Raymond. L'Existentialisme et le Théâtre de Jean-Paul Sartre. Brussels, La Lecture au foyer, 1953.

Desan, Wilfrid. The Tragic Finale: An Essay on the Philosophy of Jean-Paul Sartre. Cambridge, Harvard University Press, 1954.

——. The Marxism of Jean-Paul Sartre. New York, Doubleday, 1965.

Dort, Bernard. "Nekrassov," Théâtre Populaire, XIV (1955).

Doubrovsky, Serge. "Sartre and Camus: A Study in Incarceration," Yale French Studies, XXV (1960).

―――. "L'Echec du héros," in Corneille et la Dialectique du héros. Gallimard, 1963.

Douglas, Kenneth. "Sartre and the Self-Inflicted Wound," *Yale French Studies*, IX.

Dussane, Béatrix. Notes de théâtre, 1940–1950. Lardanchet, 1951.

Fell, Joseph P. Emotion in the Thought of Sartre. New York, Columbia University Press, 1965.

Fernandez, Dominique. "Les Séquestrés d'Altona," *La Nouvelle Revue Française*, LXXXIII (November 1959).

Fields, Madeleine. "De la Critique de la raison dialectique aux Séquestrés d'Altona," *PMLA* (December 1963).

Gassner, John. Masters of the Drama. New York, Dover, 1954.

Greene, Norman. Jean-Paul Sartre: The Existentialist Ethic. Ann Arbor, University of Michigan Press, 1960.

Grossvogel, David I. The Self-Conscious Stage in Modern French Drama. New York, Columbia University Press, 1958.

Guicharnaud, Jacques. Modern French Theatre from Giraudoux to Beckett. New Haven, Yale University Press, 1961.

Gutwirth, Marcel. "Jean-Paul Sartre à l'école de Pierre Corneille," *Modern Language Notes*, LXXIX (May 1964).

Hardwick, Elizabeth. "We Are All Murderers," *New York Review of Books*, March 3, 1966.

Hobson, Harold. The French Theatre of Today: An English View. London, Harrap, 1953.

Jameson, Frederic. Sartre: The Origins of a Style. New Haven, Yale University Press, 1961.

Jeanson, Francis. Le Problème moral et la Pensée de Sartre. Editions du Myrte, 1947. New edition followed by "Un Quidam nommé Sartre." Editions du Seuil, 1965.

―――. Sartre par lui-même. Editions du Seuil, 1955.

―――. "Le Théâtre de Sartre, ou les Hommes en proie à l'homme," *Livres de France*, XVII, 1 (January 1966).

Jarrett-Kerr, Martin. "The Dramatic Philosophy of Jean-Paul Sartre," *Tulane Drama Review*, I, 3 (June 1957).

John, S. "Sacrilege and Metamorphosis: Two Aspects of Sartre's Imagery," *Modern Language Quarterly*, XX (1959).

Kaelin, Eugene F. An Existentialist Aesthetic: The Theories of Sartre and Merleau-Ponty. Madison, University of Wisconsin Press, 1962.

Kern, Edith, ed. Sartre, A Collection of Critical Essays. Englewood Cliffs (N.J.), Prentice-Hall, 1962.

―――. "Abandon Hope, All Ye . . . ," *Yale French Studies*, XXX.

Lilar, Susanne. A propos de Sartre et de l'amour. Grasset, 1967.

Lumley, Frederick. Trends in Twentieth Century Drama. Fair Lawn (N.J.), Essential Books, 1956.

McMahon, Joseph H. "A Reader's Hesitations," *Yale French Studies*, XXX.

Manser, Anthony. Sartre: A Philosophic Study. London, The Athlone Press, 1966.

Mendel, Sydney. "From Solitude to Salvation: A Study in Regeneration," *Yale French Studies*, XXX.

Murdoch, Iris. Sartre, Romantic Rationalist. New Haven, Yale University Press, 1961.

Nelson, Robert. Play within a Play: The Dramatist's Conception of his Art. New Haven, Yale University Press, 1958.

Oxenhander, Neal. "Nekrassov and the Critics," *Yale French Studies*, XVI (Winter 1955–1956).

Paulus, Claude. "Notes sur Morts sans sépulture de Jean-Paul Sartre," *Synthèses*, II, 10 (1948).

Peyre, Henri. "Existentialism—A Literature of Despair?" *Yale French Studies*, I, 1 (1948).

———. The Contemporary French Novel. New York, Oxford University Press, 1955.

Picon, Gaëtan. Panorama de la nouvelle littérature française. Gallimard, 1960.

Pucciani, Oreste F., ed. The French Theatre since 1930: Six Contemporary Full-length Plays. Boston and New York, Ginn, 1954.

———. "Les Séquestrés d'Altona of Jean-Paul Sartre," *Tulane Drama Review*, V, 3 (March 1961).

Rabi. "Les Thèmes majeurs du théâtre de Sartre," *Esprit*, X (1950).

Ricoeur, Paul. "Réflexions sur le Diable et le bon Dieu," *Esprit* (November 1951).

Simon, John K. "Madness in Sartre: Sequestration and the Room," *Yale French Studies*, XXX.

Simon, Pierre-Henri. Théâtre & Destin. Librairie Armand Colin, 1959.

Slochower, Harry. "The Function of Myth in Existentialism," *Yale French Studies*, I.

Thierry-Maulnier. "Du premier au dernier Sartre," *Théâtre de France*, I (1951).

Thody, Philip. Jean-Paul Sartre: A Literary and Political Study. New York, Collins, 1960.

Tynan, Kenneth. Curtains. New York, Atheneum, 1961.

Will, Frederic. "Sartre and the Question of Character in Literature," *PMLA* (September 1961).

Wreszin, Michael. "Jean-Paul Sartre: Philosopher as Dramatist," *Tulane Drama Review*, V, 3 (March 1961).

Yale French Studies, XXX. Entire issue devoted to Sartre.

Index

Actor, the, 99–109, 173nn41–42, 44
Adamov, Arthur, cited, 171n7
Agamemnon, 17, 21, 22, 23
Aguerra, Jean (*In the Mesh*), 61
Aegistheus (Giraudoux, *Electra*), 58
Aegistheus (*The Flies*): murder of, 12, 13, 14, 17, 18, 19, 24, 31, 36, 42, 76; and the Occupation, 16, 17, 21, 23
Age of Reason, The (Sartre), 3, 9, 72, 172n12
Albérès, R.-M., quoted, 21, 160
Algerian War, 47, 146–49, 154, 155, 176n57
Alice in Wonderland (Carroll), 79
Alleg, Henri, 47, 148–49
Anna (*Kean*), 103, 104, 108
Anouilh, Jean, 23, 50, 60–61
Anti-Christ, Orestes as, 22
Anti-Communism: *Dirty Hands* and, 54–55, 56, 62, 92; *Nekrassov* and, 87–88, 90–92, 97, 98
Antigone (Anouilh), 23, 50, 60–61
Anti-Semite and Jew (Sartre), 81, 83
Anti-Semitism, 80, 81, 83, 132; of Genet, 90, 172n24
Apollo, 16, 17
Aristophanes, 89
Aristotle, 154
Audry, Colette, quoted, 110
Aymé, Marcel, 97

Bariona (Sartre), 1–2, 15, 160, 165n2
Barnes, Hazel, quoted, 167n21
Barrault, Jean–Louis, 168n33
Barthes, Roland, quoted, 97, 162
Bastardy, 25, 39, 97, 101, 167n29
Baudelaire, Charles, 117, 178n24; quoted, 117
Baudelaire (Sartre), 117, 178n24
Beaumarchais, Pierre Augustin Caron de, 88
Beauvoir, Simone de, 121, 150, 172n28; on *Bariona*, 1; on *The*

Flies, 16; on *The Devil and the Good Lord*, 36, 39, 168n33; on *The Victors*, 43–44; on *Dirty Hands*, 55, 62, 64; on *Nekrassov*, 94; on *No Exit*, 174n13, 175n29
Beckett, Samuel, 144–45, 161, 176n54
Being and Nothingness (Sartre), 1–2, 110, 111; on conversion, 11–12; on freedom, 34; on the look and the other, 112; on death, 122, 123, 124; on God, 138, 174n6; on the Medusa, 174n8
Bentley, Eric, quoted, 85, 124
Bergson, Henri, quoted, 87
Bernanos, Georges, quoted, 114
Black, Kitty, 174n51
Black Boy (Wright), 86
Blanchot, Maurice, quoted, 158, 178n15
Blau, Herbert, quoted, 144–45, 176nn54, 57
Bloody Five (Brecht, *A Man's a Man*), 52
Boisdeffre, Pierre de, quoted, 33, 54
Boisselot, Father, 123
Boris (*The Age of Reason*), 172n12
Bowen, Elizabeth, quoted, 42
Brasseur, Pierre, 98, 99, 108
Brecht, Bertolt, 30, 37, 86, 139; quoted, 34; Sartre on, 152, 153–54, 161
Breton, André, quoted, 150
Brook, Peter, 85
Brothers Karamazov, The (Dostoevsky), 9
Brunet (*The Age of Reason* and *The Reprieve*), 44, 72, 73, 78, 170n39
Brustein, Robert, quoted, 161

Caligula (Camus), 50
Campbell, Robert, quoted, 119–20
Camus, Albert, 15, 50, 77, 176n56; view of evil, 21; on the actor, 173n41

Canoris (*The Victors*), 44–45, 48, 49, 72, 73, 74
Carroll, Lewis, quoted, 79
Castagnié, Mme. de (*Nekrassov*), 90
Catherine (*The Devil and the Good Lord*), 28, 29
"Ce que fut la création des *Mouches*" (Sartre), 166n18
Cervantes, Miguel de, 168n33
Champigny, Robert, quoted, 3, 11, 19, 32, 33
Chapsal, Madeleine, 178n24
Chateaubriand, François René, 160
Chateaubriant, Alphonse de, 43
Chef, le, 80, 81, 82, 128, 129, 130, 133
"Childhood of a Leader, The" (Sartre), 64, 66, 80, 86–87, 128, 159
Children of Paradise (film), 99
Clamence, Jean Baptiste (Camus, *The Fall*), 176n56
Clement VII, 167n29
Clochet (*The Victors*), 47, 51
Clytemnestra (*The Flies*), 20, 23; murder of, 12, 13, 14, 16, 17, 18, 31
Cocteau, Jean, quoted, 88, 98
Collaborators, *see* Nazis
Comedy, 3, 119, 140; in *Dirty Hands*, 69–70; in *The Respectful Prostitute*, 85–86, 87, 96, 109, 158–59, 172n17; in *Nekrassov*, 87–98, 109, 158–59; in *Kean*, 98–109
Communism, 23, 41, 92, 169n22; *Dirty Hands* and, 54–55, 56, 62, 66, 68, 71, 73, 77, 130; *Nekrassov* and, 87–88, 90–92, 98
Condemned of Altona, The (Sartre), 78, 80, 127–51, 154, 158, 161, 162; *The Victors* and, 51–52, 94, 147
Condition humaine, La (Malraux), 43
Connaissance de Sartre (Audry), 110
Conversion: as image of freedom, 11–12, 33, 38, 166n8; in *The Flies*, 11, 13, 14, 18, 22, 38–39,

67, 153; in *The Devil and the Good Lord*, 25, 28, 29–30, 38–39, 40, 41, 67, 126, 153; in *Nekrassov*, 94
Cranston, Maurice, quoted, 30, 32
Creon (Anouilh, *Antigone*), 60–61
Crime and Punishment (Dostoevsky), 11–12, 18
Cross Purposes (Camus), 50
Crustacean imagery, 134, 136, 140, 141, 142–44, 146, 147, 149, 154, 158

Daniel (*The Reprieve*), 25, 113
Dellevaux, Raymond, quoted, 69
Dernière Chance, La (Sartre), 3
Devil and the Good Lord, The (Sartre), 24–42, 43, 71, 83, 99, 150, 162; nonviolence and, 34, 47; *Nekrassov* and, 93, 96; *Kean* and, 108; *No Exit* and, 121, 126, 152–53; Christian literary sources of, 167n29
Diable et le bon Dieu, Le (Sartre), see *Devil and the Good Lord, The* (Sartre)
Diary of a Country Priest, The (Bernanos), 114
Diderot, Dénis, quoted, 106, 107
Dirty Hands (Sartre), 50, 53–78, 108, 169n22; *Condemned of Altona* and, 78, 80, 128, 129–30, 137, 141, 150, 158; *Nekrassov* and, 92, 94
Doctor Faustus (Marlowe), 28
Dort, Bernard, 176n57
Dostoevsky, Fyodor, 11–12, 18; quoted, 9
Doubrovsky, Serge, quoted, 4
"Drôle d'amitié" (Sartre), 78
Dullin, Charles, 20, 166n18
Dumas, Alexandre, père, 93, 98, 99, 100, 102, 103, 104, 105–106, 107; quoted, 101–102, 104
Duncan, Ronald, 177n8
Dussane, Béatrix, quoted, 15

Ecrivains en personne, Les, 178n24
Electra (Giraudoux), 16, 58–59, 167n21

Electra (*The Flies*), 10, 14, 16, 17, 172*n*12; revolt of, 18, 19, 20, 22, 82, 83

Elena (*Kean*), 101, 103, 105, 106, 109

Eluard, Paul, quoted, 9

Emotions, Outline of a Theory, The (Sartre), 13–14, 76

Erinyes, 167*n*21 (*see also* Furies)

Estelle (*No Exit*), 111, 114–24, 126, 127, 128, 174*n*13

Etats-Désunis, Les (Pozner), 79, 171*n*1

Etre et le Néant, L' (Sartre), see *Being and Nothingness* (Sartre)

Eumenides, 167*n*21

Euripides, 154–55, 162

Eve ("The Room"), 112–13

Everyman, 114, 115

Existentialism, 12–13, 16, 34–35, 42, 54, 116, 152, 169*n*57

Existentialism and Humanism (Sartre), 34–35

Express, L' (periodical), 50, 52

Fall, The (Camus), 176*n*56

Falstaff (Shakespeare, *Henry IV*), 101, 105, 106

Fanon, Frantz, 34

Farce de Pathelin, 87

Father-figures, 19, 80, 82, 113; in *The Condemned of Altona*, 94, 128–31, 131–33, 134, 136, 137–39

Faulkner, William, 111, 157

Faust legend, 28–29, 38, 42

Faust (Goethe), 149

"Faux Savants ou Faux Lièvres" (Sartre), 56, 170*n*26

"Femmes damnées" (Baudelaire), 117

Fernandez, Dominique, quoted, 149–50

Feuerbach, Ludwig, 160

Fields, Madeleine, quoted, 129, 139

Figaro (Beaumarchais, *The Marriage of Figaro*), 88

Figaro (newspaper), 89

Figaro littéraire, Le (periodical), 89, 167*n*29

Flaubert, Achille, 130

Flaubert, Gustave, 130–31, 178*n*24

Fleurier, Lucien ("The Childhood of a Leader"), 64, 66, 80, 87, 90, 128

Flies, The (Sartre), 9–24, 50, 93; *The Devil and the Good Lord* and, 31, 33, 36, 37, 38–39, 42, 43, 121, 150, 152, 153, 162; *The Respectful Prostitute* and, 80, 82, 83, 172*n*12

Force of Circumstance (Beauvoir), 168*n*33, 172*n*28

"Forgers of Myth: The Young Playwrights of France" (Sartre), 50, 125, 165*n*1

France: Occupation, 3, 15–16, 20–24, 37, 38, 53, 125, 141–42, 143, 146–47, 153, 156, 166*n*n15,18, 174*n*13, 177*n*3 (*see also* Resistance); Algerian war and, 47, 146–49, 154, 155, 176*n*57

France-Soir (newspaper), 89

Franco, Francisco, 49

François (*The Victors*), 44, 45, 51

Franz (*The Condemned of Altona*), 51–52, 80, 94, 128–51, 152, 154, 158, 162

Fred (*The Respectful Prostitute*), 79–87, 90, 128

Freedom, 2, 34, 44, 138, 152–53, 166*n*8, 178*n*28; in *The Flies*, 9–14, 15, 18, 20, 22–23, 24, 31, 33, 76, 153; in *The Devil and the Good Lord*, 31–33; in *Dirty Hands*, 58, 73; in *The Respectful Prostitute*, 83; in *No Exit*, 116; art and, 155–63

Freud, Sigmund, 40, 120, 150, 174*n*8

Furies, 21, 167*n*21

Gaillard, Pol, quoted, 54, 60

Gandrey-Rety, Jean, quoted, 51

Garcin (*No Exit*), 111, 114–24, 126, 127, 128, 136, 152

Gassner, John, quoted, 82

Gavley Gay (Brecht, *A Man's a Man*), 139

Genet, Jean, 159, 161, 178*n*24; characters of, 24–25, 32, 117; as model of Goetz, 25, 39–40;

Genet, Jean (*Continued*)
quoted, 27, 38, 117; *Kean* and, 102, 173*n*42
Genius, 40
George (*Dirty Hands*), 55, 59, 65, 69, 74, 141
Gerlach, von (*The Condemned of Altona*), 131, 132, 133, 136–39
Gesture: act and, 5–6, 18, 40, 44, 66, 73, 77–78, 98–109, 113–22, 123, 124, 127, 132–33, 144–45, 152, 157, 162, 168*n*34, 173*nn*41–42
Ghost Sonata (Strindberg), 127
Ghost of Stalin, The (Sartre), 63
Gide, André, 11, 150; quoted, 171*n*7
Gilbert, Stuart, 165*n*1
Giraudoux, Jean, 16, 167*n*21
Goblet (*Nekrassov*), 95, 96, 97
Goebbels, Joseph Paul, 132
Goethe, Johann Wolfgang von, 35, 149
Goetz (*The Devil and the Good Lord*), 34, 64, 93, 96, 98; God and, 24–30, 31, 32, 33, 34, 38, 40, 42, 66; heroics of, 35–38, 39, 41, 42, 43, 66, 67, 73, 107–108, 113, 121, 126, 152, 153, 154, 162
Goetz von Berlichingen (Goethe character), 35
Gomez (*No Exit*), 122, 123
Gomez (*Troubled Sleep*), 157, 178*nn*14, 23
Gomulka, Wladyslaw, 55
Good Woman of Setzuan (Brecht), 30, 154
Grand Inquisitor (Dostoevsky, *The Brothers Karamazov*), 18
Gris, Ramon ("The Wall"), 49
Guicharnaud, Jacques, quoted, 22–23, 121–22

Hamlet (Shakespeare), 59
Hegel, Georg Wilhelm Friedrich, quoted, 121
Heidegger, Martin, 166*n*15
Heimburger (trial of Henri Martin), 75–76

Heinrich (*The Devil and the Good Lord*), 29, 40, 41, 93, 96, 108; evil of, 26–27, 28–29, 31, 32
Hell, 28; *No Exit* on, 113–27, 128, 133, 141, 150, 158
Henri (*The Victors*), 44, 45, 48, 49, 72, 74
Hernani (Hugo), 100
Hilda (*The Devil and the Good Lord*), 30, 32, 33, 47, 125, 167*n*29
Himmler, Heinrich, 131
Hitler, Adolf, 15, 20–21, 129, 130, 142, 147, 148, 166*n*10; bourgeoisie and, 128, 129, 131–32, 133
Hoederer (*Dirty Hands*), 5, 50, 53–78, 94, 108, 150, 171*n*42
Hugo (*Dirty Hands*), 50, 53–78, 107–108, 113; Franz compared with, 80, 94, 129, 141, 150, 152, 158
Hugo, Victor, 100
Huis-Clos (Sartre), see *No Exit* (Sartre)
Humanisme et Terreur (Merleau-Ponty), 33

Incest, 128, 134, 150, 172*n*12
Inez (*No Exit*), 111, 114–24, 126, 127, 128, 136
"Inhumanism," 29
In the Mesh (Sartre), 61
Ivich (*The Roads to Freedom*), 65, 172*n*12

Jean (Strindberg, *Miss Julie*), 4
Jean (*The Victors*), 45, 46, 48
Jeanne d'Arc (Péguy), 166*n*15
Jeanson, Francis, quoted, 13, 24, 25, 63–64, 66–67, 72, 102, 111, 156, 166*n*1, 171*n*42
Jeriah Jip (Brecht, *A Man's a Man*), 139
Jessica (*Dirty Hands*), 53, 54, 56, 59, 60, 65, 68–72, 74, 76
Joan Dark (Brecht, *Saint Joan of the Stockyards*), 34, 154
Johanna (*The Condemned of Altona*), 128, 129, 133, 134; judg-

ment of, 134, 135, 136, 137, 143, 144
John of the Cross, saint, 167n29
Journals of André Gide, The, 171n7
Joy, as *émotion*, 13–14, 166n8
"Judgment, The" (Kafka), 168n35
Jupiter (*The Flies*), 13, 14, 16; Zeus and, 10–11, 165n1; on freedom, 15, 18; symbolic murder of, 17–20, 31, 93, 138; as father-figure, 80, 82, 138

Kafka, Franz, 111, 157, 168n35
Kant, Immanuel, 33, 47
Karsky (*Dirty Hands*), 57
Kean, Edmund, 99, 100
Kean (Sartre), 93, 98–109
Kean, ou Désordre et Génie (Dumas), 99, 100, 101–102, 103, 104, 105
Keres, 167n21
King Lear (Shakespeare), 24
Knock (Romains, *Knock*), 96
Krapp's Last Tape (Beckett), 144–45, 176n54
Kyo (Malraux, *Man's Fate*), 145

Landrieu (*The Victors*), 47, 51
Language, 125–26: in *The Flies*, 14, 22, 82, 172n12; in *The Devil and the Good Lord*, 40–41, 108; in *Dirty Hands*, 69, 71, 78; in *The Respectful Prostitute*, 86; in *Kean*, 101–102, 104–105, 108; in *The Condemned of Altona*, 144–45; in *The Trojan Women*, 155; action and, 155–63
Lapoujade, 51
Last Judgment, 123–24, 136–37, 141 (*see also* Look, the)
Lawrence, T. E., 44
Lemaître, Frédérick, 99
Lemarchand, Jacques, quoted, 89–90
Leni (*The Condemned of Altona*), 128, 130, 133, 134, 135, 136, 137, 145, 148
Lettres Françaises, Les (periodical), 54, 89
Levine, Isaac Don, 55–56

Libération, La (newspaper), 88
Lindsay, Howard, quoted, 93
Literature, action and, 6–7, 155–63, 177n13, 178n19
Littérature engagée, or committed literature, 2, 109, 156–57, 159, 161, 178n19
Lizzie (*The Respectful Prostitute*), 80–87, 94
Look, the, 24–34, 38, 40, 42, 66, 111–14, 118–19, 121, 122–23, 126, 174n8; as Last Judgment, 123–24, 136–37
Louis (*Dirty Hands*), 55, 56, 57, 59, 60, 62, 63–64, 68, 71; Brunet and, 170n39
Loyola Ignatius, quoted, 53
Lucie (*The Victors*), 46, 48, 49
Lucien Drelitsch (*In the Mesh*), 61–62
Lucien Fleurier ("The Childhood of a Leader"), 64, 66, 80, 87, 90, 128
Lumley, Frederick, quoted, 27

McCarthy, Joseph, 89
McMahon, Joseph, quoted, 49
Madeleine (*Nausea*), 156
Magic: *The Flies* imagery of, 10, 14, 17, 18, 20; *émotion* as, 76; racist, 84; literature and, 156, 157; theatre and, 125
Mains sales, Les (Sartre), see *Dirty Hands* (Sartre)
Mallarmé, Stéphane, 56, 161, 178n24
Malraux, André, 44, 150; quoted, 24, 41, 43, 77, 117, 123, 145
Man's Fate (Malraux), 145
Man's Hope (Malraux), 123
Man's a Man, A (Brecht), 52, 139
Marcelle (*The Age of Reason*), 127
Maritain, Jacques, quoted, 26
Marlowe, Christopher, quoted, 28
Marriage of Figaro, The (Beaumarchais), 88
Martin, Henri, 75–76
Marx, Karl, 40, 74, 160
Marxism, 34–35, 41, 59, 92, 130

Mathieu (*The Roads to Freedom*), 3, 45, 67, 72; freedom and, 9, 166n8; the stone and, 10–11, 142

Mauvaise foi, or self-deception, 22, 23, 116, 117, 119

Medusa image, 112, 113, 118, 126, 141, 174n8

Mephistopheles (Marlowe, *Dr. Faustus*), 28–29

Mercader, Ramon, 55–56

Merleau-Ponty, Maurice, quoted, 33–34

Meursault (Camus, *The Stranger*), 77

Michelet, Jules, quoted, 97

Mind of an Assassin, The (Levine), 55–56

Miss Julie (Strindberg), 4

Moatti, Jacqueline, 155

Monde, Le (newspaper), 178n19

"Mon Faust" (Valéry), 110

Monstres sacrés, Les (Cocteau), 98

Montherlant, Henry de, 97

Mouches, Les (Sartre), see *Flies, The* (Sartre)

Mourning Becomes Electra (O'Neill), 16

Mouton (*Nekrassov*), 98

Murdoch, Iris, quoted, 5–6, 120, 152, 174n8

Myth: *The Flies* use of, 16–17, 22, 50, 153, 167n21; *No Exit* as, 111–12; of Medusa, 112, 113, 118, 126, 141, 174n8

Myth of Sisyphus, The (Camus), 173n41

Nagy, Imre, 55

Napoleon Bonaparte, quoted, 53

Nasty (*The Devil and the Good Lord*), 25–26, 27, 29, 40, 41–42

Nausea (Sartre), 1, 3, 71, 81, 110, 111, 127, 128, 149, 168n46; crustacean imagery of, 142, 143; art and, 156, 161

Nazis, 143, 146–47, 166n15; collaborators, 15, 16, 20–22, 23, 128, 129, 131–30, 140

Negro, The (*The Respectful Prostitute*), 79–87

Nekrassov (Sartre), 85, 87–98, 102, 109, 158–59

Nelson, Robert, quoted, 105, 107

Nobel Prize, 55

No Exit (Sartre), 5, 50, 78, 94, 110–27, 152–53, 157–58; *The Condemned of Altona* and, 127, 128, 133, 136, 141, 149, 150, 158

Nonviolence, 34, 47

Notes de théâtre (Dussane), 15

O'Brien, Justin, 176n56

Occupation, France, *see* France: Occupation

Odilon of Cluny, quoted, 167n29

Olga (*Dirty Hands*), 53, 54, 59, 62, 68, 69, 70, 76, 77, 170n39

O'Neill, Eugene, 16

Oresteia (Aeschylus), 16

Orestes (Euripides), 17

Orestes (*The Flies*), 64, 66, 73, 93, 107, 113; liberation of, 2, 9–14, 15, 18, 19, 20, 31, 35–36, 38–39, 42, 43, 67, 76, 82, 121, 138, 152, 153, 154, 162; as the Resistance, 16, 17, 20–24, 37, 42

Othello (Shakespeare), 99, 103, 105, 106, 107, 108

Pablo ("The Wall"), 49, 112

Palotin (*Nekrassov*), 90, 94, 95, 96, 98

Paradox of Acting, The (Diderot), 106

Parain, Brice, quoted, 125–26

"Paris sous l'Occupation" (Sartre): on guilt, 21–22; on the Nazis, 143; on the Resistance, 177n3

Parisien, Le (newspaper), 92

Paulhan, Jean, 162

Péguy, Charles, 166n15

Pellerin (*The Victors*), 47, 51

"Père et Fils" (Sartre), 130

Perken (Malraux, *The Royal Way*), 77

Pétainistes, 21

Peyre, Henri, quoted, 83

Philebus (Plato), 11

Philippe (*The Reprieve*), 170n33

Philoctetes (Gide), 11

Picon, Gaëtan, 162; quoted, 111, 126–27

Pierre (*The Reprieve*), 174n14

Pierre ("The Room"), 113, 127

Piscator, Erwin, 166n10

Plague, The (Camus), 21

Plato, 11

Poésie et Vérité (Eluard), 9

"Popular, the Absurd, and the Entente Cordiale, The" (Blau), 176n54

Poseidon (*The Trojan Women*), 155

Pozner, Vladimir, 171n1; quoted, 79

Prime of Life, The (Beauvoir), 16, 165n1, 174n13, 175n29

Prince Hal (Shakespeare, *Henry IV*), 101, 106

Prince of Wales (*Kean*), 101, 103, 105

Proust, Marcel, 156

Pucciani, Oreste, 146; quoted, 72–73, 134

Putain respectueuse, La (Sartre), see *Respectful Prostitute, The* (Sartre)

"Qu'est-ce qu'un collaborateur?" (Sartre), 20–21

Racine, Jean, 177n15

Racism, 79–87, 88, 93

Raskolnikoff (Dostoevsky, *Crime and Punishment*), 11–12

Rassemblement Démocratique Révolutionnaire, 92

Réflexions sur Lekain (Talma), 173n44

Reprieve, The (Sartre), 174n14; *The Flies* and, 9, 10, 25, 113, 166n8, 170n33

Resistance, the, 1–2, 3, 147–48, 174n13, 177n3; *The Flies* and, 15–24, 37; *The Victors* and, 43–52, 94; *Dirty Hands* and, 55, 78

Respectful Prostitute, The (Sartre), 79–87, 128; *Nekrassov* and, 85, 88, 93, 94, 96, 108, 109, 158–59

Responsibility, 17, 20, 30, 33, 60, 83, 138, 139; guilt and, 15, 22–23, 25

Revolution, 25, 33, 41–44, 58, 60, 61, 63–64, 73–74, 153, 154, 155–63, 178n19

Rimbaud, Arthur, 74

Rire, Le (Bergson), 87

Roads to Freedom, The (Sartre), 3, 44, 65, 170n39

Romains, Jules, 96

Romanticism, 13, 100–101, 103, 105, 108

Romeo and Juliet (Shakespeare), 99, 105, 106

"Room, The" (Sartre), 112–13, 149

Roquentin (*Nausea*), 2, 3, 45, 71, 81, 126; sickness of, 142, 143; salvation of, 156

Royal Way, The (Malraux), 77

Rufio Dichoso, Il (Cervantes), 168n33

Sade, Donatien, marquis de, 118

Saint Genet (Sartre), 178n24; *The Devil and the Good Lord* and, 24, 39–40; on the traitor, 27; on evil, 38; on identity, 66; on revolution, 73–74; on racism, 84; on gesture, 101, 173n42; on guilt, 142; on art, 159; on property, 172n24

Saint Joan (Shaw), 166n15

Saint Joan of the Stockyards (Brecht), 34

Saint Just, Louis Antoine de, quoted, 54

Salaud, le, 80, 87, 89, 90

Sartre, Jean-Paul: childhood, 6, 36, 65–66, 67, 100, 163n34, 170n36, 173n42; experience as prisoner, 1–2, 15, 24, 160; beginnings as playwright, 1–4; idea of theatre, 1–7, 50, 100, 124–25, 140, 152, 160, 162, 166n18; changes in idea of freedom, 1–2, 12, 14, 15, 34–35, 73–74, 83, 172n28; belief in salvation, 153, 155–57, 161–62, 168n34; relation to Com-

Sartre, Jean-Paul (*Continued*)
munists, 41, 54–55, 56–57, 63–64, 92, 172*n*28
Sartrean hero, 4–6, 31, 38–39, 66–67, 73–74, 90, 93–94, 107–108, 121, 152–55, 162
Sartre (Jeanson), 165*n*2
Sartre (Murdoch), 152
"Sartre: The Janus of Modern Dramatists" (Brustein), 161
Satire: in *The Flies*, 15, 20, 21; in *The Respectful Prostitute*, 80, 85–86, 158, 172*n*17; in *Nekrassov*, 87–98, 158
Savonarola, Girolamo, quoted, 167*n*29
Schneider ("Drôle d'amitié"), 78
Scottsboro case, 79
Search for a Method (Sartre): on Marxists, 130; on Flaubert, 130; on existentialism, 169*n*57
Senator, The (*The Respectful Prostitute*), 80–87, 90, 94, 128
Séquestrés d'Altona, Les (Sartre), see *Condemned of Altona, The* (Sartre)
Shakespeare, William, 59, 99, 105, 107, 178*n*15; quoted, 24
Shaw, George Bernard, 166*n*15
She Came to Stay (Beauvoir), 121
Sibilot (*Nekrassov*), 85, 90, 95, 96, 97, 98
Simon, Pierre-Henri, quoted, 22, 41
Slick (*Dirty Hands*), 55, 59, 65, 69, 74, 141
Slochower, Harry, cited, 16
Socrates, 11
Sophocles, 17
Sorbier (*The Victors*), 44, 45–46, 51
Spanish Civil War, 49, 157
Staging, 2–3, 5; *Bariona*, 1; *The Flies*, 20, 166*nn*10,18; *The Devil and the Good Lord*, 37; *The Victors*, 51, 169*n*13; *Dirty Hands*, 59; *The Respectful Prostitute*, 85–86; *No Exit*, 114, 126, 127, 174*n*13, 175*n*23; *The Condemned of Altona*, 149–50, 176*nn*56–57
Stalin, Josef, Trotsky and, 55, 56

Stone imagery, 10–11, 17, 95; and the Medusa, 112, 113, 142
Strasberg, Lee, quoted, 99
Strindberg, August, quoted, 4, 19, 127
Sylvia, Gaby, 174*n*13

Talma, François Joseph, quoted, 173*n*44
Tertullian, quoted, 27
Tête des autres, La (Aymé), 97–98
Théâtre Populaire (periodical), 14, 125, 152, 176*n*57
Thief's Journal, The (Genet), 27
Thierry-Maulnier, 89
Thody, Philip, quoted, 50, 55, 78
Tito (Josip Broz), 55, 56–57, 170*n*26
Tolson, M. B., 175*n*23
Torture: in *The Victors*, 43–52, 94, 147, 169*n*13; in *The Condemned of Altona*, 133, 135–36, 137–39, 140–41, 143–44, 146–47; Algeria and, 146, 147–49, 155
Triolet, Elsa, cited, 37
Trojan Women, The (Euripides), 154–55, 162
Trotsky, Leon, 55–56, 57
Troubled Sleep (Sartre), 141–42, 157, 178*nn*14,23
Tynan, Kenneth, quoted, 32, 93

United States, the: *The Respectful Prostitute* and, 79–87, 88; anti-Communism of, 89; Sartre in, 125, 165*n*1; war in Viet Nam and, 176*n*57
"Unprivileged Painter, The" (Sartre), 51

Valéra, Georges de (*Nekrassov*), 87, 88, 89–91, 93–98, 107
Valéry, Paul, quoted, 110
Veronique (*Nekrassov*), 90, 91, 93, 94, 95
Vichy Government, 15, 21–22, 23, 51, 166*n*18
Victors, The (Sartre), 43–52, 78, 82, 83, 94, 147

"Victory, A" (Sartre), 47, 148–49
Viet Nam: French war in, 75;
    American war in, 176n57
Vilar, Jean, quoted, 32
Vision, A (Yeats), 110
Voie royale, La (Malraux), 24

"Wall, The" (Sartre), 1, 49, 112–13
Weight, imagery of, 14, 66
Werner (The Condemned of Altona), 128, 130, 133, 134
What is Literature? (Sartre): on the Occupation, 15; on torture, 43; on literature, 157, 161
Words, The (Sartre): on gesture, 6, 109, 173n42; on heroics, 36, 42, 67, 70, 100, 159, 168n34, 177n4; on bourgeois ritual, 65, 170n33; on the look, 113; on crustaceans, 143; on salvation, 153, 155–56; on theatre, 160; on literature, 161–62, 163; on incest, 172n12
World War II, 141, 147; Sartre's experience as prisoner, 1, 2, 43–52; Resistance and, 23 (see also Resistance); Dirty Hands and, 62, 78; industrialists and, 129, 130, 136
Wreszin, Michael, quoted, 48
Wretched of the Earth, The (Fanon), 34
Wright, Richard, 86, 87

Yeats, William Butler, quoted, 110

Zeus, see Jupiter